COPPA MUSSOLINI
PREMIO DELLE NAZIONI
ROMA
4-11 MAGGIO 1935
A - XIII

IX CONCORSO IPPICO INTERNAZIONALE

SAMSUNG
NATIONS CUP
SERIES

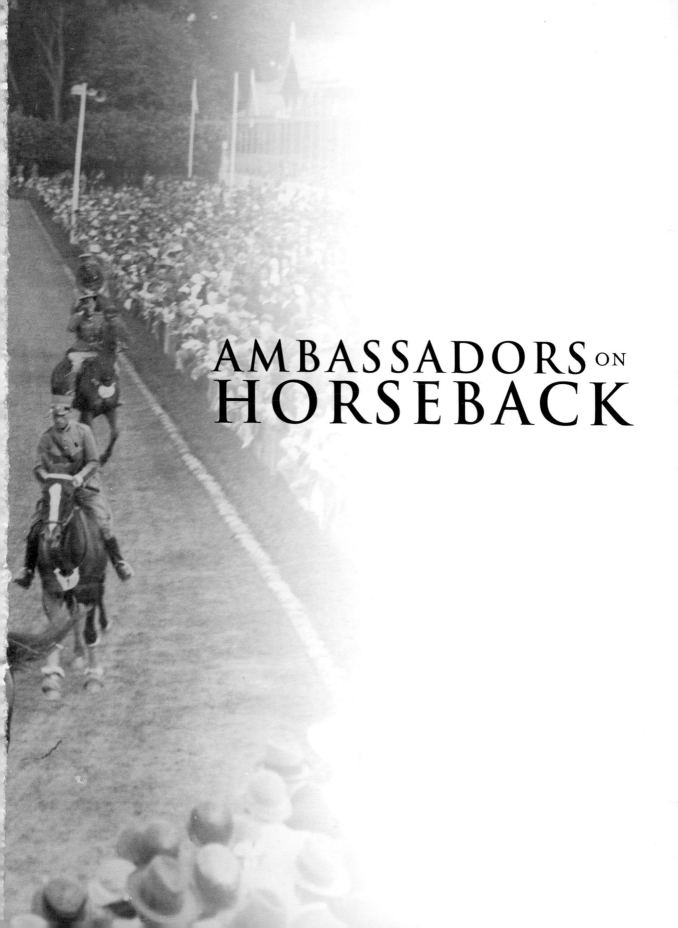

# AMBASSADORS ON HORSEBACK

**Michael Slavin:** Born in 1931, Michael Slavin has been a keen observer of horses since the time they were worked on his family's farm in Cavan in the thirties and forties. When he moved to Dublin after the Second World War, the horse shows at the RDS became an annual pilgrimage. In the late sixties he began a career as an equestrian journalist and commentator. He has written for the *Irish Field*, *Irish Farmers Journal*, *Horse and Hound*, plus other equine publications in six countries. He acted as RTÉ Radio's showjumping and eventing commentator for twenty years. His previous books include *Irish Show Jumping Legends 1868 – 1998*; *The Ancient Books of Ireland* and *The Book of Tara*. He now runs an antiquarian bookshop at the Hill of Tara, where he also makes his home with his wife, Katie.

**Louise Parkes:** worked at the semi-State body, Bord na gCapall, the original Irish Horse Board, and in the mid-1980s she set up the equestrian photographic agency, EPS, while also supplying reports and articles to high-profile publications including *Horse and Hound* magazine and *Horse International*. In 1995 she became equestrian reporter for the *Irish Independent* newspaper and subsequently contract journalist to the international governing body for equestrian sport, the Swiss-based Federation Equestre Internationale – roles she continues to fill. She also has experience as a broadcast journalist, providing radio reports and television interviews for RTÉ and TV3. Her work has taken her to European and World Championships and to the Olympic Games in Atlanta, Athens and Hong Kong. A keen amateur rider and Connemara pony enthusiast, she lives with her husband, Tony, on a small-holding in County Kildare.

# AMBASSADORS ON HORSEBACK

## THE IRISH ARMY EQUITATION SCHOOL

### Michael Slavin and Louise Parkes

THE O'BRIEN PRESS
DUBLIN

First published 2010 by The O'Brien Press Ltd,
12 Terenure Road East, Rathgar, Dublin 6, Ireland.
Tel: +353 1 4923333; Fax: +353 1 4922777
E-mail: books@obrien.ie
Website: www.obrien.ie

ISBN: 978-1-84717-213-6

A catalogue record for this title is available from the British Library

1 2 3 4 5 6 7 8 9 10
10 11 12 13 14 15 16

Printed and bound in Poland by Białostockie Zakłady Graficzne S.A.
The paper in this book is produced using pulp from
managed forests.

This book was a great collaboration between many gifted people
and key organisations in the world of horses. Thank you to the
authors, Horse Sport Ireland under Chair Joe Walsh, the
magnificent RDS and particularly CEO Michael Duffy, and
a lot of impressive army staff at the Army Equitation School and
elsewhere, especially Lieutenant Colonel Gerry O'Gorman, who
headed up and steered this ambitious book project with humour,
skill and diplomacy.
*Michael O'Brien, Publisher*

The lines from Patrick Kavanagh's 'The Man after the Harrow'
from *Collected Poems*, edited by Antoinette Quinn (Allen Lane,
2004) are reproduced by kind permission of the trustees of the
estate of the late Katherine Kavanagh through the Jonathan
Williams Literary Agency.

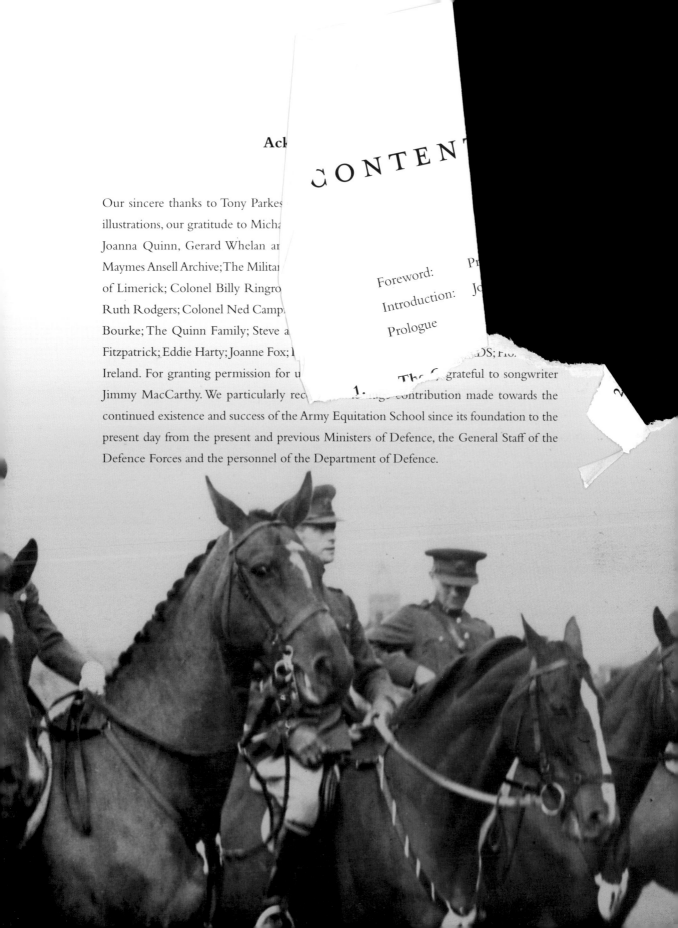

**Ack**

Our sincere thanks to Tony Parkes
illustrations, our gratitude to Micha
Joanna Quinn, Gerard Whelan an
Maymes Ansell Archive; The Militar
of Limerick; Colonel Billy Ringro
Ruth Rodgers; Colonel Ned Camp
Bourke; The Quinn Family; Steve a
Fitzpatrick; Eddie Harty; Joanne Fox; 
Ireland. For granting permission for u
Jimmy MacCarthy. We particularly rec
continued existence and success of the Army Equitation School since its foundation to the
present day from the present and previous Ministers of Defence, the General Staff of the
Defence Forces and the personnel of the Department of Defence.

# CONTENT

T S

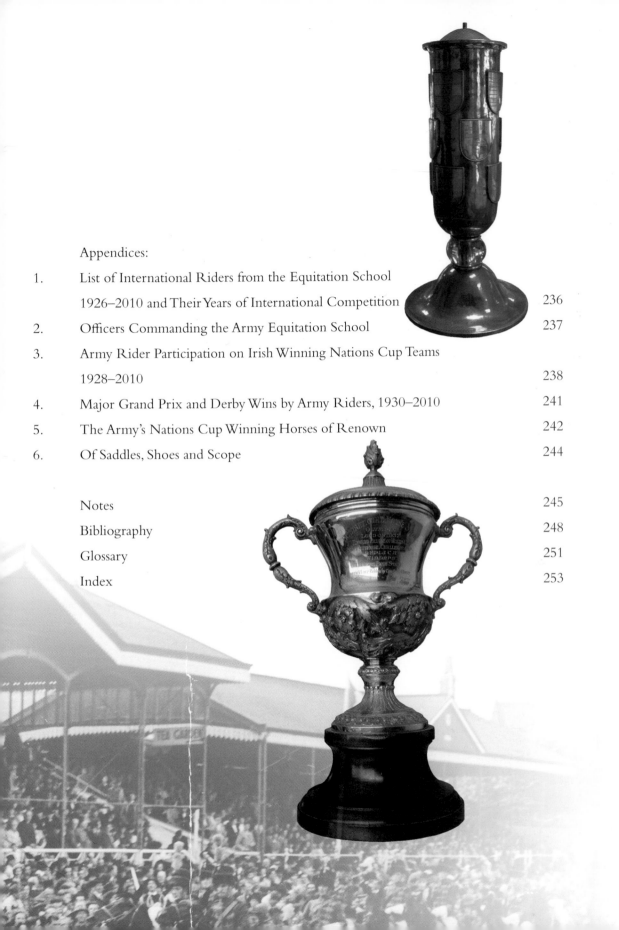

Appendices:

# FOREWORD

It was due to his admiration for the values and standards of the Irish Army Equitation School that my late father, King Hussein, sent me to Ireland to train during my early showjumping career. He once told me that the School was 'one of the very best examples of how the military and horses could celebrate history and work together for a peaceful future by inspiring people around the globe' – and this is exactly what it continues to do today.

I was delighted when I heard that Michael Slavin and Louise Parkes had joined forces to record the story of this great institution. It has played a pivotal role in the sport of Nations Cup jumping which, in 2010, is beginning its second century, and it has provided us with some of the greatest horsemen of all time.

I congratulate the authors on a job well done, and I commend the foresight and wisdom of the Irish Government and Irish Defence Forces in continuing to support the army riders who represent their country with such great pride and passion.

To Commanding Officer, Lieutenant Colonel Gerry O'Gorman and all his team I send my best wishes for many more successful years ahead. May Irish ambassadors in uniform continue to fly the flag for your wonderful nation and for its most treasured possession – the Irish horse.

*HRH Princess Haya*
*FEI President*

# INTRODUCTION

**Opposite:**
*Where it all begins:
on an Irish farm a
new foal is born.*
(Irish Farmers Journal).

A wonderful blending of the versatile Irish horse with our innate talent for horsemanship made possible the founding of the Army Equitation School back in 1926. Those same two vital elements have ensured the survival of this important institution down to the present day. As the school looks forward to its centenary in less than sixteen years' time, it can now claim to be the world's only remaining military equitation school still participating in top class international equestrian competition.

Founded to promote both Ireland and the Irish horse around the world, it has fulfilled both these missions to a superb degree because in each generation it has had the excellence of our home-bred jumpers and eventers at its disposal.

Down the centuries, successive intakes of bloodlines had our equines grow into the useful working and riding horse that suited the unique Irish farming style. In contrast to the heavier animals developed in Britain and the Continent, the horse of the Irish countryside was lighter, more versatile and could be yoked, driven or ridden. It had the quiet, easy temperament that matched its environment. Termed the Irish Draught by dealers coming home from abroad, it was just right for crossing with the purer drop of selected thoroughbred that had been perfected during the seventeenth century. The crossing of the naturally performance-tested working horse with the speed, stamina, athleticism and courage of the thoroughbred produced the world-famed Irish cross-country hunter and cavalry horse of the eighteenth and nineteenth centuries.

It is no wonder that a sport admirably suited to our Irish hunter, that of showjumping, had its birth right here when the Royal Dublin Society (RDS) ran its first Dublin Horse Show at Leinster House in 1868. As this sport spread to countries all across Europe, a whole new market evolved for our mounts, and by the time international military-team showjumping contests came into being during the early part of the twentieth century, Irish horses were being jumped under the flags of nations right across the Continent of Europe.

When a military Nations Cup, the Aga Khan, was first run at the RDS in 1926, most of the horses on the visiting teams were Irish bred. In fact, during the run-up to that event, the Swiss Colonels Richard Zeigler and Ernst Haccius declared, 'We will bring our Irish horses to Dublin and will win your cup.' That they did in 1926 and at show's end they bought an additional seventy-five Irish horses to take home with them. It was Colonel Zeigler's contention that the introduction of Nations Cup events at Ballsbridge, along with the formation of the army jumping team, would ensure that the export trade to other countries would be vastly increased as well.

What happened next is the wonderful, varied and exciting story of the fortunes both of the Irish horse and the Army Equitation School that is graphically told in this well-documented book. So well did the Irish horses do their job, within ten years Ireland was the top showjumping nation in the world. Down the decades since then, great Irish-bred jumpers, like *Limerick Lace*, *Blarney Castle*, *Red Hugh*, *Ballyneety*, *Loch an Easpaig*, *Rockbarton*, *Kilbaha* and more recently the superb mare, *Mo Chroi*, have helped keep the army team competitive at the very top level of the sport. In addition, army horses such as *San Carlos*, *Inis Meain*, *Kilkishen* and *Jump Jet* have done us proud in the sport of eventing. The exploits of these and other great Irish mounts for the more than forty international army riders that have represented Ireland and the school so superbly during the past eighty-four years are all recorded here in words and pictures to delight both the historian and the horse-lover alike.

This is a unique 'good news' Irish story that is worth the telling. And it is not over yet. As the school heads towards its centenary, it enters a whole new phase of its history – one in which it is more and more a part of the evolution of the Irish horse. Both the sport of equestrianism and the horses taking part in it have been undergoing dramatic change in recent decades. In order to keep pace, both Irish breeding policy and the training of our young horses have to undergo a renewal which will keep us competitive in the years ahead. In conjunction with Horse Sport Ireland, the RDS and the many breeders and producers around the country, the school is now playing its part in this renewal. As the current Officer Commanding the School, Lieutenant Colonel Gerry O'Gorman has noted: 'We have done it before and can do it again. A turnaround is taking place and a number of breeders are going the right way about it for the demands of today.'

Through our climate and our rich soil, Ireland is one of the most horse-friendly places in the world. Down the centuries we have been able to bring in bloodlines from abroad, make them better and make them our own. This evolutionary process continues right now as we incorporate strictly selected jumping blood from Continental Europe. Crossed with our performance mares, this will help produce the kind of Irish horse needed by our main shop window, the Army Equitation School, as it aims for its second century.
*Joe Walsh, Chairman, Horse Sport Ireland*

# PROLOGUE

The establishment of the Irish Army Equitation School in 1926 was an extraordinary step by any measure. The previous ten years had seen relative complacency about Ireland's status within the British Empire replaced by a fire-storm of nationalism leading to the formation of the Free State in 1921. During that decade of conflict and change, the Irish Army evolved.

Its roots were in revolutionary organisations like the Irish Republican Brotherhood, the Irish Citizen's Army and the Irish Volunteers. Through the Easter Rising of 1916 and the War of Independence (1919–1922) these groups gradually coalesced into the national army that took over after the Treaty with Britain was ratified in 1922. With Michael Collins as Commander-in-Chief, this army fought on the pro-treaty side in the Civil War that followed. When it ended in May 1923 the peacetime army was reorganised. In July 1924 the Transport Corps was established to control and administer all army transport, mechanical and horse. It was within this Transport Corps that the Army Equitation School was born in 1926.

*Above*:
*Insignia of Ireland's Defence Forces*

On opposite sides amid the maelstrom of the Easter Rising were two men whose united influence would, ten years later, be pivotal to the formation of the Army Equitation School. They were the then thirty-five-year-old King's Counsel William Evelyn Wylie and the thirty-six-year-old Irish Volunteer Lieutenant William Thomas Cosgrave.

From a Coleraine Presbyterian family, Wylie graduated with honours in law from Trinity College, Dublin, and was part of the Officer Training Corps that defended the college against the rebels during Easter Week. Cosgrave was a Dublin City Councillor from James's Street, who had attended Christian Brothers' schools in James's Street and Marino. He joined the Irish Volunteers in 1913 and during the Rising he saw sustained fighting against British forces. He was Adjutant to Commandant Eamonn Ceannt with the 4th Dublin Brigade in the South Dublin Union (now St James's Hospital). His step-brother, Goban Cosgrave, was killed during the action there.

Following the ceasefire, Wylie was appointed by General Sir John Maxwell to create a legal presence as Crown Prosecutor at the subsequent Military Court Martial Tribunals

that tried the captured rebels. Wylie found this role very disagreeable since he objected both to the secrecy of the trials and the absence of counsel for the defence. When the South Dublin Union surrendered, Cosgrave was arrested and then tried before Maxwell's Tribunal at Richmond Barracks. Based on his active participation in the Rising, Lieutenant Cosgrave was sentenced to death. However, in attempting to fill the defence vacuum, Wylie presented mitigating evidence on his behalf which resulted in his sentence being commuted to penal servitude for life. (Wylie is also credited with having similarly saved the life of Éamon De Valera).

Over the next four years Wylie served as Law Advisor to the Government at Dublin Castle. In 1920 he travelled to Westminster to argue the case for an equitable treaty with

*Above:*
*Judge William Wylie and President William T. Cosgrave in step at the 1923 Dublin Horse Show.*
*(RDS Library Archive)*

Prime Minister Lloyd George, Leader of the House Bonar Law, and Secretary of State Winston Churchill. When his view that the Irish could govern themselves was rejected, he resigned his position at the Castle in protest. Subsequently appointed a High Court judge, he concentrated his energies on the land question and the betterment of farmers, issues which he saw as central to both the peaceful transfer of power and future prosperity in Ireland.

Having been interned for a year, Cosgrave was released in 1917 and then elected as a

Sinn Féin MP in a Kilkenny by-election. After the Treaty was signed, he was a member of the Provisional Government and became its acting Chairman after the death of Arthur Griffith. When Michael Collins was killed, he was called upon to take charge. Following the enactment of the Irish Free State Constitution in December 1922, W. T. Cosgrave became leader of the government as President of the Executive Council, a position he held until 1932.

Under the new Free State Administration, Wylie was again appointed High Court judge. But in addition to his professional and family interests, he was also a passionate horseman and very much involved in the equestrian events at the Royal Dublin Society in Ballsbridge. It was as an RDS Council Member and organiser of the great Dublin Horse Show that Judge Wylie joined with President Cosgrave to help bring about the establishment of the Army Equitation School in 1926. In conjunction with the then fully established army, the two former belligerents were now involved in the most peaceful of pursuits through the wonderful unifying force of the Irish horse.

*Left (l to r):*
*Key figures in the introduction of Military Jumping for the Aga Khan Cup – RDS Director Edward Bohane, Council member Judge William Wylie and Prince Aly Khan, son of the donator of Ireland's Nations Cup, His Highness The Aga Khan.*
*(RDS Library Archive)*

I

# THE CALL TO HORSE

## 1926 to 1927

*'Boot, saddle, to horse, and away!'*
Robert Browning

In April 1926 a still fledgling Irish Free State Government took the daring decision to establish an Army Equitation School. Its first mission was to field an international showjumping team to compete against the best military squads in the world during the following August's Dublin Horse Show. At the time, they had neither trained horses nor riders at their command. So, it was a most extraordinary 'mission impossible'. Only through the innate ability of the Irish horse and our native talent for riding, could it ever be accomplished.

The proposal even to contemplate such a risky task back in 1926, came from the Royal Dublin Society (RDS). Recognised as the inventor of the sport, the RDS had been running national horse jumping competitions at its annual Dublin Horse Show since 1868. However, for its 1926 show, the Society's Council decided to vastly expand its programme by including the then growing spectacle of Nations Cup contests, which featured military teams of three from Europe and the Americas. At that time, cup events were run annually in Rome, Nice, London, Brussels, Strasbourg, The Hague, New York and Toronto. In addition to the team Nations Cup events at these shows, a series of individual military jumping contests were also included and the most important of these was the Grand Prix. The RDS wanted Dublin to become part of that circuit. But in order to achieve this, they needed to have an Irish Army team competing. Hence, in autumn 1925, RDS officials proposed to President W T Cosgrave's government that the formation of an army showjumping team would help promote both the new Irish Free State and the Irish horse around the world. [1]

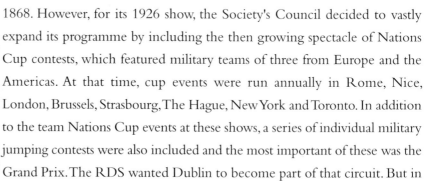

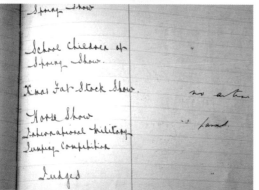

## THE RDS

The Royal Dublin Society was founded in 1731 to help improve 'Agricultural Husbandry, Manufactures and Other Useful Arts' in Ireland. At the time of its hundredth anniversary, in 1831, the RDS began to run an annual Spring Show on the grounds of its then headquarters, Leinster House on Kildare Street, Dublin. Then, in 1868, the RDS had its first show completely devoted to the horse at the same venue. In a far-reaching decision, the RDS Council took the advice of Lord Howth and included 'lepping' contests in the programme. [2]

This innovation is credited in the *Guinness Book of Showjumping* and in equestrian historian Max Ammann's authoritative volume, *The FEI Championships*, as being the birthplace of the sport. So popular did the Horse Show become, it was moved to a new arena at Ballsbridge in 1881. It has thrived there ever since. Their first Nations Cup was held in 1926 and the Dublin venue is second only to Rome in terms of the number of cups hosted since then (Rome 80 and Dublin 73). The cup presented to the winning nation at Dublin is named after His Highness the Aga Khan, who was the spiritual and temporal head of the Ishmaeli Muslims. He had a deep interest in horses and an abiding love of Ireland. Thus, he donated the first cup in 1926. Any team taking it three years in a row is allowed to keep it, and the Aga Khan made a commitment that it would always be replaced.

*Opposite top: McKee Barracks.*
*Opposite bottom: Minute from RDS Shows and Sales Committee meeting of 15 October 1925, which passed a resolution to run international military jumping at its 1926 show. (RDS Library Archive)*
*Top: Waiting for the Irish – a gathering of competitors at Lucerne Show in 1926. The new team first travelled there in 1927. They had a difficult time then, but ten years later they won the Swiss Cup three years in a row. (Max Ammann / FEI Archive)*

*Above:* A variety of
military uniforms worn by
visiting teams. *(RDS Library
Archive)*

International military team-jumping, or Nations Cup competitions, began at London Olympia in 1910. Abandoned during the war years, it gained new vigour in the 1920s. A similar type event had been included for the first time at the 1912 Stockholm Olympic Games and again at the post-war Olympiads of Antwerp in 1920, and in Paris in 1924. Many of the horses taking part in these competitions on British, Italian and Swiss teams were bred on Irish farms. Thus, promotion of the Irish horse, along with flying the flag of the new nation, were the most telling arguments in favour of forming an Army Equitation School that would send teams to compete at prestige venues on both sides of the Atlantic. Reflecting back on that time, President Cosgrave's son and later Taoiseach (1973–1978) Liam Cosgrave notes, 'Until Ireland joined the UN the only consistent mention of Ireland abroad was through the achievements of the Army Jumping Team.' [3]

In the 1920s Judge William Wylie, a most talented and adept negotiator, was in charge of the Dublin Horse Show at the RDS. He was also an inveterate promoter of hunter sales at the show, and it was during his conversations with a Swiss Army buying team in the autumn of 1925 that the idea of holding a Nations Cup competition at the 1926 show was first seriously mooted. Swiss Colonels Zeigler and Haccius noted that each year between five hundred and a thousand Irish sport and cavalry horses were bought into their country. It was their contention that this trade could be vastly expanded to other countries through the introduction of military Nations Cup contests. Despite the difficult political times, Wylie had actually been daring enough to run non-Nations Cup military jumping at the RDS in 1921, hence his heart was with the idea. But he next had to convince both the RDS and the Irish Government to be as daring as he. For such an undertaking to be fully successful, an Irish Army team *had* to take part. According to Wylie's own memoir,[4] he got a sympathetic ear from both RDS Director Edward Bohane and Free State President William Cosgrave, who was himself a horse-loving man. (At this time the head of the Irish Free State Government was referred to as 'President'; only after the Constitution of 1937 would the title 'Taoiseach' be used.)

However, within bureaucratic circles, a positive response was much more difficult to come by. As the new state struggled with all of the financial demands being made upon it, expenditure on men riding horses was not that easily justified. Hence there was some understandable delay within the Government.

At the start of 1926, Wylie was under pressure to make final preparations for the new competition. He had to send invitations to teams he hoped would take part from around Europe, but there was still no definite word from the Government. Supreme diplomat Wylie took the initial 'Yes' from President Cosgrave as a given, and proceeded to arrange the Nations Cup, come what may. Minutes of the Executive Council meetings of that time indicate that Minister for Agriculture Patrick Hogan was consistently listed as 'in attendance'; it is known that he saw the project as one that would encourage small farmers in the breeding of horses, and his support was a given. One way or another, the go-ahead came in April 1926 to form a jumping team for the following August's Dublin Horse Show. It was a matter of going ahead for the time being within the already existing horse transport unit at Marlborough Barracks, and let matters evolve after that. One of the school's first recruits, then Captain Gerald (Ged) O'Dwyer, later noted of this beginning, 'With untrained horses and riders, it was a very ambitious undertaking.'[5]

From that decisive moment in April, matters moved very quickly. Much had to be done. A base for the new school had to be selected. Riders, horses and grooms had to be found. Suitable saddles, uniforms and tack had to be bought. A workable organisation had to be put in place – all of this in the space of just three months. But, reflecting the energetic can-do spirit which then prevailed in the new nation, it was done.

The former Marlborough Barracks in the Phoenix Park (renamed McKee Barracks), with its stables and indoor arena, was chosen as headquarters for the school. Judge Wylie put all of his horse-buying expertise at the disposal of the army as it began the task of

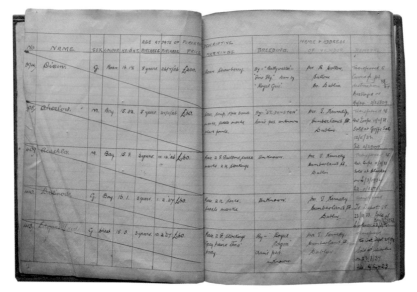

*Above: A page from the Army Equitation School's first* Horse Purchase Book *showing some of the jumpers bought in 1926 in the months prior to the first ever international outing of the new army team in August of that year.*
(Army Equitation School)

finding suitable showjumpers. Major Liam Hoolan, who was in charge of the estimated six hundred horses the army had at that time within the Transport Corps, was named Officer Commanding the new school. The first part of the 'mission impossible' had been accomplished.

## McKEE BARRACKS

Initially known as Grangegorman Barracks, McKee was built by the British Army between 1888 and 1892 on twenty-five acres at the edge of the Phoenix Park in north west Dublin city. It included a riding school and stables on the west side of its redbrick quadrangle. It was renamed Marlborough Barracks after Winston Churchill's grandfather and former Viceroy of Ireland, the Duke of Marlborough. During Queen Victoria's 1900 visit to Dublin, the First Dragoon Guards from Marlborough was one of the units providing her mounted escort. Down through the years, it also served as a headquarters for the Royal Irish Lancers. Units of the Lancers saw action during the 1916 Rising.

On 17 December 1922, following the formation of the Irish Free State, the barracks was handed over to Irish troops. The following year, it served briefly as a training school for the new Garda Siochána. In 1926, the barracks was renamed McKee in honour of Dick McKee, who had been Commandant of the Dublin Brigade during the War of Independence – captured on the evening of Bloody Sunday, he died in captivity at Dublin Castle. Also in 1926, McKee Barracks became the home of the newly created Army Equitation School.

When Raidio Éireann began its broadcasts as the national radio station in 1926, its transmission mast for the next five years operated from McKee.

The Army School of Music was also stationed there for a period.

In his *Brief History of McKee*, Commandant E Kiely notes: 'These were hard times in McKee, there being harsh discipline and poor food for both officers and men.'[6] But matters gradually improved after that, and since 1941 McKee has been home to the Army School of Catering.

In 1931 a new mounted escort called the Blue Hussars was formed at McKee. With Major Ged O'Dwyer of the Equitation School in command, it made its first public appearance at the Eucharistic Congress of 1932. During the Second World War, the 1st Anti-Aircraft Battalion was based at McKee. The barracks suffered some minor damage when German bombs were dropped on the Phoenix Park in 1940. Today, the barracks provides Army Headquarters and also houses the Directorates of Supply, Transport, Ordnance and Engineering. It has also been a training ground for many of the Irish Army units preparing for peace-keeping duties around the world.

Think of it: just four years after the ceasefire in the War of Independence and the setting up of the Irish Free State, Ireland was to join with the great nations of Europe in fielding a national equestrian team. Just three years from the ending of hostilities in the terrible Civil War that divided families and townlands around the country, soldiers of the new state were being called upon to form the nucleus of a most peaceful endeavour in promoting both Ireland and its horses. There can be no doubt that from the time the RDS put forward the idea of forming a team in autumn 1925, a degree of networking went on within the army in the hope of finding soldiers with some riding experience as candidates for the proposed equitation school. Major Liam Hoolan, who was appointed first OC of the new school, had seen action with the flying columns of North Tipperary during the War of Independence. Following the truce, he was appointed OC of the Free State garrison in Nenagh, where his second-in-command was Captain Ged O'Dwyer from Limerick (one of the first selected riders). When the Civil War ended in 1923, Liam was called to Dublin and assigned to then Marlborough Barracks.

*Above: One of the first recruits to the team – Captain Cyril Harty, who was a National Hunt jockey and father to racing legends Eddie Harty, Buster Harty and John Harty. (Army Equitation School)*

Another man who played a major role in the early days of the school was Colonel Michael Hogan, brother of Minister for Agriculture Patrick Hogan. From Loughrea, County Galway, he had served in the War of Independence, and in the Free State Army during the Civil War. One of his close comrades-in-arms was another first recruit, fellow Galway-man Captain Daniel (Dan) Corry. When stationed together at the Curragh in 1924–1925, Michael and Dan were founder members of the Naas Harrier Hunt. Influence also came from a future OC of the school, Colonel Liam Hayes; he was a cousin to Ged O'Dwyer and his close companion during the War of Independence. These three men – Hoolan, Hogan and Hayes – had much to do with the 'call to horse' in April 1926 of the two men who would become legendary figures in the early army teams, Captains Ged O'Dwyer and Dan Corry. Also called up was a neighbour of Ged's in Limerick, Captain Cyril Harty, a National Hunt jockey who had joined the army in March 1923. All three of these soldiers were known for their interest in riding. But Ged O'Dwyer himself once described the three of them as 'hunting and racing men, who knew nothing about showjumping.'[7] A fourth member called up, but who never jumped internationally, was point-to-point rider Commandant Tom Mason.

So these were the first selected riders. Now, what of the horses? The new Free State Army did have some re-mounts for ceremonial and transport purposes, but it did not have a cavalry unit, as such. Captain Dan Corry later recalled of his arrival at McKee, 'When we got to the barracks, the only horses I saw there were pulling carts in the yard.' Having first proposed the idea of fielding an army showjumping team and then seeing it through to the point where riders were actually in place, Judge Wylie of the RDS stepped in to play a major role in finding the horses for them to ride. He was a hunting man, a former showjumper and a judge at shows all around the country, so he had a good idea what was out there in terms of jumping talent. During the months of May and June, he and Liam Hoolan accomplished the second element of the 'mission impossible' when five potential jumpers arrived at the stables in McKee.

*Above:* Gun practice by Captain Dan Corry at Galway during the Civil War in 1922, just four years prior to his call-up for the new jumping team.
(Donal Corry)

An Army Transport Corps Memorandum on 'The Development of the Force 1923 – 1927' gives a succinct summary of what had happened up to this point:

In the spring of 1926 the Dublin Horse Show committee approached the Army Authorities on the matter and as a result a special grant was made for the purchase of six animals suitable to compete. The animals purchased had but little training in show-yard jumping and the training of both animals and officers who rode them was carried out by the Horse Transport Depot and furthered by competing at a number of local shows. The results became more and more satisfactory… It is thought that the fact of army personnel and animals taking part in such competitions against representative horsemen from the world's excellence cannot but have a salutary effect, if only as an advertisement of one of the principal products of the country ie Hunters.[8]

Beginning in May 1926 and over the following months, a total of £1,615 was spent on the purchase of potential showjumping horses. Reflecting the patriotic ethos of the time, the newly arrived mounts at McKee were given names from heroic ancient Irish folklore and literature: *Cuchulainn, Finghin, An Craobh Ruadh, Roisin Dubh* and *Ferdia*. Just a few short weeks prior to the opening of competition at the Dublin Horse Show, a fine, big roan gelding was bought. He was appropriately named *Oisin*, after the hero of the Fianna legends who was said to have ridden off into the Otherworld, the Land of Victories. *Oisin* was soon to be part of a magical moment when the new army team took to the international field for the first time at the RDS on Tuesday, 3 August 1926.

Mid-April to the beginning of August is a very short time. But back then, in 1926, it had to be time enough for raw young riders and equally raw jumpers to prepare for the immense test of the first Aga Khan Cup at the Dublin Horse Show. Daily training began. Fences similar to those at the RDS were set up in a small practice area at McKee. There were long hacks in the Phoenix Park and exercises in the indoor school. As later recalled in Thomas Toomey's memoir of Ged O'Dwyer, *Forgotten Dreams*: 'in addition to continuous daily practice over jumps, the riders went through various exercises to get to know their mounts. The horsemen short-listed to ride on the new team hardly saw home from the time they arrived at McKee until after completion of the show in Ballsbridge.'[9] When asked by this author how they coped with this intense period of preparation, Ged O'Dwyer's brief but honest answer, 'It was a struggle.'

Struggle or not, the team's newfound talents were soon put to the test in country shows during June and July at places like Tullamore, Dundalk, Clones, Bray and Ballinasloe. From that time until now, it has been part of the school's mission to give constant support to local shows around the country. Of course, in those early days, not all the reaction was positive. A somewhat cryptic remark in *Forgotten Dreams* is revealing: 'The *knowing* ones, both within and without showjumping circles, were waiting for Humpty Dumpty's great fall.'[10] The amount of falling they did appears to have been amazingly slight since they did record wins and seconds at Tullamore and Bray. Corry netted prize money totalling £55 at Clones, Dundalk and Ballinasloe on his horse *Finghin*.

But that was all by way of introduction. The truly seminal moment was to come in the very first international competition on the opening day of the Dublin Horse Show. Every available seat at the massive arena was filled. In this Confined Military Class, two riders jumped the course together. The best from each heat went forward into the second round. First into the ring were Lieutenant Boudouin de Brabandere of Belgium and Ireland's Captain Ged O'Dwyer. De Brabandere was a rider with long experience, and just one month previously he had jumped on his country's winning Nations Cup team at Nice. Off went the two riders – the Belgian in his dark uniform on his Nations Cup horse, *Acrobate*, and Ireland's Captain Gerald 'Ged' O'Dwyer in his newly tailored green riding outfit on the very recently purchased roan gelding, *Oisin*.

During three of his previous six years, Ged had known only the terror of war and had seen his family home in Fennor burned down in a reprisal raid by British forces. It is little wonder that Ged later said of that starting moment, 'I had a strong feeling that at least half of the packed stands on opening day were hoping for a win by Britain.'[11] He may well have been right, since the *Irish Times* report of the show on the following Saturday, 7 August, noted that when the British team took a temporary lead in Friday's Aga Khan Cup 'there was tumultuous applause all around the ground'.[12] But when the starting bell rang out for this opening competition, this was no time for looking back. History, for an instant, stood still. This was the moment Judge Wylie, President Cosgrave, Minister Hogan and Major Liam Hoolan had dreamed of and worked for. What the Army Equitation School has done so successfully for more than eighty years had begun.

The winners of the International Military Jumping Competition (over the course). From left to right—Captain Weid (Switzerland), 1st Prize; Captain G. O'Dwyer (Ireland), 2nd Prize; Captain Bühler (Switzerland),

[IRISH LIFE photo]

Lieut. Baudouin de Brabandère (Belgium), Capt. G. O'Dwyer (Ireland), on "Oisin," 2nd prize. MILITARY JUMPING. [Irish Sketch.

*A unique collage created by Ged O'Dwyer using* Irish Life *and* Irish Sketch *pictures of the very first international military jumping competition at the RDS on Tuesday, 3 August 1926. The circular picture shows, first into the ring, Ged on* Oisin *heading out over the bank against Lieutenant Baudouin de Brabandere of Belgium.*

*In the presentation picture, Captain Van der Weid of Switzerland is in first place with the Irish-bred stallion* Royal Gris *and Ged is second on the gelding* Oisin, *bought just two weeks before the show. (Noel O'Dwyer)*

As reported in the army publication, *An t-Óglach*, of that week: 'They went off at a rattling pace and cleared every obstacle without a fault.'[13] After two rounds, twelve horses had jumped well enough to qualify for the final. Among them were *Finghin* for Captain Dan Corry and *Oisin* for Captain Ged O'Dwyer. In the end, the winner of the competition was Captain Henri Van der Weid of Switzerland on the Irish-bred *Royal Gris*. Dan Corry took fourth place. But there had to be a jump-off for second and third between Ged and Captain Hans E Bühler of Switzerland. It was the young twenty-seven-year-old Irish soldier's second big test of the day. O'Dwyer had been commended for coolness under fire during the Civil War; he needed that quality again now in this sporting battle as he took on Olympic medal winner Bühler. Ged was first to go and, to a huge reception, he crossed the finish line with all fences standing and a high mark from the judges. The pressure was now on the Swiss rider and it showed when he came to the water jump – a hesitation there, and it was all over. Ged and *Oisin* had won the jump-off. The joyful reaction from the stands made it appear as though he was the overall winner of the whole tense competition! In fact, he had secured second place behind Van der Weld on *Royal Gris*. Amazingly, it turned out that big grey *Royal Gris* was an Irish-bred stallion and that he was the sire of *Oisin*'s dam, hence *Royal Gris* stood ahead of his own grandson in the prize line-up.

In that week's *An t-Óglach* report, there was unrestrained pride in the army riders' accomplishments on this, their first major outing: 'Events have proved that we were right when we foretold that the Irish Army competitors would make a good display in the International Military Jumping Competitions at this year's Dublin Horse Show.'[14] It certainly was a fairytale beginning. But no more than that – as the week progressed much stiffer tests were soon to come.

In Friday's Nations Cup, the Irish side of Corry, O'Dwyer and Harty came up against crack squads from Britain, France, Belgium, Holland and Switzerland. So great was public interest in the event, the outer doors to the RDS had to be barred in order to prevent any more people cramming into the already crowded show grounds. A record 34,000 thronged every available space around the arena. Heightening the spectacle was the first ever public performance by the newly established Army Band. They led each of the visiting teams into the enclosure and then played their National Anthem as they stood before the Governor General's box. There to take

ARMY HORSEMEN'S SUCCESS.
Fine Performance on Opening Day of Dublin Show.
SECOND AND FOURTH IN INTERNATIONAL COMPETITIONS.

CAPTAIN D. CORRY (left), and CAPTAIN G. O'DWYER, who secured Fourth and Second places respectively in the International Jumping Competitions, on the opening day of this year's Dublin Horse Show.

the salute was the man who had made it all possible – President William T Cosgrave. It was utterly apt that when the Irish team of Captain Dan Corry on *Finghin*, Captain Cyril Harty on *Cuchulainn* and Captain Ged O'Dwyer on *Oisin* entered the enclosure, the band struck up 'A Nation Once Again'. That tradition is maintained to this day in the Aga Khan parade and never fails to stir emotion in the expectant crowd.

For this inaugural Aga Khan, the set Ballsbridge course was being used. Its banks, stone wall and water-jump may have given a slight edge to the home side, and in the years to come this was to become a bone of contention between the RDS authorities and the newly formed ruling body of the sport, the Federation Equestre Internationale in Switzerland.

But on this occasion, the Swiss and their Irish-bred horses were well up to the task and they quickly became the ones to beat. At this time, the

PARADE INTERNATIONAL JUMPING CHAMPIONSHIP ROYAL DUBLIN SOCIETY.

event was judged on an accumulative scoring system devised by Judge William Wylie. Points were awarded for good jumping at each obstacle around the arena. Even when a fence was knocked, a rider could still gain points for his riding style. The Swiss side of Van der Weid, Bühler and Kuhn put in a masterful first round performance for a score of 85.50 out of a possible 90. Ireland scored a creditable 82 and at the break between the two rounds they were lying fourth behind Switzerland, with France at 84 and Belgium at 83. It was all to play for in the second round. This time, with their nerves calmed and determination at its highest point, the Irish put in a brilliant rally. Having jumped all of its three riders, Switzerland had an overall total of 174.5. With their crowd-pleasing second round, Britain had moved up to the runner-up slot on a score of 166. For the home team, Captain Cyril Harty on *Cuchulainn* went clear and got maximum points.

*The first official dinner for visiting teams at McKee Barracks during the 1926 Horse Show. Key people included are Colonel Michael Hogan (front row, second from left), who was instrumental in the formation of the army team; next to him Colonel Zeigler of Switzerland, who put forward the idea of running military jumping at Dublin; (front row, far right) Lieutenant de Brabandere, who was first into the ring along with Ged O'Dwyer; (top row, second left) Dan Corry, Commandant Tom Mason (fourth left); between him and Ged O'Dwyer (sixth left) is Captain Van der Weid of Switzerland, who won the opening event. (RDS Library Archive)*

Captain Dan Corry and *Finghin* had just one mistake as they took a top stone off the wall. Ireland's fate in the competition then rested on Captain Ged O'Dwyer and *Oisin*. Once again, the new partnership delivered. They produced a cool clear, to give the Irish a two-round total of 169.5 and second place behind Switzerland (174.5) and ahead of Britain (166), France (165), Holland (159) and Belgium (138). Just as in the first class on opening day, a second was greeted as though it was a win. The *Irish Times* report of the event said, 'The feature of the international jumping competition for the magnificent Challenge Cup presented by his Highness The Aga Khan … was the manner in which Captain O'Dwyer brought the Irish team up into second place on the last circuit.'[15]

In addition to the good showing in the Aga Khan, the Irish were further heartened by news that Swiss Army buyers had purchased seventy-five horses at the show. The Equitation School's twin objectives of advertising the Irish nation and the Irish horse had been well and truly fulfilled on this, its first international outing.

Euphoria has to be the word to describe the reaction to this success. And in its glow, Government officials were lulled into thinking that this young Irish side was ready to take on the even greater challenge of competing abroad. During the official dinner for the visiting teams at McKee Barracks, invitations were extended for shows in the countries taking part. Despite reservations on the part of Officer Commanding Major Liam Hoolan and the riders, the invitations to Olympia, London, in June 1927 and to Lucerne soon afterwards were accepted. It has to be remembered that Olympia was jumped indoors and the courses there, and on the Continent, had become much more complicated and technical than those in Ballsbridge. This time the 'mission impossible' was truly that!

With generous aid from British team members, like Captain Joseph Hume Dudgeon and Major Edward T Boylan of Drogheda, the army men began their preparations for their first venture abroad. A course somewhat similar to that at Olympia was set up at McKee. Then, for three weeks before the show, they practised at the British Army Equitation School in Weeden, Northamptonshire. Prior to their departure, President Cosgrave called them to his office and reminded them that they were the first army officers to wear the Irish uniform outside Ireland. Dan Corry later recalled that he said: 'No matter where you go, never do anything that would dishonour the uniform you are wearing.'[16]

Despite the practice at McKee and Weedon, nothing could have prepared them for what they faced in the London competition. Their first visit there was a total disaster that nearly ended the army school's adventure before it had a chance to take root. Reflecting on what happened, Dan Corry colourfully declared, 'We were kicking poles back into the Irish sea.' In this author's interview with Ged O'Dwyer at the time of his ninetieth birthday, his face clouded at the memory of it: 'We were just plain embarrassed by what happened. Our big, striding horses could not cope with the confined space and tight distances. We were hunting men riding hunters. We did have the naive idea that there would be some open distances between fences and that there would be wings to the fences so that a horse would not run out. But it was like galloping inside a house and our horses were not trained to turn that sharp. So we knocked everything in sight. To say the least, we did not like it and felt rather foolish to be in that position.[17]

The competition was judged under a negative faults system rather than the accumulative points approach used in Dublin. So, in this, their first attempt at the Prince of Wales Cup, the Irish picked up a total of 75.5 faults for last place behind Britain (5), France (10.5), Italy (20.5), Poland (26.6), Belgium (31.5) and Sweden (38.5). A disaster, indeed, before a packed British audience! No wonder Ged used the word 'foolish' in his memory of the event. But he also added, 'We swore we would be back and that matters would be different.'

Matters did not improve when the Irish team moved on from London to Lucerne. Courses there were even more difficult than at Olympia. The fences varied both in number and construction for each competition. Once again, the team just could not cope. Their highest placing over four days of jumping was twelfth. So deflated were they when it came to Nations Cup day, they did not participate against sides from France, Switzerland, Belgium and Hungary. A member of the winning French team on that occasion – Captain Camille Montergon – later recalled his memory of Ireland's innocent effort at entering the world of international showjumping: 'It was at Lucerne in 1927 that I saw Ireland's competitors for the first time. None of them had any experience in international competition. How fine the courage of the young Irish Army, thus flinging itself boldly into the water in order to learn to swim'.[18]

It was a dispirited side that came home from Lucerne to jump at that year's Dublin Horse Show. An attempt by Judge Wylie to bring the Ballsbridge course somewhat into line with those on the Continent did not help matters. Neither did the very wet weather of 1927. As it turned out, before a disappointed home crowd, Ireland was placed last in the Aga Khan. Nor did the Irish riders feature well in the individual contests. This definitely was the end of the beginning. But was it also the end of the whole innovative Equitation School project? With the possibility of being disbanded staring it in the face, the school had to come up with one more daring initiative if it was to survive.

# THE RODZIANKO RESCUE

## 1928 to 1931

*'I have no spur to prick the sides of my intent but only vaulting ambition, which o'erleaps itself'*
*William Shakespeare,*
*Macbeth, i, VII*

The Irish Army team's failure to perform on their first trip abroad did not go unnoticed in the home press. At the time of their London disaster, Irish peer, The Mcgillicuddy, wrote a stinging letter to *The Irish Times* declaring that the team needed expert training if it was to take on the task of international showjumping. At that very same time, however, Colonel Michael Hogan, who had travelled with the team to Olympia, was already in the process of finding a solution to the problem. He knew very well that the team was on probation, with little time to redeem itself. At the London event, either by design or by chance, Hogan had met up with world-famed Russian riding expert Colonel Paul Rodzianko, and out of that meeting evolved the Army Equitation School's salvation.

There can be no doubt that members of other military teams wanted the new Irish squad to prosper. None more so than the British, who had two riders on their side with strong connections to Ireland – Colonel Joe Hume Dudgeon and Major Edward Boylan. Dudgeon, who would soon after establish a progressive riding school in Dublin, may well have been the one who introduced the two colonels.

In August 1927, Colonel Michael Hogan was appointed Assistant Quartermaster General within the army and this promotion was a further help towards executing a rescue. Among his responsibilities was the Equitation School, and soon after his new appointment came an important change in the school's status within the army structure. Up to this point, since its founding in April 1926, the school had been a subordinate unit within the Army Transport Service. But from 1928 onwards, it was to become a separate unit, reporting directly to the Quartermaster General's office. Also established was an Advisory Group to the Minister of Defence on matters relating to the school.

Early in 1928 Hogan made contact once more with Rodzianko and hired him as team

*Above:* Colonel Paul Rodzianko's Italian teacher, Frederico Caprilli, demonstrating his innovative forward seat.

trainer. It was Ged O'Dwyer's view that Hogan, whom he regarded as 'a brave and impulsive man' may have had to pull all sorts of strings to hire Rodzianko. But in order to avert a crisis in the unit and knowing that he would have the full backing of his brother, the Minister for Agriculture, hire him he did.

Rodzianko's fee is said to have been in the region of £50 a week – about fifteen times the average wage of an ordinary soldier at the time. On an annual basis, it was equal to the full travel budget for both horses and riders of the Equitation School during the previous year.[1]

Rodzianko was more than just a riding instructor. He was, in fact, a world class expert in the new methods of equitation that had recently evolved in Europe. Up to that point, horsemanship had focused largely on a comfortable seat for the *rider*. But in studies conducted at cavalry schools of the time, it was concluded that this did not sufficiently consider comfort for the *horse*. Because the traditional hunting and racing seat put a great amount of pressure on the mount's loins and kidneys, it stressed the horse and sapped its stamina. Setting about correcting this error in the early twentieth century were two great equestrian innovators, James Fillis of Scotland and Captain Frederico Caprilli from Italy. Fillis became Director of the Russian National Cavalry School in St Petersburg and Caprilli was instructor at the Italian Cavalry College in Pinerola. Caprilli contended that the traditional riding methods 'caused discomfort and pain to the horse and consequently disgusted him with his work.'[2]. The solution put forward – separately – by these two great innovators was the revolutionary *forward* seat. But the new system also demanded greater discipline on the part of the rider, who, instead of just sitting comfortably, was forced to work at maintaining a forward balance in a posture that required a great deal of practice.

Colonel Paul Rodzianko had benefited from training under both Fillis and Caprilli. Thus, in him the young Irish Army team had an amalgam of all that was best and most up to date in the art of competition horse-riding. This is what Colonel Hogan was paying high wages for and the Russian proved to be worth every farthing of it.

When Rodzianko arrived at McKee, he first began a series of preliminary courses that involved the school's administrators – these courses were intended to give those in charge

*Below: Colonel Michael Hogan, who saved the Army Equitation School through employing Colonel Paul Rodzianko. Colonel Hogan was a good friend of Captain Dan Corry and together they formed the Naas Harriers in the early twenties.*
(Army Equitation school)

## COLONEL PAUL RODZIANKO

Paul Rodzianko was born into a land-wealthy Ukraine family with a distinguished military history – it has been said that the island of Ireland would fit neatly within the former Rodzianko estates. His father was equerry to Tsar Nicholas II. Thus, as a young officer, Paul became part of the famed Cossack regiment and was assigned to the Tsar's elite Household Cavalry. Following training with James Fillis at the Russian Cavalry School in St Petersburg and with Federico Caprilli at the Italian Cavalry College in the pre-World War I years, he competed internationally with the Russian military showjumping team. He was part of the side that won the Prince of Wales Cup at Olympia, London, in 1912, 1913 and 1914. In the latter victory he was riding an Irish horse called *Macgillicuddy Reeks*. During World War I, Rodzianko served first on the Russian border and then on the Italian front. After the armistice he returned home and saw action with the White Army during the Russian Civil War. Following their defeat by the Bolsheviks, he was forced to flee abroad and in 1921 he took up the position of riding instructor at his old *alma mater*, the Italian Cavalry School. However, Mussolini's Blackshirts had him thrown out and from then until his appointment to the Irish Army Equitation School, he lived in England and survived by his teaching skills. His Irish tour began in 1928 and ended at the beginning of 1931. Soon afterwards, he married Anita Leslie, a member of the literary Glaslough County Monaghan Leslie family; he then returned to England and took up a teaching career there once more. During World War II he served with the British troops in North Africa and Italy. In 1951, and again in 1952, he came back to the Army Equitation School to instruct a whole new group of riders. Commandant J J O'Neill, who rode there at that time said of him, 'He was a magnificent instructor with a great control and understanding of horses.'[3] His legacy remains with the school to this day.

some idea of the training, pain and dedication required to become a proficient showjumper. The group included the officers who had been instrumental in the school's birth – Liam Hoolan, Michael Hogan and Liam Hayes – along with a future OC, Fred Bennett. Also attending were current team members Ged O'Dwyer, Dan Corry and Cyril Harty, plus three new recruits: Lieutenant Fred Aherne from Meath, Tom Finlay from Laois, and Kerryman Dan Leonard.

But as 1928 progressed, Rodzianko's concentration was solely on the retraining of Captains O'Dwyer, Corry and Harty. As later recalled by Ged O'Dwyer, their redemption from possible oblivion was also a crucifixion: 'He turned us inside out, but it hurt. We were in the saddle for six hours a day and while the new seat was easy on the horse, it was very uncomfortable for us. I can remember many nights dragging myself back to our barracks and just about having the energy to fall into bed only to wake up sore the next morning. Then it was back into the grind once more – heels down, toes out, knees in, hollow back and light hands – for six more hours.'[4]

There can be no doubt that Rodzianko would have felt under pressure to produce some early results worthy of his pay. And there could be no better way to do this than in a winning performance on home ground at Ballsbridge. With this in mind, he all but confined the team to barracks for the first seven months of 1928 while they practised the severe lessons of the forward seat over and over again. So, it was not really until the opening day of Dublin Horse Show, Tuesday, 7 August, that a transformed threesome emerged once more from behind the walls of McKee. For anyone with a true eye for horsemanship, they had a more polished riding style which began to show when Harty, Corry and O'Dwyer took part in the early classes. O'Dwyer and *Cuchulainn* came a close second in the first military competition. On the Wednesday, Cyril Harty and *An Craobh Ruadh* scored a morale-boosting first-ever international win by the school when taking the popular Puissance or High Wall Competition ahead of Commandant Chandeleon of Belgium. But Rodzianko was holding fire for Friday's Nations Cup. The tactics of experience were at work and instead of throwing their best at every competition as in previous years, the team mounts were saved as much as possible for Friday's big occasion.

In the Aga Khan competition, teams from Britain, France and Belgium lined out against the new-look Irish side. And right from the start, it became obvious that Rodzianko's charges were well up to the task. In the first round, Harty on *An Craobh Ruadh*, O'Dwyer on *Cuchulainn* and Corry on *Finghin* took the lead with a combined score of 138 points. This compared well with a first round, last place total of only 107 the previous year. Pressed by the British, who trailed by just two points, the Irish had to hold their nerve in the second round. This they did, to record an even better combined total of 139 for an overall score of 277 – and their first ever Nations Cup win. Britain came second at 272, and a crack French team were third with 265. To the strains of the 'Soldier's Song', the Aga Khan Trophy was presented to the Irish trio by the Governor General of the Irish Free State, James McNeill.

So impressed were Government officials with the team's dramatic improvement, that at the traditional dinner for visiting teams in McKee Barracks, hosted by Chief of Staff Lieutenant General Dan Hogan (himself a horseman) and Minister for Defence Desmond FitzGerald, it was announced that in the years ahead Nations Cups would be contested in Britain, France, Belgium and the USA. The Army School of Equitation and Ireland's international showjumping team had well and truly survived the crisis and had been reborn.

*Ireland's first Nations Cup win: presentation of the Aga Khan trophy 1928 (right to left) Captains Cyril Harty on* An Craobh Rua, *Dan Corry on* Finghin, *Ged O'Dwyer on* Cuchulainn.

The team's first away outing after their Aga Khan win was to Biarritz in mid-October 1928. On Rodzianko's advice, the horses were shipped to France a full three weeks in advance. En route, both they and the riders made a stopover at the famed French Cavalry School of the Cadre Noir in Saumur. Colonel Michael Hogan was in charge of the group that included the three regulars, O'Dwyer, Corry and Harty, along with new recruit Lieutenant Fred Aherne. Another new recruit, Captain Tom Finlay, was in reserve at home.

Tall and stately, Fred Aherne was an experienced rider from north County Meath, where he had participated in the War of Independence. After a distinguished career with the Army team during the thirties, he returned to the school as OC in 1949. Laois man Tom Finlay was a powerful athlete, who had won All Ireland hurling medals with both his native county and with Dublin during the early twenties. He was described as a most reliable rider who never let the big occasion get to him. These two additions to the squad in 1928 indicate that Rodzianko's training courses were beginning to bear fruit. The search for new horse talent was also reaping results. Added to the team was a Carlow bred mare named *Roisin Dubh* that had recently been purchased for £70 through Judge Wylie.

Despite the well planned itinerary, this French trip was not without its hitches. On the way from Saumur to the south of France, Ged O'Dwyer was hit with a severe stomach bug. This meant that Aherne was immediately in at the deep end as a replacement. In his very first class, he took a fall and saw no further action at the event. On opening day, Dan Corry won *Roisín Dubh*'s purchase price when placed second on the little brown mare in the Grand Military International. By Thursday, O'Dwyer had recovered enough to ride *Oisin* to second in a jump-off class. He was then part of the team that was placed third behind Belgium in the Nations Cup, but he saved his best for the Sunday. With the difficult enough ride, *Oisin*, he won the main individual event of the show, the Loewenstein Cup. Even sixty-five years later, Ged still referred to this win as the most memorable moment of his career.[5] Unfortunately, at the Grand Prix prize-giving ceremony, the band played 'God Save the King' instead of 'The Soldier's Song', an indication of how little-known the Irish nation was at that time.

The team's improvement did not go unnoticed by its previous critic, Captain Montergon. He now commented:

> Ireland has indeed begun to swim and its swimming master, Colonel Rodzianko, chose the proper method: short leathers, firmly seated, and at the same time forward– watching closely for the 'short ones'. In a word, thoroughly up to date. The Irish have good jumpers, some of them remarkable jumpers, and they are trained to jump properly. They have thus gotten away from the uncontrolled and random jumping, that of taking fences in their stride, which I have observed in the English teams. We

shall see arise in the international sky new stars or rather a new constellation – the Irish Horse.

Kind words, indeed, that in time proved prophetic.[6]

The team had a further six months of intense instruction under Rodzianko prior to their next away trip, a return to France for the Nice show in April 1929. In the meantime, two more officers were selected to join the school – Lieutenant Jack Lewis from Crecora, County Limerick, and Tralee man, Lieutenant Dan Leonard. Jack Lewis had seen service in both the War of Independence and, on the Treaty side, in the Civil War. He became one of the most successful riders with the army team during the thirties. In the post-war years, he served as OC of the school from 1945 to 1949.

Jack later went on to be the first Director General of the Showjumping Association of Ireland. Dan Leonard's early military experience was during World War I with the British Army, in which he held the rank of Captain. He joined the Irish Army in 1922 as a private, but was commissioned a Lieutenant prior to his appointment to the Equitation School in 1929. A most dapper man, he was one of the first

army riders to sport the new dress uniforms in 1935.

Named on the team for Nice, along with O'Dwyer and Corry, were recent additions Fred Aherne and Tom Finlay. They had eleven horses with them in the care of eight grooms under the command of Tipperary man Sergeant Major Paddy Dunne, who was to become something of a legend within the school. His keen sense of a horse's needs made him a most valuable advisor, not only to the Irish riders but to those of other countries as well.

## GROOM, PADDY DUNNE

Like so many of the men and women who have looked after the army horses down the years, Paddy Dunne combined a love of the horse and a great deal of common sense with a wonderful sense of humour to accomplish what, at all times, is a most responsible job. Born in Tipperary in 1898, Paddy worked on a number of local stud farms prior to joining the army in 1922. Four years later, when the Equitation School was set up, he became one of its first grooms. Promoted to Sergeant Major, he headed up the grooming section during the twenties and thirties. He was given great credit by the riders for his management of the horses during the team's early trips to the USA and Canada. Ged O'Dwyer, in particular, never failed to give him mention whenever he was interviewed. He once told this author that during their many trips abroad,

Paddy acquired a worldwide reputation for finding solutions to equine problems. On one occasion he was called upon to help with a horse owned by Queen Wilhelmina of Holland. So happy was she with the outcome, she invited the whole Irish team to her hotel for a celebration. During the evening the bauld Paddy offered to buy the queen a drink. 'Whatever you are having yourself,' she said, so he got her a Guinness. He was held in such esteem by the riding officers that at his funeral in November 1946, Dan Corry, Ged O'Dwyer, Tom Finlay and Fred Aherne acted as pall bearers.

Among the well known names that followed Paddy Dunne in the role of head groom were Sergeant Majors James Daly, Walter Smith, Steve Hickey, Paddy Watters, Martin Smith, and Company Sergeants Jimmy Dwyer,

Declan O'Connor and Paddy Byrne.

Up until the year 2000, head grooms at the school held the rank of Sergeant Major. Since 2000 Company Sergeants have held the post. Sergeant Major Steve Hickey, who was head groom from 1964 until 1984, describes the role played by this key person within the team: 'It was my responsibility to ensure that all grooms fulfilled their duties to the highest level. I inspected stables every morning and made sure both the horses and their tack were in proper order for the morning ride. The same applied to trips abroad when I also had the added responsibility of making travel arrangements for both horses and grooms.'

Being such a responsible and travel- demanding job, the selection of grooms from among the Non Commissioned Officers from within the Artillery and Transport Corps was taken very seriously. Down through the years, all of these grooms have had one main purpose: to place the horses under their care at the disposal of the riders in the best form possible. The Irish Army grooms, both male and female, have retained a superb reputation among their confrères on the international circuit. Their green fatigues became a familiar sight at shows abroad, and, along with the riders and horses they serve, they are part of the good image that the Irish Army Equitation School has consistently presented, both at home and abroad.

The 1929 trip to Nice proved to be something of an early turning point in Rodzianko's relationship with army management. Apparently for financial reasons, the Colonel was not allowed to travel with the team. His absence at this early stage of the team's transformation proved to be a devastating psychological blow. In the Nations Cup they placed last of the seven countries taking part.

Dispirited, they returned home for two weeks prior to heading out again in early May for their first attempt at the Belgian Cup in Brussels. During this break, they must have made a very strong plea to have financial difficulties put aside in order that Rodzianko could travel with them for the rest of the season. He was allowed go to Brussels and immediately put his stamp on proceedings by ordering that the team horses be walked the twelve miles from the city to the show grounds at Genval. Among the group was a young gelding called *Finghin Og*, that just three months previously had been pulling a cart on the Curragh. He was, in fact, to give a great morale boost to the side when he and Ged O'Dwyer won the opening event of the show. Using other new mounts, like *Ballinagore, Slievenamon* and *Mourne Abbey*, the team got well into the prizes throughout the tournament. The team of Aherne, O'Dwyer, Corry and Finlay came third in the Nations Cup behind Italy and France. Their total winnings for the week amounted to 6,000 Belgian francs. All in all, the show proved a good build-up to the next big test at Olympia, where they were making their return two years on from the disaster of 1927.

At this time, not only were the riders on a stiff learning curve, the same could be said of the school's administrative staff. Colonel Liam Hoolan still held the post of OC, but he did not travel with the team. Instead, there was a series of what might be called 'travelling OCs'. Colonel Michael Hogan served in this role for Biarritz in 1928. Commandant Tom Foxe was in charge at Nice in 1929. For Brussels, Colonel JJ 'Ginger' O'Connell, a legendary army figure, was given this duty. A most colourful individual, Ginger had a master's degree in Education and had done a tour with the US Army before taking part in the Easter Rising. He served a period of internment and was an assistant Chief of Staff during the War of Independence. In 1922 his imprisonment by the anti-Treaty forces in the Four Courts precipitated the start of the Civil War. When peace came, he remained in the army and rose to the rank of Colonel. For a short period he was OC to the school. He was also author of the military history book, *The Irish Wars*.

O'Connell's trip to Brussels was not without incident. At show's end, he presented a tricolour to the manager of the hotel where the team stayed. When the item appeared on the expense sheet, it was severely questioned by the financial controller and Ginger ended up having to pay for it out of his own pocket. This was symptomatic of the administrative problems the team faced in those early years. There were great demands on the country's finances from every direction, and it is understandable that for some of those controlling the purse strings a request for a new piece of ordnance or better food in the canteen would supersede the sometimes ad hoc needs of the new equestrian school. One constant irritant between the school and the Department of Finance was the matter of out-of-pocket expenses incurred by both riders and grooms during trips abroad. The riders were put up by each show in top-class hotels. That was fine, but it meant rubbing shoulders with well-financed officers from other teams. Their own daily allowances came nowhere near covering the incidental outlays for clothes, food and city travel. Another expense was the traditional but very costly 'filling of the cup' for trophies they won. Eventually, after an exchange of many letters with the Department of Finance, the daily rate for riders was raised from five shillings to seven shillings and sixpence. The grooms' allowance went from two shillings to half a crown.

For the London Olympia trip in mid-June of 1929, Captain Ged O'Dwyer was put in charge of the squad, along with Rodzianko. It proved to be their most successful away action to date – a far cry from their neophyte efforts just two years previously. Over eight days of jumping, they took first, second or third placings no less than thirty-four times. Included in the wins was the prestigious Duke of Connaught Cup, won, appropriately enough, by Connaught man Captain Dan Corry on *Slievenamon*. Dan also won a military competition with *An Craobh Ruadh*. In another military event, Ged O'Dwyer scored again on his big Biarritz winner, *Oisin*. And instead of coming last in the Prince of Wales Cup, the Irish were third this time.

In another bit of good news from this season, the team returned home to compete at Tipperary and Tullamore shows with a string of horses that were all different from those used in London. The McKee stable was growing.

Next was Dublin, where O'Dwyer on *Finghin*, Cyril Harty on *Turoe* and Tom Finlay on *Cuchulainn* hoped to retain the Aga Khan Trophy. They came very close to doing just that when, after two rounds, they pushed the French to a tie-breaking jump-off. The French won the jump-off by a single point: 140 to 139. But for the home crowd it amounted to a moral victory to see their team come so close once more, ahead of five visiting sides from Sweden, Switzerland, Britain, Belgium – and the USA, who were jumping at Dublin for the first time.

That autumn, following successful visits to the Ennis and Moate shows, the team made their first trip to the tough North American circuit. In terms of their core purposes of advertising both Ireland and the Irish horse, this was an important next step in their development. At shows in both Boston and New York, the emigrant Irish turned out in

big numbers to give them the most loving of warm welcomes. In both cities, the team was the subject of civil receptions. However, from a competition point of view, the trip proved to be something of a bridge too far. While it served as a stiff learning mission, it did not bring any top prizes. Just as with Olympia, the team promised they would be back and that things would be different.

On their return from the States, the team's gruelling training regime under Rodzianko resumed once more as they prepared for the 1930 season. New Recruit Lieutenant JJ Lewis had his first significant win on an army horse when he took one of the main competitions at that year's Spring Show on *Edgar's Pride*. At about the same time, Dan Leonard made his international debut at Brussels, where the team began its 1930 season. With *Roisin Dubh*, he was narrowly beaten in an opening day jump-off. Throughout the week-long event, the Irish won a total of 7,000 Belgian francs. In the Nations Cup, Fred Aherne on *Aherlow*, Tom Finlay with *Moonstruck*, Cyril Harty on *Slievenamon* and Ged O'Dwyer on *Finghin* came third behind Switzerland and Italy.

Following their return from Belgium, it was announced on 12 June that Colonel Liam Hayes would take over as OC of the school. He was a distant relative of Ged O'Dwyer and had been closely involved with him during both the War of Independence and the Civil War. His son, the great rider of the fifties and sixties, Seamus Hayes, would become trainer of the army team in the late fifties. His grandson, Captain William Hayes, was a member of the school in the 1990s.

From the start, Liam Hayes had taken the keenest possible interest in the new venture and had scouted for a number of horses for the school. He now took a very hands-on approach during his two-year term as OC. A two-show trip to Olympia and Lucerne was next on the 1929 schedule. In a very specific memorandum from the Quartermaster General, Colonel EV O'Carroll, it was noted that Ged O'Dwyer should be team leader, while Rodzianko would have responsibility for instruction and the selection of riders for the Nations Cups. At London, the team of Finlay on *Turoe*, Corry on *Slievenamon* and O'Dwyer on *An Craobh Ruadh* put up a good fight but they finished third. At Lucerne the Irish came fourth out of five.

Looking at these results – two thirds and a fourth – the administration at home might well have once again questioned the value of their expensive instructor. A delay in Rodzianko's travelling from London to Lucerne did not help matters. The reason given was illness, but when medical certificates were demanded, they were not forthcoming. Another difficulty arising at the time was over dress uniforms for the team. When they travelled, both Rodzianko and the team itself had to attend dress functions in their regular riding gear, while others had ornate uniforms at their disposal. It was to be five more years before this problem was solved and officers' dress uniforms were procured.

It is obvious from reading the archives of the time that the riders had full confidence in Rodzianko. They were hungry to learn what he had to teach and they wanted his expertise with them, not only at home in McKee, but at shows abroad as well. Their views were not fully shared by those controlling the army purse. Reading between the lines in a number of exchanges during 1930, it would appear that the Russian was seen as something of a handful, whose aristocratic lifestyle added extra costs to his already expensive basic wage. As the year progressed, it became rather obvious that, despite the great value placed upon him by the riders themselves, Rodzianko's differences with the administration meant that his days at McKee were numbered. One comment found in the Advisory Group minutes of 15 December 1930 says it all, 'He is a very difficult man to get on with.' However, at that same time he was offered an extension of his tour. He did get to be an Irish Colonel – a rank he had also attained in Britain, but for some reason he did not reply to the offer of a tour extension.[7]

At Dublin that year the newer faults system rather than the accumulative points scoring was used for the first time. This did not help Ireland and they finished in fourth place on a score of 26, behind Switzerland who won with 17. On that year's American circuit

*Below*:
*Capt. Dan Leonard and
Miss Ireland jumping
the wall at 1931
Tralee Show.*
*(Joan Parker)*

they won more prize money than on their inaugural tour but the Nations Cup results were still fairly disappointing as they came third in the Nations Cup at both Boston and Toronto, and fourth in New York. This was a bit less than the expectant Irish in those three cities would have hoped for.

Sometime between the team's return from the States and the start of the 1931 season, Rodzianko's term came to an end. His leaving was much like his arrival – without any degree of documentation. But his legacy has lived on in the Army Equitation School's riding method to this day. International rider and later OC of the school, Colonel Billy Ringrose, put it this way: 'He introduced the latest and the best developments to the school during this period. After his contract terminated his methods were adhered to by the riders he had trained and this was one of the telling factors in their success.'[8]

But at the time, for the young, still relatively inexperienced officers at the school, Rodzianko's leaving must have been like losing a father figure, and no doubt they wondered how they could survive without his constant instruction and correction.

# 3
# LIFE AFTER RODZIANKO

## 1931 to 1933

*'Right or wrong, keep going'*
*Ged O'Dwyer[1]*

It is no great exaggeration to say that following the departure of Colonel Rodzianko, the still young Army Equitation School was like a family orphaned. They had, indeed, learned much during the three short years that he had been with them as mentor and instructor in the art of modern riding, yet within each of the still-novice officers, there was a sense of dependency that lingered after his leaving. But, in the spirit of the times, they saddled up and soldiered on. Captain Ged O'Dwyer was appointed school instructor and team leader. Some forty-five years later, Ged had this down-to-earth recollection of that time of change: 'From the floor of our School, in between riding my horses, I endeavoured to ensure that the Maestro's teaching received strict adherence. We had been competing at international shows since 1926 with little success, but all the while our knowledge of training and riding had been improving.'[2]

At the end of 1930, three new riders joined the school – Lieutenants James Neylon, George Heffernan and Louis McGee. McGee was from Dublin, Neylon hailed from Corofin, County Clare, and Heffernan was a native of Athy, County Kildare. Along with Neylon, Heffernan had been in the first ever cadet class of 1929. The two men had both got top ranking, and they came to the Equitation School together. At the time of the school's fiftieth anniversary, then Colonel James F Neylon (retd.) recalled his days of joining: 'Colonel Paul Rodzianko, in addition to training the existing riders, also sought new blood. On passing out as a cadet in the first cadet class, recruited by competitive examination in 1929, I was selected for a trial in the Equitation School. During our

*Above:*
*Having taken over as trainer of the army team after Colonel Rodzianko's departure in 1932, Ged O'Dwyer described the methods used in this booklet.*

officer training it was necessary to do a two-month riding and driving course with the horse artillery. At the final parade, two of us, George Heffernan and I, were selected for further equitation training under Colonel Rodzianko. Having done advanced training at McKee Barracks from November 1930, I won my first competition on a horse called *Edgar's Pride* at the RDS Spring Show in May 1931.' [3]

Ged O'Dwyer's lifelong motto was, 'Right or wrong keep going', and never was that resolve more tested than during the team's first show of 1931 in Nice. Just about everything conspired against them – rider injuries, new and more technical competitions and the first use of a fixed time allowed in each event. Even prior to their departure, Captain Dan Corry sustained a serious injury and was unable to travel. Making up the side were Captains O'Dwyer and Finlay, along with Lieutenants Fred Aherne and Dan Leonard. Soon after their arrival at the show, Fred Aherne hurt his arm and was just about able to continue. In every competition entered, they finished well down the line. Tom Finlay took the wrong course in the Nations Cup and the Irish four accumulated a massive total of 232 faults for second-last place out of the nine countries taking part. To say they were obviously missing Rodzianko is an understatement.

Despite some new intakes of horses during 1930 they still had only a small number at their disposal. O'Dwyer referred to this concern in an article published early the following year in *An t-Óglach*: 'Our position has been and still is very difficult. Owing to the shortage of horses, the same mounts must be used indoor and outdoor.' [4] Nice was jumped outdoors, and it has to be said that the results from there in 1931 did not fully reflect the team's true form. This fact was borne out during their next series of shows to Brussels, London and Lucerne. Having arrived home from Nice at the end of April, they were due in Brussels by 12 May. During the interval they had a chance to become more familiar with some new horses that had recently arrived at the school.

Included among them was a future legend named *Limerick Lace*. This six-year-old chestnut gelding, by the thoroughbred sire *Forest Prince*, had been purchased at Roscrea fair by Limerickman Joe Hogan, and sold on to the army in November 1930 for £275. He was to win that amount many times over during a sterling career that lasted until 1939.

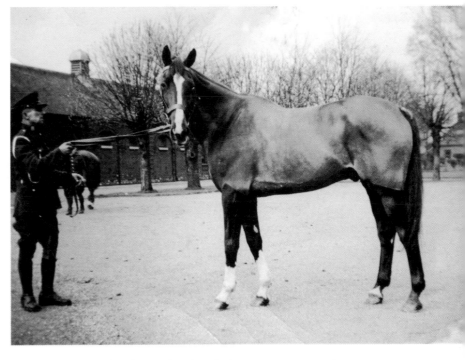

*Above:*
*A young* Limerick Lace, *soon after he arrived at McKee Barracks in 1931.*
(Joan Parker)

At the Brussels show of 1931, matters improved for the Irish side of Aherne, Harty, Leonard and O'Dwyer. In the opening four-horse relay competition, the Irish had a morale-boosting win. Throughout the ten-day show, they were placed in every competition entered and accumulated winnings of 11,000 Belgian francs. But their best result came in the five-team Nations Cup. After two tough rounds, they were tied for first place with the Italians, whose hugely experienced side finally won out in the jump-off. At the show's conclusion, all the official teams were presented to the King and Queen of Belgium. But Ged insisted that the grooms attend as well. In his report of the trip in the school's log book he had particular praise for the grooms, whom he described as 'the smartest of soldiers that left nothing to be desired.'[5]

It was on to London after that, and one more bid at winning the prestigious Prince of Wales Cup. For the first time, five riders were sent – Captains Dan Corry and Tom Finlay, along with good Brussels performers O'Dwyer, Aherne and Harty. Colonel Liam Hayes was in charge. Lieutenant Aherne on *Blarney Castle* began well by sharing first place with Lieutenant Zavier Bizard of France in the Holland Cup. This wonderful bay gelding would bring Fred some of his greatest wins in the years ahead. The Irish challenged well in the Prince of Wales and were lying a close second after the first round, but dropped back to fourth behind France, Holland and Britain. In his school log report, Colonel Hayes gave full credit to the team's efforts at Olympia, but, oddly enough, he expressed the view that as a result of his severe injury earlier in the year Captain Dan Corry had lost some of his nerve. Dan did not take long to prove that theory wrong in the months ahead.

The outdoor event at Lucerne was next and travelling there were Captains Corry, Finlay and Harty, along with Ged O'Dwyer, who had just been promoted to Commandant. Following the Rodzianko tactic, the Irish exercised remarkable restraint during the early days of the show and held their fire for the big one. As if to celebrate his promotion, Ged delivered a superb first clear round on the not-overly talented *Rosnaree*. Cyril Harty jumped a clear and a twelve on *Kilmallock*. Tom Finlay had had eight faults in the first round and four in the second on *Moonstruck*. The final result came down to Ged. For the second time in the contest, he steered *Rosnaree* clear and gave Ireland its first away Nations Cup win. In what was a high-scoring event, Ireland took

first place, with 24 faults. Switzerland came second at 28, and the Italian team that had just beaten them in Brussels were third, with 32. Further down the line came Belgium, France and Hungary. It was an exultant jumping team that arrived back at McKee Barracks in mid-July to begin preparations for Dublin. Included in their build-up was a trip to the Clonmel Show, where Commandant Ged O'Dwyer jumped the great *Limerick Lace* in public for the first time. Despite being just a young six-year-

*Above:*
*After winning their first away Nations Cup at Lucerne in 1931, the Irish team of Ged O'Dwyer, Dan Corry, Tom Finlay and Cyril Harty celebrate with a trip to the Lido.*
*(Donal Corry)*

old, the talented gelding was included among the school's entry for Ballsbridge.

Living up to their well-publicised Lucerne success was going to be difficult at Dublin Horse Show, which, for the first time, had eight visiting teams taking part. Captain Dan Corry got the Irish off to a very good start in the Puissance competition. Determined to contradict criticism of his London performance, he powered to a win on *Finghin* ahead of Olympic gold medalist for Italy, Captain Tomaso Lequoi. Corry also had a second to Britain's Major Joe Hume-Dudgeon in Thursday's Swiss Cavalry Cup.

The Aga Khan that year was a closely fought affair, which Britain won with 16 faults, ahead of Sweden at 21. The Irish side of O'Dwyer, Harty and Aherne came third, with 23. As evidence of the popularity of the Irish horse at this time, a full 50 percent of the mounts taking part in this competition had been bred in Ireland.

Determined to make amends for two previous disappointing trips across the Atlantic, the team of Corry, Harty, O'Dwyer and newly promoted Captain Fred Aherne next headed out on a tour that would take them to Boston, New York and Toronto. At Boston Garden, they had wins in the pairs competition and in the Myopia Cup (for which they rode borrowed horses from members of the famous Myopia Hunt Club in Essex County). But in the Nations Cup there they were placed a disappointing fifth. At New York their best result came in the three-horse relay Westchester Cup, in which they took both first and second.

At the Great Toronto Winter Fair, the Irish were all but invisible over the first five days of the show. But when it came to the Nations Cup, they were very much in view. In a re-shuffle of mounts, O'Dwyer took up the ride on Fred Aherne's usual mount *Turoe*; Cyril Harty was on Dan Corry's *Shannon Power*, while Aherne went with the six-year-old *Blarney Castle*. The re-shuffle worked as they convincingly won the Nations Cup Ferguson Trophy. Over the two rounds, the Irish did not knock a single fence and ended on a total of only two time penalties. This, their second away win, and in the same year at that, was a very satisfying end to the 1931 season. It certainly gave members of the Equitation School additional confidence as they entered into a time of great challenge, change and uncertainty in Irish history.

The year 1932 was a period of change both in Irish politics and in the Equitation School itself. The men at McKee had to deal with the new Fianna Fáil government that came to power in March of that year. And over the following twelve months there were three changes of Officers Commanding. In January 1932, Colonel Liam Hayes was promoted to the rank of Major General and appointed to the post of Adjutant General of the Army. Commandant Ged O'Dwyer was named Acting OC until a replacement was appointed later that year. One of his first actions in this new post was to seek what was to be a pivotal meeting with the Quartermaster General, Colonel EV O'Carroll. His aim was to gain greater exposure for the team in the most important international competitions. 'I made the following suggestion, viz, that our team should try to win only the most important events at future international shows. My reason was that the Nations Cup, the Puissance and big speed competitions get press coverage in many countries. Apart from prestige value, such press coverage should create a wider market for Irish horses. My suggestion was approved and it remained our policy until World War II.'[6] Although not mentioned at that time, it is clear from what happened over the next few years that his ultimate goal was of Olympic proportions. But more of that later.

Joining the school at the beginning of this new year was a most enthusiastic Ennis, County Clare, man, Lieutenant Tom Quinn. He competed for the rest of the 1930s, served with the army during the World War II years and retired with the rank of Commandant in 1945. From that time on, he was always a gracious host in his home town whenever the army team visited there for the annual County Clare Agricultural Show, on 15 August each year. His nephew, Jimmy, rode with the team during the sixties.

The coming to power of Éamon De Valera's Fianna Fáil Government in March 1932 created uncertainty within McKee Barracks as to the school's future. It is difficult for us in another century to place ourselves in the mindset of that time, which was less than ten years on from the end of the Civil War, but one cannot forget that many of the riding officers had fought on the opposite side to Dev during that war, which left such divisive memories throughout the whole country. It must be remembered too that within a very short time (19 February 1933) Equitation School founder Colonel Michael Hogan was arrested in a dramatic midnight raid on his home and put on trial under the new Official Secrets Act. The charge was that he had passed some sensitive documents from the previous Cosgrave government on to his brother James, who was a professor of history at University College Cork. In what has been described as 'a farcical trial' Hogan was found not guilty.[7] Thus, during this period of transition, some, including Acting OC Ged O'Dwyer, were fearful that Dev's new Government might close the school. The feeling of that time within McKee is well reflected in Thomas

Toomey's memoir, *Forgotten Dreams*: 'February 1932 saw the ascent to power of Fianna Fáil under the leadership of Éamon de Valera and for many in the army it was an uneasy time as only nine years previously they had claimed victory in a very bitter Civil War against many of those who had now come to power. The newly appointed Minister for Defence was Frank Aiken, who had been Chief of Staff of the IRA at the time of the ceasefire, at the end of the Civil War.'[8] Some sixty years later, in an interview for the *Farmer's Journal*, Ged O'Dwyer still maintained that Dev was not a great friend of the school.

Despite all of this, the school did survive, and indeed thrive, during the early years of the new Fianna Fáil Government. On 15 March, when he took office De Valera himself said: 'We heard of frightful things that would happen the moment Fianna Fáil came into power. We have seen no evidence of these things. We have had a peaceful change of government.'[9]

During the early days of his new administration, Dev made a point of inspecting troops on horseback. Also, at that time, the mounted ceremonial Blue Hussar unit was initiated. With Commandant Ged O'Dwyer at its head, it had its first official outing at the great Eucharistic Congress which took place in June of 1932. Just as it still is, the horse was central to the image of Ireland at that time and as part of that important image the Equitation School was perhaps more secure than it realised. In addition, as already mentioned, the two away wins, one of which had happened in the important zone of North America, must have helped bolster the position of the school at this time of change. However, it has to be said that later on in the mid-thirties, the Army Equitation School's role would be politicised to a degree that it had not known under the Cosgrave administration.

## THE BLUE HUSSARS

At the end of 1931, a mounted unit known as the 'Blue Hussars' was formed and trained at McKee Barracks. It was composed of soldiers from various corps, including the Transport and Artillery section, which at that time was still using some horses. Separate from the Equitation School, it was intended to be used as an escort for visiting dignitaries and to present a special equine image of

Ireland on ceremonial occasions. Its most remembered role was that played in the Eucharistic Congress of 1932 when it acted as escort for the papal legate, Cardinal Lorenzo Lauri, who arrived at Dun Laoghaire on 20 June. From there, he was escorted to the Phoenix Park by the Blue Hussars, led on this occasion by Comdt. Ged O'Dwyer, who had just returned from jumping with the Irish team at Rome. The Blue Hussars continued in existence until the beginning of World War II. It was re-constituted in 1946, but soon after the coming to power of Taoiseach John A Costello's coalition government, it finally came to an end in 1949. One of its riders in those later years was Sergeant Major Steve Hickey, who went on to be head groom with the Equitation School and later one of the world's leading showjumping course builders between 1975 and 2000. He built the courses for the World Championships at the RDS in 1982.

For the Nice, Rome and Brussels tour of 1932, some new ground was broken in terms of both riders and horses. Lieutenant Jack Lewis was having his first major international outing with the team and so were horses like *Kilmallock*, *Miss Ireland*, *Ireland's Own* and *Limerick Lace*. Lewis clearly indicated his worth by winning the Prix Pierre Gautier at Nice with *Kilmallock*, and then taking the Trofeo Campodoghlio in Rome. So too did *Limerick Lace*, who jumped well to be runner-up in the Nice Grand Prix. However, apart from these good successes, this three-show tour was not a great advertisement for a team that was anxious to prove its worth with the new Government: at least three horses and two riders were temporarily injured during the events. In terms of Nations Cups, the side of O'Dwyer, Lewis, Lieutenant Dan Leonard and Dan Corry were placed last of eight in Nice, and with injuries to both horses and riders not yet mended, they did not even start in the Cup competition at Rome. However, despite a harrowing train journey through Switzerland and Germany, during which visas and travel permit checks were constant irritants, they improved to be joint second in Brussels. Whatever about the Government as a whole, there was still strong support for the team's efforts within the army administration. For example, we have this assessment of their progress from keen equestrian observer Colonel J J O'Connell, who acted as OC of the Equitation School from March to June of 1932: 'And where do our own officers – and horses – stand. The fairest test of them is not in Dublin, but elsewhere. They are regarded as quite respectable adversaries; as a team they must be taken into account and they manage "to get in on the money" with reasonable regularity. Give them time and reasonable facilities and they will be all right.'[10]

During this spring 1932 tour, the team fulfilled one of its many diplomatic duties when it was presented to Benito Mussolini. Ged O'Dwyer later noted of this meeting that it was not a happy experience since he felt the Italian leader exuded a 'sense of arrogant aggression'.[11]

*Above*:
*The Mussolini medallion presented to the Irish team at Rome Show.*
*(Pat Quinn)*

But as part of its brief, particularly within a Europe going through major changes, the officers of the Equitation School were ambassadors on horseback and they fulfilled that role even in situations that were not all that pleasant.

During this period of profound political change in Ireland, the team's diplomatic role on the home front was no less difficult. For example, that spring, 1932, the army received an unprecedented invitation from the Royal Ulster Agricultural Society for the team to compete at its upcoming Balmoral Show in Belfast. However, the invitation was turned down and a further sixty years would go by before a uniformed army officer would showjump north of the border (see Chapter 10). Other incidents illustrating the strained Anglo–Irish relations of the time happened at the Olympia show in London, which the team next attended in July 1932. In charge of the team was Colonel Fred Bennett, who had just taken over from Colonel J J O'Connell as the fourth OC of the school. Armagh-born Bennett had served with Frank Aiken during the War of Independence. He took the Treaty side in the Civil War and entered the army as a captain in 1923. On two occasions during the London event he was called upon to assert Ireland's identity as a new nation. Early in the show, when Captain Fred Aherne won the prestigious Holland Cup on *Ireland's Own*, instead of playing 'The Soldier's Song', the military band in attendance played 'St Patrick's Day' in what was considered to be a fast, undignified jig pace. When Colonel Bennett protested to show director Lord Lonsdale, it appears he was told in no uncertain terms that there was only one national anthem for the British Isles and that was 'God Save the King'. The matter became something of a diplomatic incident and was referred to the Irish High Commissioner in London. Later in the show, there was further controversy when on the advice of the Irish Department of External Affairs, headed by President De Valera himself, the Irish team did not participate in the Duke of Connaught Cup. This cup was confined to horses and riders from the British Commonwealth and any hint at this time that Ireland should be treated as a member of the Commonwealth was anathema to the new Government in Dublin[12] Oddly enough, Dan Corry had won the Connaught Cup back in 1929 without a word being said about it.

It has to be remembered that all of this happened just weeks after De Valera had informed Britain that his new Government was abolishing the Oath of Allegiance to the king. There was also his declaration at Arbour Hill cemetery on 23 April: 'Let it be made clear that we yield no willing assent to any form or symbol that is out of keeping with Ireland's right as a sovereign nation. Let us remove these forms one by one so that this state that we control may be a Republic in fact.'[13] For the next four years, the British did not jump at the Dublin Horse Show, and this may well be another result of the strained Anglo–Irish relations at that time.

The team of Aherne, O'Dwyer, Tom Finlay and George Heffernan were placed third in the 1932 Prince of Wales Cup behind France and Britain, before returning to McKee in preparation for Ballsbridge. And they reaped rewards; for, in addition to a number of good placings throughout the week, the three-member Irish selection side of Fred Aherne on *Ireland's Own*, Dan Leonard on *Miss Ireland* and Ged O'Dwyer on *Limerick Lace* won the Aga Khan Cup for Ireland's second time. Ged and the now brilliantly coming-of-age *Limerick Lace* also took the Grand Prix, and, for good measure, Ged was second as well on *Kilmallock*. It was a stunning home performance.

Buoyed by this home success and despite financial constraints, the team again took on the North American circuit in the fall of that year. For the first time in his career, Ged O'Dwyer did not travel with the squad. Instead, at home in McKee, he awaited results recorded by his team mates Dan Corry, Fred Aherne and Jim Neylon. The news was good as the trio swept to victory in the Nations Cup at Boston. The Irish had been knocking at the door there for a couple of years, but this time they took the cup after

an exciting jump-off with France. In that jump-off, Corry was the hero as he delivered a final, winning, clear round on *Shannon Power*. The win was greeted with a standing ovation from a Boston crowd that included a large contingent of emigrant Irish. It also got detailed coverage in both the Boston and the home newspapers. Such a win in such a place as Boston must have been sweet music to the ears of a new Government that looked so much to the USA for support in these difficult times. In his St Patrick's Day radio address to the people of the USA earlier that year, Dev had sought that support.

In addition to the Nations Cup win, the Irish also took the pairs event at Boston Garden. And the grooms had their moment of glory as well when the Irish lads came out on top in a special grooms' competition.

Nations Cup wins eluded the Irish in both New York and Toronto that year. But at Madison Square Garden they did take the three-horse relay Westchester Cup for the second year in a row. Then, before a cheering crowd of eleven thousand, Dan Corry swept to victory in the International Military Sweepstake with *Shannon Power* – a horse aptly named for the progress being made at that time in bringing electric power to the Irish countryside.

*Above*:
Captain Dan Corry helping unload the team horses at Boston prior to their Nations Cup win there in 1932. Left to right: Sliabh na mBan, Shannon Power, Gallowglass *and* Blarney Castle.
*(Donal Corry)*

*Opposite top*:
Westchester Cup, won
three times in a row by
the Irish at New York in
the thirties and which
now resides at
McKee Barracks.
(Army Equitation School)

**Opposite bottom**:
Despite desperately
missing the guidance of
Colonel Rodzianko,
Captain Ged O'Dwyer
puts on a good show as
he leads out the Irish
team that includes James
Neylon, Dan Leonard
and Fred Aherne in the
parade at Nice 1931.
(Joan Parker)

At the Great Winter Fair in Toronto, Corry, Aherne and Neylon each delivered a win that made up for the fact that they did not retain the Ferguson Cup. However, with a Nations Cup win and five other quality firsts to their credit, this 1932 American tour had been the army side's most successful to date. Even forty-four years later, this, his first international outing still held very positive memories for Colonel Jim Neylon: 'This US–Canadian tour was noted for the fact that it was the first time a team from our Equitation School had won a large number of first prizes on a tour. As I write, on the mantelpiece is a silver cigar cassette presented to the team at a dinner in the RDS on 12 January 1933. The inscription reads: PRESENTED BY IRISH FRIENDS TO COMMEMORATE THE TEAM'S NOTEABLE SUCCESSES.[14]

All in all, the year of change, 1932, had turned out quite well with two Nations Cup wins plus firsts in ten other international competitions. Colonel J J O'Connell's words of 'give them time and they will be all right' were beginning to ring true. As members of the school mulled over these results during the Christmas break, the kernel of a new dream began to take more definite shape: an equestrian Olympic medal for a new nation. Hence it was that the very first show attended by the Irish Army jumping team in 1933 was Berlin, venue for the next Olympic Games in 1936. From that moment on, team plans in terms of both horses and riders were focused on one main glorious goal – that of beating the Germans on their home ground for Olympic gold. On this occasion, in January 1933, just weeks prior to Adolf Hitler's coming to power, they had an encouraging start to that campaign as the home team beat them by only a single fence.

That long 1933 season was a new learning curve for the army side, as they took in more shows than in any of their previous years – Berlin, Nice, Rome, Brussels, Lucerne, Dublin, Chicago, New York and Toronto. It was also a year of struggle as they tried new horse-and-rider combinations, and along the way, injuries, both human and equine, hindered their path. Fourth in Nice, seventh in Rome, sixth in Brussels, fifth in Lucerne tells its own story. But matters began to improve after that as the Irish came second to France at Dublin.

With finance still a problem, just three riders were sent on the 1933 North American tour. Captain Dan Corry, who was in charge, was joined by Captains Fred Aherne and Cyril Harty. Matters went well enough for them on their first visit to Chicago as Corry on *Shannon Power* and Aherne on *Ireland's Own* scored individual wins, while Corry on *Slievenamon* and Aherne on *Ireland's Own* teamed up to take the pair event. However, their curtailed team of three hit a major snag at Madison Square Garden when it was discovered that the relay event there had been changed to teams of four. The matter was solved when Corry called on one of his grooms to fill the extra slot. Twenty-seven-year-old Cavan man William Finlay did the honours on the difficult ride *Ireland's Own* to help Ireland win the event. On this, the first and only occasion in which one of the grooms rode an army horse in major international competition, Captain Corry insisted that Private Finlay ride forward to receive the Westchester Cup. According to newspaper reports of the event, Finlay got a massive reception from the packed Madison Square crowd.

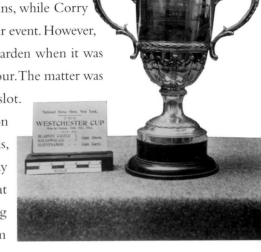

They saved the best until last as Aherne on *Blarney Castle*, Corry on *Shannon Power* and Harty on Ged O'Dwyer's usual ride *Limerick Lace* took the Ferguson Cup in Toronto ahead of Sweden, USA, Canada and Czechoslovakia.

In many ways, the years 1932 and 1933 had been transition years – dealing with the new Government, changes of Officers Commanding, new shows, new horses and the initiation of new riders. But overall, while not as successful (three firsts) in terms of Nations Cup competition as the team would have hoped or would have wished, over the two seasons they did score a total of forty individual international wins. That had to give the riders extra hope as they faced the season of 1934.

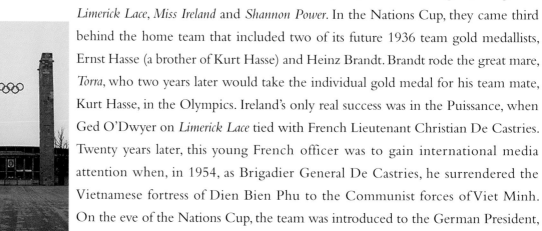

# 4

# THE OLYMPIC DREAM

## 1934 to 1936

*'Forget the worm's opinion too*
*Of hooves and pointed harrow pins,*
*For you are driving your horses through*
*The mist where Genesis begins.'*
*Patrick Kavanagh*[1]

**B**y the beginning of 1934, the Olympic dream had well and truly taken hold within the Army Equitation School. As proof of this, they again made the Berlin show their first outing of the season – they had to test themselves once more in the very place that would be the Olympic crucible of 1936. In Berlin, they experienced the highly charged atmosphere of Nazi Germany where Olympic glory in all disciplines, not least in the equestrian, was to be promoted as evidence of German superiority in all things. At a dinner on the eve of the 1934 show, their host, General Hermann Goering, stated: 'This tournament should not only promote the cause of international sport, but will also provide the foreign guests with a view of the modern Germany as well.'[2]

For this exploratory outing, Commandant Ged O'Dwyer, and Captains Aherne, Corry and Leonard travelled two of their newer mounts, *Sarsfield* and *Gallowglass*, along with

*Limerick Lace, Miss Ireland* and *Shannon Power*. In the Nations Cup, they came third behind the home team that included two of its future 1936 team gold medallists, Ernst Hasse (a brother of Kurt Hasse) and Heinz Brandt. Brandt rode the great mare, *Torra*, who two years later would take the individual gold medal for his team mate, Kurt Hasse, in the Olympics. Ireland's only real success was in the Puissance, when Ged O'Dwyer on *Limerick Lace* tied with French Lieutenant Christian De Castries. Twenty years later, this young French officer was to gain international media attention when, in 1954, as Brigadier General De Castries, he surrendered the Vietnamese fortress of Dien Bien Phu to the Communist forces of Viet Minh. On the eve of the Nations Cup, the team was introduced to the German President,

Lt. Leonard     Cd. O'Dwyer     Cl.e t Hogan     Cpt. Ahern     Cpt. Corry

Paul Von Hindenburg. This stately man was in very ill health at the time; he died later that year at the time of Dublin Horse Show and was honoured with a special ceremony in the Ballsbridge arena when Germany won the Aga Khan Cup.

The disappointment in Berlin in 1934 did not dampen the enthusiasm for gold in 1936. Recalling that time, Ged O'Dwyer said, 'We wanted that medal, and none more than me.'[3]

Following Berlin, there appears to have been a clear-cut decision to stay on home ground for a time, bringing on some newer mounts that might well help realise the golden dream. On an annual budget of about £2,000, the school was buying between four and seven horses annually. So, new names began appearing on their show entry sheets – *Owen Roe*, *Duhallow* and *Red Hugh*. For the Dublin spring show in May of that year, they entered a total of twenty-three horses. Later in the season at other shows around the country, they brought out *Kilmallock*, *Beann Eadair* and *Glendalough*. O'Dwyer later wrote: 'Our horses were bought on their appearance only and none of them would have done any showjumping prior to purchase by us. Out of the horses acquired in this way, one in four emerged as an international winner. This we considered a very satisfactory average.'[4]

The team's next international appearances of 1934 were not until Olympia and Lucerne, in June and July. At both events they had superb individual results. In London, Captain Jack Lewis opened with a win on *Tramore Bay* in the Irish Army Cup, which

*Below:*
*Commandant Ged*
*O'Dwyer jumping*
*Limerick Lace to win*
*the Saorstát Éireann*
*Cup in 1934.*
*(RDS Library Archive)*

was donated to the show by Minister of Defence Frank Aiken; Cyril Harty and *Kilmallock* took the Bedlington Challenge Cup; Commandant Ged O'Dwyer, on *Blarney Castle*, beat British legend Colonel Mike Ansell in one main event, and was second in another. Over the duration of the show, Ged emerged as leading rider. Though the Irish had to settle for second place to a brilliant French side in the Prince of Wales Nations Cup, overall the show was an encouraging outing.

The good form continued at Lucerne, where Lewis and Aherne both scored wins and O'Dwyer swept to victory on *Blarney Castle* in the important Swiss Cavalry Cup. Once again, they slotted into second place behind France in the Nations Cup. But it was a team with growing confidence that returned home to face six visiting sides at Dublin. Despite heavy rain on Aga Khan day, the traditional pageantry was in no way dampened. The scene is beautifully described here in one onlooker's memory of the show:

It was a thrilling and memorable moment when, in the presence of twenty thousand people, with the flags of the seven nations fluttering from their standards, the first nations entered the famous arena. To the music of a stirring martial tune, the German team of horsemen came slowly down the ground. Then, wheeling, they faced the thousands of distinguished people filling tier upon tier, with Lord Powerscourt, the

Society's President and President De Valera in the centre. After Germany came Sweden, the Netherlands, Belgium, France, Switzerland, each in turn saluted by the anthem of their country and each cheered to the echo by people deeply moved by the grandeur of this symbolic pageantry. But the appearance of the Irish team let loose all the pent-up emotion of twenty thousand people as Commandant O'Dwyer and his brother officers came down the enclosure like conquering heroes. When they wheeled into position,

the strains of the country's own national anthem came, vibrant and strong, and the other nations honoured the nation of which they were guests by coming to the general salute. On the stands and around the entire enclosure, the people too were paying eloquent and respectful homage to the anthem of the young state.[5]

On this occasion, the Germans beat the French, who up to that point had dominated the 1934 Nations Cup series with their wins in London, Lisbon and Lucerne. In what was a close battle on soft ground, the Irish side of O'Dwyer, Aherne, and Leonard, with Olympic hopefuls *Limerick Lace*, *Blarney Castle* and *Miss Ireland*, came third. But the best was yet to come in an historic moment that brought old Civil War enemies Commandant Ged O'Dwyer and now-President Éamon de Valera face-to-face in a unique meeting. O'Dwyer, who had won the Cavalry Cup earlier in the week, lined out on *Limerick Lace* in an entry of ninety civilian and military riders for the beautiful, newly-

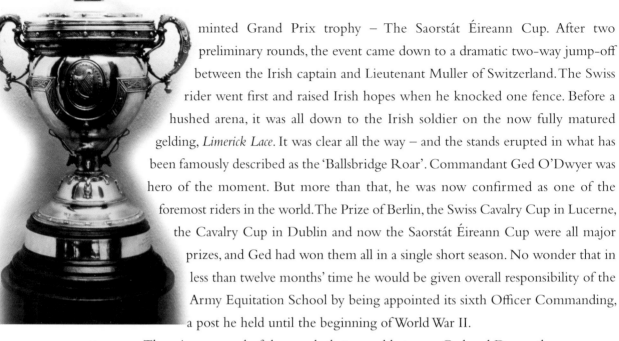

minted Grand Prix trophy – The Saorstát Éireann Cup. After two preliminary rounds, the event came down to a dramatic two-way jump-off between the Irish captain and Lieutenant Muller of Switzerland. The Swiss rider went first and raised Irish hopes when he knocked one fence. Before a hushed arena, it was all down to the Irish soldier on the now fully matured gelding, *Limerick Lace*. It was clear all the way – and the stands erupted in what has been famously described as the 'Ballsbridge Roar'. Commandant Ged O'Dwyer was hero of the moment. But more than that, he was now confirmed as one of the foremost riders in the world. The Prize of Berlin, the Swiss Cavalry Cup in Lucerne, the Cavalry Cup in Dublin and now the Saorstát Éireann Cup were all major prizes, and Ged had won them all in a single short season. No wonder that in less than twelve months' time he would be given overall responsibility of the Army Equitation School by being appointed its sixth Officer Commanding, a post he held until the beginning of World War II.

*Above:*
*Saorstát Éireann Cup*
*presented for the Grand*
*Prix winner at the RDS*
*in 1934.*
*(Army Equitation School)*

There is no record of the words that passed between Ged and Dev as the army man rode forward to receive the Saorstát Éireann Cup from the President. These two men, who, just twelve years previously, had vehemently supported opposite sides in the Civil War, now shook hands in the most peaceful and joyous of circumstances. When 'The Soldier's Song' rang out around the arena, both past enmities and possible future conflicts – at least for a moment – were put aside as an Irish victory was rightly celebrated.

Following Dublin, Captain Dan Corry made a blitz of the provincial show circuit, scoring top wins at Ennis, Limerick, Wicklow and Gorey. He was then joined by Jack Lewis and Fred Aherne for the winter tour to New York and Toronto. All three had individual victories at both events. They came a close second to the USA at Toronto.

While the team was away, Ged O'Dwyer, for the first time, formally announced the school's intention of fielding a team for the 1936 Olympic Games to a consultation meeting of the Minister of Defence's Advisory Board. At this time the intention to compete would have been communicated to the Berlin Olympic committee, but definitive entries of the exact horses and riders to take part would not be due until some three weeks prior to the start of show jumping at the games.

But just at this very time back in 1934 dark clouds were gathering on the Irish athletic sports scene that would have a profound bearing on the army team's Olympic hopes. In November of that year a Congress of the National Athletic and Cycling Association of Ireland (NACAI) all but voted itself out of the 1936 Olympics. From that moment on, pressure would be brought to have all Irish competitors, including the showjumping team, withdrawn from Berlin.

To understand the circumstances that prevailed at the time, we must briefly delve back into the history of Irish athletics. Almost from the time that this sport was first organised within the Irish universities in the mid-nineteenth century, it was under the governance of an all-island body, the NACAI. Even after partition in 1922 and the setting up of the Irish Free State, the NACAI continued to be the governing body for the whole of Ireland. This apparently caused no problems until the coming into power of Éamon De Valera's new government in 1932. Around this time, there were pressures from British interests to have Northern Ireland athletes compete under the British Amateur Athletic Board (BAAB). This was like a red rag to the De Valera Government and to the NACAI. They both wanted the All-Ireland governance of athletics to continue. Eventually, the overall world-governing body, the International Amateur Athletics Federation (IAAF), took a hand in the matter by siding with the BAAB. In August 1934 the IAAF made the rule that 'jurisdiction of members of the International Amateur Athletics Federation is limited by the political boundaries of the country or nation they represent'. This meant that the NACAI could only govern the sport within the twenty-six counties and not in the thirty-two counties as had formerly been the case. In November 1934 the matter truly came to a head at the NACAI Congress in Dublin. A proposal was put before the fifty-three delegates to accept or reject the new 'political boundaries rule'. A Yes vote would allow the NACAI to remain affiliated to the international federation, the IAAF; a No vote would leave them out in the cold, with their members banned from international participation. The No vote won by a margin of three – 27 votes to 24. According to expert on the subject, Dr Cyril M White of UCD, 'reason and practicality failed to prevail and sentiment carried the day.'[6] In essence, from that moment, Irish athletes and cyclists were barred from participation in all international events, including the 1936 Olympic Games. (The International Amateur Athletics Federation made this fact official in March of 1935.) It is of interest to note that at the regressive November

1934 Congress, the Army and Garda delegation had voted No in their combined seven votes. From that point on, the army jumping team's participation in the 1936 Olympics was under threat. How could one section of the army go counter to their confrères within the NACAI? In sympathy with the athletes, a strong campaign was mounted to have no Irish participation in Berlin.

But these developments do not appear to have been taken very seriously by the Equitation School's riders at this time. Interviews given in the years ahead by Ged O'Dwyer and Dan Corry, clearly indicate their belief that they were still on course to compete at Berlin in August 1936. Their preparation for the games remained on track during the 1935 season.

Joining the side at the beginning of the new year was a tall Cork man, Jack Stack. At age twenty-three, he had entered the Cadet school in 1932. When commissioned in 1933 he first served with the Signals and Transport Corps before being transferred to McKee. With a horse called *Red Hugh*, he would be part of a dramatic team victory at Aachen in 1937. He had five individual wins under his belt by the time war began and returned to compete again when peace arrived. In the great military tattoo at the RDS in 1945 Jack had a moment in the spotlight when, on *Red Hugh*, he played the part of British General Monroe during the superb re-enactment of the Battle of Benburb.

It has been said that beginning in 1935 the Irish Army jumping team could be likened to a great orchestral piece building toward a crescendo – third in Rome, Brussels and London; second in Nice and Amsterdam, and then four Nations Cup wins in a row at Lucerne, Dublin, New York and Toronto. In the nine events they met just about all the teams that were also preparing for the following year's Berlin Olympics. At every one of these shows the Irish were within what would be a medal position of first, second or third. So, hopes grew in the team that their golden dream could come true.

At Nice, where Fred Aherne won the Grand Prix on *Ireland's Own*, the side came second to the German A team. At Rome Lieutenant Tom Quinn made his debut and took a fourth on the opening day with *Red Hugh*. Joining Ged O'Dwyer, Fred Aherne and Dan Leonard, he had his first taste of team competition as the Irish were third behind France and Italy in the beautiful Piazza di Siena. Ged and *Limerick Lace* came close in the two main jump-off competitions, as he was placed second in both.

The team was again third in Brussels, before travelling on to Amsterdam, where they came second to a German side that included Olympic champion team members Kurt Hasse and Heinz Brandt. At London, Captain Jack Lewis got the Irish off to a brilliant start when, with *Tramore Bay*, he scored Ireland's first ever win in the prestige King's Cup. In the Daily Mail Cup, Ged O'Dwyer, on *Limerick Lace*, did battle with the future 1936 Olympic individual gold medallist, Hasse, and after a tense third round O'Dwyer emerged the winner. O'Dwyer again featured prominently in the Prince of Wales Cup. Clear the first time out – and the final outcome all came down to his second round. Another faultless score and he would have forced the British into a jump-off, but it was not to be – he went clear all the way to the last fence, but with that down, Ireland again had to be content with third place behind Britain and Germany. However, there was compensation for the Limerick man at show's end as Ged received word that he had been appointed replacement for Colonel Michael Hogan as Officer Commanding the Equitation School – Hogan had taken up the post for his second time in August 1933, six months after his name had been cleared in the Official Secrets court case. Ged would take command during the Dublin Horse Show of 1935.

So pleased were the Irish with the performance of their horses in London that on their way to Lucerne they were brave enough to make a pact that they would bid to win every class available to them at the Swiss venue. Ged O'Dwyer's recollection of this coming-of-age moment goes like this: 'On the train from Paris to Lucerne, Aherne, Corry and Lewis said, "Skipper, let's have a go here and win the lot." I fell for the suggestion immediately. We really had a go and won eight out of a possible eleven firsts.'[7] Included in their unique haul were a number of speed wins, plus the Swiss Cavalry Cup and Prix de Pilatus (Ged O'Dwyer on *Limerick Lace*), Prix St Gothard (Fred Aherne on *Ireland's Own*); St George Cup (Fred Aherne on *Gallowglass*). But the best performances of O'Dwyer, Aherne and Lewis were still to come in the Nations Cup as they jumped clear over a total of ninety fences to win on zero penalties – 24 ahead of second-placed Switzerland. What a contrast that was to their first visit there seven years previously when they were so demoralised they did not even jump in the team competition.

It was surely as conquering heroes that the side returned to do battle once more on home ground at Dublin Horse Show. It is a measure of the respect in which the team

was now held that just prior to the opening of competition in Ballsbridge, Lieutenant Kurt Hasse of Germany is quoted as saying, 'The Irish have tip-top horses and equally good riders – no team in the world can beat them.'[8] The future Olympic champion's words certainly proved prophetic on Friday of that week as the side of Commandant Ged O'Dwyer on *Limerick Lace*, Captain Dan Corry on *Miss Ireland*, Captain Fred Aherne on *Blarney Castle* pulverised the opposition in a display that had them incur just one penalty in the first round and then go on to win with 44 points to spare over the following year's German Olympic champions. In addition, Fred Aherne won the Puissance on *Ireland's Own*, and O'Dwyer on *Limerick Lace* took first in Thursday's jump-off. He and *Limerick Lace* were second to Kurt Hasse in the Swiss Cavalry Cup and to Heinz Brandt in the Grand Prix.

To finish what had been a plateau year of 1935, the Irish also dominated the North American tour as O'Dwyer, Aherne, Corry and Lewis took the Nations Cups at both New York and Toronto, plus six other individual firsts. They were definitely ready for the Olympic year of 1936! However, it is odd that in the minutes of meetings by the Advisory Board to the Minister for Defence held in late 1935 and early 1936, there is no mention of the Olympic Games as one of the venues to be attended in 1936. It is also odd that in the main sporting and daily papers during the first half of that year, there is not a single mention of the team's Olympic hopes. Yet, at the same time, activities of the Equitation School still had all the hallmarks of Olympic preparation. Perhaps they felt that if their results continued to be top-quality, then the threatened pull-out of other organisations from the games could not be applied to their team, which had a sure chance of winning an Olympic medal for Ireland.

Going into the Olympic year, they had ten Nations Cup horses in regular use and eleven riders with international experience to call on.

The 1936 season began with a morale boosting early win at Nice. James Neylon joined Fred Aherne, Dan Corry and Ged O'Dwyer for the trip. Between them, they had six individual wins: Neylon on *Miss Ireland* and *Kilmallock*; Aherne on *Gallowglass* and *Ireland's Own*, and O'Dwyer on *Blarney Castle* and *Limerick Lace*. In the Nations Cup they took first place, ahead of Spain, Portugal, Poland, France, Switzerland and Czechoslovakia, all of whom were using the event as an Olympic trial. When it ended, the newly appointed Irish ambassador and horse enthusiast Art O'Briain drove his car into the arena to collect the host of Irish prizes.

Brussels was next on the Irish calendar in mid-May. That was followed shortly afterwards by London, which, in the Olympic year, had been brought forward to June. The school made these two events into Olympic trials and different teams were fielded for both. Corry, Neylon and Lewis went to the Belgian fixture, where, with *Tramore Bay*, *Miss Ireland* and *Kilmallock*, they took second place by 11 faults to future Olympic silver medallists, Holland. Lewis and Corry joined up with O'Dwyer and Aherne in London. The Irish opened well on the Tuesday, filling the top three places in the King's Cup, which was presented by Sir Anthony Eden. Following in Jack Lewis's footprints of the previous year, O'Dwyer won it on *Limerick Lace*, while Lewis, on *Tramore Bay*, came joint second with Aherne on *Blarney Castle*. As ever before, the Prince of Wales Nations Cup again eluded the Irish.

This time, they were second to the French by a mere three penalties. But then came Amsterdam and a bid for top honours there in the presence of their good friend Queen Wilhelmina. For the Nations Cup, they fielded what must have been emerging as their four preferred mounts for Berlin: *Blarney Castle*, *Miss Ireland*, *Kilmallock* and *Limerick Lace*. This time there was no thought of second place as they powered home to win the Dutch Cup ahead of Belgium, London winners France, Japan and the home side. They had little time to celebrate this superb win before regrouping for the 4 July start to Lucerne. At this point, there were just about six weeks to go until the Olympic equestrian competitions in Berlin.

For the Swiss Cup, James Neylon took up the ride on *Limerick Lace*. Dan Corry switched to *Red Hugh* while Ged and Jack Lewis remained with *Blarney Castle* and *Kilmallock*. On the opening days the Irish were winners in all of the main individual events. But again their best came in the Nations Cup as the quartet on their selected mounts came through as popular winners for the second year in a row.

With the two great wins at Amsterdam and Lucerne behind them, and just three weeks to go until the day of showjumping competitions in the Olympic Stadium, the team arrived back at McKee as truly potential gold medal winners. But instead of a happy homecoming and word that their final entries for the games had been made, they were hit with the devastating news that they were definitely not travelling to Berlin. Disbelief, disgust, disappointment, pure horror are the reactions later expressed by the riders at what appeared to them as an utterly negative and inexplicable decision. 'We were devastated,' is how Ged O'Dwyer responded when this author asked him about it over fifty years later. Still smarting at the memory, he exclaimed: 'We were up against a hostile Government. It was De Valera stopped us.' And that was this great rider's firm belief until the day he died. However, it may not be that simple. I have recently spoken to a superb Irish athlete of the time, Jim Reardon, who was captain of Ireland's running team at the 1948 Olympics. He told me that he had once raised this very question with President De Valera and the response he got was: 'My name was being used about this matter, but it was not me. I could not take sides.'

Somehow the Army Equitation School had been dragged into the bitter NACAI dispute. The Minister for Defence at the time, Frank Aiken, has been quoted as saying that if it was left to him he would have been against the withdrawal of the army jumping team. No one has ever taken responsibility for the decision, but it appears that someone, somewhere felt that, given the circumstances of the time, there would be other option but to pull the plug on the showjumping team.

However, since the army riders were operating in a completely different sphere, there is no indication that they had had any understanding of the depth of problem that faced them. When it did finally sink in, it was devastating; it was ugly. Ireland's greatest possibility of winning showjumping Olympic gold was smashed in a welter of unproductive politics.

Regardless of the circumstances or the hurt felt, the riding officers had no option in the short term but to put it all behind them and take on the task of flying the flag on home ground at that year's Dublin Horse Show. This they did to a commendable degree by winning the Aga Khan for the second year in a row, while using their second string of horses. The non-use of top mounts like *Limerick Lace*, *Miss Ireland* and *Blarney Castle* was explained as a 'sporting gesture' in deference to the fact that visiting teams from France, Belgium and Holland would already have their top horses saved for the games.[9] The team of Commandant Ged O'Dwyer on *Clontarf*, Captain John Lewis on *Glendalough* and Captain Dan Corry on *Red Hugh* took the cup by a single fault ahead of Britain, France, Belgium and Holland.

Afterwards, Major Ged O'Dwyer fulfilled his assignment as an observer of the equestrian Olympic competitions. Dublin Horse Show ended on Saturday, 8 August. The showjumping competition was not due to take place in Berlin until 15 August, so he headed out on Monday, the 10th. There he met both Hermann Goering and Adolf Hitler, who greeted him with the words, 'You are the greatest rider in the world.' There too he walked all of the courses in the Olympic arena, but to his utter sadness he was not able to do what he had dreamed of and planned for over the previous three hard seasons. During this author's interview with him over fifty years later it was evident that the hurt still remained: 'I sat in my dress uniform unable to jump a fence. In the previous twelve months our team had won eight Nations Cups. I was looking at the ninth one for sure. But here I was on my two flat feet. I reckoned the most we would have had was 16 to 24 faults. The Germans won it with 44 faults. Holland was second with 51 and

Portugal third on 56 – all teams that we had beaten during the season. It was heartbreaking and in the long run, the reason why I left the army after serving with the 18th battalion during the early war years.'[10]

Two facts emerge from this sad 1936 Olympic saga. One, based on their form both before and after Berlin and barring any unforeseen mishap, the Irish Army show jumping team would have won a medal. Two, given the retrograde state of Irish sporting politics at the time, they were never going to get that chance. The army jumping team's Olympic dream of 1936 had been brutally killed by the blows of unproductive politics.

*Below*:
*When Ged O'Dwyer limited his travel abroad following the Olympic withdrawal, it fell to Captain Fred Aherne to take over a leadership role on trips abroad. He is shown jumping* Ireland's Own *at Aachen, where Ireland won the Hitler Cup in 1937.* (Joan Parker)

*Above*:
*Although heartbroken about having the army team withdrawn from the 1936 Berlin Olympics, Commandant Ged O'Dwyer still had to travel as an Irish representative to the Games, where he met both Adolf Hitler and Hermann Goering. He is shown here with Vice Chancellor Goering and a British representative at the Games.* (Noel O'Dwyer)

# 5

# SOLDIERING ON IN THE SHADOW OF WAR

## 1937 to 1945

*'Too late now to retrieve*
*A fallen dream, too late to grieve'*
*Francis Ledwidge*[1]

Writing about the army team's 1936 Olympic withdrawal, Limerick historian Liam Meade quoted Captain Dan Corry as saying, 'Such was their feeling of disillusionment, many of the riders gave serious consideration to resigning from the army in protest.'[2] But, in fact, neither the practical Dan himself nor any of his comrades did immediately resign. Dan was a resilient type of individual, who could bounce back from disappointment in a way that the more serious Ged O'Dwyer found difficult. Dan's son, Donal, recalls that his dad's attitude was a philosophical one, which aimed at proving that the team could have won that much-desired medal if they had been given the chance.

After the Olympic heartbreak, the squad soldiered on for the rest of 1936. Corry scored three impressive wins on the North American tour at New York and Toronto on *Red Hugh*. With him on that team were Fred Aherne, Jack Lewis and Cyril Harty, who was making his final winter tour. Croom, County Limerick man Cyril came from a strong racing family. Before joining the army he rode successfully in National Hunt and shared the Irish Amateur title with Cecil Brabazon in 1920. He was also the last ever winner of the Grand Military Cup at Punchestown. After his retirement from the army he became a race-horse trainer near the Phoenix Park. Three of his sons, Buster, Eddie and John, excelled in both racing and equestrian sport.

At Madison Square Garden in 1936 the army team of Harty, Aherne and Lewis were involved in a unique two-team jump-off tussle with Britain for the Nations Cup – they tied on a zero fault score after the first round. The two sides tied again in the first jump-off and only in the second tie-breaker did Britain win by a single penalty. This is the kind

of in-the-arena battle that month-by-month fuelled the school's enthusiasm to keep going.

If the driving force behind the team in 1936 was the dream of Olympic gold, the engine of their 1937 season was surely the effort to say to the world 'We are the champions.' To this end, they went hunting the Germans. At the first meeting of the two sides in Paris, Ireland had to be content with second. Their next chance would be in London where they blossomed for one of their most memorable victories, by taking the long sought-after Prince of Wales Cup at Olympia. And they did it in style, not only ahead of the Germans, but by the best score recorded in the more than twenty-year history of the cup till then. Captains Dan Corry on *Red Hugh*, John Lewis on *Tramore Bay* and Commandant Ged O'Dwyer on *Limerick Lace* gave of their very best in this most convincing and satisfying of wins. And there to celebrate with them was their mentor, Colonel Paul Rodzianko, who attended the show with his Irish wife, Anita Leslie!

In that same week, a second team simultaneously gave a distinguished performance at Amsterdam. There, the side of Captain George Heffernan and Lieutenant James Neylon, along with novice Lieutenant Jack Stack, tied with France for first place in the Nations Cup and were only narrowly beaten in the jump-off by three faults. Heffernan on *Kilmallock* had two individual wins, including the Grand Prix and was leading rider of the show. Jack Stack had an encouraging debut when taking second place in the Grand Prix with *Owen Roe*.

From Amsterdam and London, it was on to Lucerne with a side made up of Lewis, Aherne, Neylon and Corry, whose partnership with *Red Hugh* had now reached a peak of perfection. Corry and *Red Hugh* were to be stars of the show, with three wins, including the Grand Prix. Jack Lewis on *Owen Roe* also had a win in the Lido Cup. The team's Nations Cup performance there was equally superb as they swept to victory ahead of France, Italy, Switzerland and Belgium. This was their third consecutive win in Lucerne and it gave them possession of the prestige Swiss Cup, which still resides at McKee Barracks.

Ged O'Dwyer rejoined the team with *Limerick Lace* for Dublin where, along with Fred Aherne on *Duhallow* and the red hot Dan Corry on *Red Hugh*, they won the Aga Khan for the third time in a row. Their winning margin was all of 24 faults ahead of France. The Irish would have dearly loved to have beaten Germany here at Ballsbridge before their own home crowd, but the Germans opted not to compete at Dublin that year. So, in order to make their point once more, they had to hunt them to their home ground at Aachen. OC Ged O'Dwyer sat this one out and sent the team of Capt. Jack Lewis with *Limerick Lace*, Captain Fred Aherne on *Ireland's Own*, Lieutenant George Heffernon on *Duhallow*, and Lieutenant Jack Stack on *Red Hugh*. Their score of 24 faults over the Olympic-type course matched Ged's assessment of what they might have done at Berlin in 1936 – and it was good enough to beat the German champions by eight faults to take the Hitler Cup. Putting a final stamp on their dominance at this time, this Aachen win brought to eight the number of Nations Cups won by Ireland during the two seasons of 1936 and 1937 – more than any other country.

For many of the school's riding officers at the time, this win over Germany went

*Opposite bottom:*
*One of three valuable replicas of the Prince of Wales Cup presented to the victorious Irish team at Olympia in 1937. Only six of them were ever made. The other three went to the Dutch team that won in 1936. The practice was discontinued after 1937.*
*(Donal Corry)*

*Below:*
*The Hitler Cup, won by the Irish team of Jack Stack, Fred Aherne, George Heffernan and Jack Lewis at Aachen in 1937. Presented by Adolf Hitler himself, it still resides at McKee Barracks.*

some way toward expiating the Olympic disappointment. But for Ged O'Dwyer the hurt lingered and this was to have a telling effect on his participation in the months ahead. In fact, during the rest of 1937 and the whole of 1938 he jumped in only two of the eleven Nations Cups in which the Irish took part. In him, the feeling of loss ran deep and it took the sensitive efforts of his trusted friend, Quartermaster General Edward V. O'Connell, to bring him back into the competitive fold at the start of 1939.

Despite the absence of Ged from the team, they still came out in winning form for the opening fixture of 1938 at Nice. Aherne was joined by Corry, Lewis and Stack and from the very first day they were dominant. In all, they had four individual firsts and scored Ireland's second winning of the Nice Nations Cup ahead of France, Holland, Poland, Rumania, Turkey and Olympic bronze medallists, Portugal.

Rome was next and best of the Irish there was Capt. John Lewis, who scored Ireland's first ever win in the Gran Premio di Roma. With *Limerick Lace*, he took the colourful Romulus and Remus Trophy that was not to be won by an Irish rider again until Captain Billy Ringrose took it in 1961.

Ged O'Dwyer turned out for London, along with Corry, Aherne and Heffernon. Some top horses, like *Red Hugh*, had just returned from Rome and were being rested for Dublin. Thus, the Irish had mixed results in Olympia. In the Prince of Wales Cup, they were placed second to Britain by 16 faults. Dan Corry had a double of wins on *Duhallow*. Fred Aherne did the same with *Ireland's Own*. But, despite having five horses qualified, the King's Cup, that they had won in both 1935 and 1936, eluded them this time.

After a much-needed break, Lucerne, Amsterdam and Dublin came next on the 1938 schedule, followed by their last pre-war visits to New York and Toronto. At their most favourite Continental venue of Lucerne, the side of Corry, Aherne, Lewis and Neylon came first or second in every major event when winning seven and being runners-up in a further four. Their very best result was in the Grand Prix, when Jack Lewis and *Limerick Lace* took the cup ahead of Dan Corry on *Red Hugh*. Their run of success did not hold in the Nations Cup, however. Despite clears from Lewis on *Limerick Lace* and Fred Aherne on *Ireland's Own* they were second to France by five and a half faults.

The in-form Lucerne side was joined by 'skipper' Ged O'Dwyer for the home test at Dublin. Having had to be content with second placings during the first three days, the team of Fred Aherne on *Blarney Castle*, Dan Corry on *Duhallow* and Ged O'Dwyer, who was rejoined with *Limerick Lace*, lined out for the Aga Khan. Present on that day,

along with Taoiseach Éamon De Valera, was the newly elected first President of Ireland, Douglas Hyde. A crowd of 29,000 turned out to watch what ended as a very close-fought Nations Cup battle between Ireland and the Olympic Champions, Germany. After the first round, these two superbly matched teams were tied on a score of just six faults. Fences fell in the second, and the German score rose to 24. Corry and Aherne kept Ireland in the lead, but for one more time it was still all down to Ged O'Dwyer on *Limerick Lace*. They did all that was needed for Ireland to win their fourth Aga Khan in a row – a feat that Ireland has never equalled since. For the first of many times since then, the President of Ireland stepped forward to present the gleaming gold cup to the Irish team. Topping a good home performance, Fred Aherne, riding *Blarney Castle*, won the Dublin Grand Prix for his first and only time.

Following a return trip to Aachen, where they finished fourth, a three-man team of Dan Corry, Jack Stack and Jim Neylon ended that season in style when they won the Nations Cups in both New York and Toronto. An interesting feature of these two events was the fact that Captain Corry rode two horses in both cups. With *Tramore Bay* and *Duhallow*, he delivered two clear rounds that helped bring victory in Madison Square Garden. The ever-maturing Jack Stack, on *Blarney Castle*, also went clear, to have Ireland win on a zero score. Mexico and USA tied for second on four points. Matters were equally tight at the Great Winter Fair in Toronto, where the Irish score of nine had them take the Canadian Cup by just two faults ahead of USA. Before they took the boat back home, team leader Dan Corry was made an offer of $700 for James Neylon's ride *Clontarf*. He turned it down. Sadly, after the outbreak of war, this good jumper was auctioned off for a mere 35 guineas.

The fateful year of 1939 began on a happy enough note for the school when Fred Aherne and founder team member, Dan Corry were both promoted to the rank of Commandant. With the threat of war in Europe becoming ever more real, the team's first campaign of the new season was to Nice at the end of April. As if to take advantage of the last few months of peace, a record nine countries took part. The side of Lewis, Corry, Neylon and Stack had four major class wins. Capt. Lewis proved his good relationship with the great *Limerick Lace* by taking the Grand Prix. Continuing his brilliant run of form, Dan Corry also had a double of firsts with *Red Hugh*. They were fourth in the

Nations Cup, behind France, Britain, Belgium, and ahead of Turkey, Poland, Portugal, Rumania and Latvia. For the Latvian riders it would be another fifty years before they would have another equestrian outing as representatives of a free nation.[3]

The newly promoted Commandant Fred Aherne replaced James Neylon for Brussels in mid-May, where the team came second behind Belgium in the Nations Cup. Again, Commandant Corry was the bright spot at the show as he won the pairs with *Red Hugh* and *Duhallow*. He also received the silver trophy for outstanding rider of the show. But in his report of the event, Corry expressed grave worries that the school's dwindling supply of horses was rapidly losing form through the stress of constant travel – one has to remember that with two seas to cross, the Irish have always been at a disadvantage in this regard and never more so than at this pre-war time when long border delays put extra strain on the animals.

Ged O'Dwyer came out to replace Jack Stack for the Olympia show, but first prizes eluded them there and they were a disappointing fourth in the Prince of Wales Cup. James Neylon, with some fresh horses, travelled out for the last two Continental shows that the school would attend prior to Europe becoming a war zone – Amsterdam and Lucerne. From then on, most of these officers on horseback would become enemies in vicious combat rather than friends in sporting competition. This author is old enough to remember the feelings of helpless dread that pervaded those mid-months of 1939. Any thoughts of the future were shrouded in the fear that only bad things were about to happen. But Ireland's horsemen had two more promises to keep before returning home for Dublin 1939.

In Holland, Major Ged O'Dwyer said farewell to Continental competition in the most glorious of ways: with *Limerick Lace*, he first made it to the jump-off for the Amstel Priz and was only narrowly beaten on time by the great German hero of world showjumping Captain Hans Heinrich Brinckmann – only one fifth of a second separated the famous Irish partnership from victory.[4] But they were not to be denied their win in the main individual prize of the show, the Grand Prix of Amsterdam. They scored Ireland's second win in that prestige event. Germany's crack team got the better of Ireland in the Nations Cup, but the Irish side retained their confidence as they headed for a re-match in Lucerne, where they had scored their first ever away victory eight years earlier.

Right away, Captain James Neylon struck form there and scored two wins on *Duhallow*. But, as Ged would later recall, 'It was the Cup we were after.' Lining out for that were top sides from France, Belgium, Germany, Switzerland, Italy and Hungary. But, in the end, it came down to a close battle between Ireland, Switzerland and Germany. After the first round, just five faults separated these three contenders. In the second round, the Irish and Germans pulled away. A clear from Neylon on *Duhallow* and a four from Jack Lewis on *Kilmallock* left the sides neck-and-neck. So once more it was up to Limerick man O'Dwyer and *Limerick Lace* to deliver the final winning clear. In his brilliant, stylish way he did just that to give Ireland the win by a single penalty – 12.5 to Germany's 13.5.

That sweet Swiss victory was the Irish Army team's last win abroad for ten long years. After the war, with a different team, they would win Harrisburg in 1949, when the world had become a very different place.

But in the meantime, there was Dublin 1939 – the last international show there until 1946. This was an occasion of emotional reunion for riders, who knew that it was their final chance for a very long time of being together on such a wonderful, peaceful mission. As the great equestrian writer and poet of the time, Stanislaus Lynch, put it in his report of the show for a British magazine: 'In these days when European events are threatening to turn people's lives into a nightmare, it is refreshing to find Ballsbridge an oasis of international peace.'[5]

Happily joining the Irish for the event was Colonel Paul Rodzianko, who, despite a broken leg, made his way to Dublin. Also on hand was the original proposer of international jumping in Ireland, Colonel Richard Zeigler of Switzerland. Teams from Britain, Germany, France, Belgium and Switzerland had entered. Even now, it is heartbreaking to think that in less than a month these visiting officers would be at war. But all of this did not stand in the way of excellent competition, described as 'magnificent horsemanship and the highest standard of jumping'.[6]

Captain Dan Corry led the Irish attack. With *Red Hugh*, he won the opening military event; he also closed the show in style when, with the same great jumper, he took the Grand Prix for his second time. In the Aga Khan, the Germans powered into an early first-round lead, with just five faults against them. But their advantage was not to hold in the second round. Germany ended up third on a total of 21. The door opened for the home side to score its fifth consecutive Aga Khan victory when both Fred Aherne on *Duhallow* and Ged O'Dwyer on *Limerick Lace* had superb second-round clears. But in the end they had to give way to France, who were the proud winners by just three faults. This event was Ged's last team appearance with the great *Limerick Lace*, on which, over six seasons, he had won 29 international firsts and contributed to nine Nations Cup wins.

Leading the winning side as Chef d'Equipe was a lifelong friend of Ged O'Dwyer's, Captain Zavier Bizard. During the thirties, Bizard had been a star on the world circuit with his King's Cup winner, *Honduras*. This great, big jumping horse was captured by the Germans during their occupation of France; he was later re-captured by the Americans as they pushed into Germany. After the war, *Honduras*, renamed *Nipper*, became part of the West German-based USA Army showjumping teams that won at both London and Dublin in 1948. *Honduras/Nipper* is a wonderful symbol of the sport's survival of the destructive world conflict.

After Dublin 1939, the school returned briefly to the national circuit. Fred Aherne and

*Below*:
*The winning French team at Dublin in 1939. The Irish side, which came second, separates them from the third-placed Germans, out of the picture to the right. Within a month, France and Germany would be at war and both officers and horses would become part of that conflict. (RDS Library Archive)*

*Above:*
*A parade of army*
*troopers, led by Col. Jack*
*Lewis at the RDS*
*Showgrounds, which was*
*occupied by the army*
*during World War II.*

Jack Stack jumped at Sligo Show on 15 August. Two days after the outbreak of war, James Neylon joined Aherne at Ballaghaderreen on 5 September. And there it ended. It is noted in the archives that entries had been made for the end-of-season show at Ballinasloe during the first week of October, but there is no indication that any of the officers jumped there. Very soon after the start of hostilities in Europe, the school began to wind down. The RDS had hoped to continue its Horse Show into 1940 – and had actually printed the schedule for it. But then it, too, had to be cancelled. The Irish Army took over a large part of its showgrounds for the 'duration' and instead of the pounding hooves of showjumpers, the arenas and walkways at the Ballsbridge grounds now echoed to the sound of parading troops.

During 1940 and early 1941, the school's personnel and horses were gradually dispersed. At first, a determined effort was made to retain a training programme at the school, but this was discontinued in April 1940. A new unit known as An Marc Sluagh (The Horse Troop) had by this time been formed to control all horse transport throughout the army. At a conference held in the Acting Quartermaster General's office on 19 June 1940, attended by Major Ged O'Dwyer as OC of An Marc Sluagh, it was stated that the Minister for Defence had, the previous day, decided that 'during the present emergency all activities of the school should cease and that all commitments be cancelled.'[7] Ged was ordered to have all the class one horses put out to grass at Áras an Uachtaráin and at the Royal Hospital, Kilmainham. At the time, there were twenty-five mounts in this category of top showjumpers. When Major O'Dwyer was given command of the 18th Battalion, Commandant James Finlay took over as OC of An Marc Sluagh. He was then ordered to sell off thirteen class one and forty-eight class two horses.

Among the well-known jumpers to come under the hammer at Clarke's Horse Repository in Dublin on 9 January 1941, was the wonderful mare, *Miss Ireland*. Along with her went the likes of *Clontarf*, *Man of Aran*, *Downpatrick*, *Armagh Hills*, *Yellow Ford*, *Lough Foyle*, *Kylemore*, *Finola*, *Boyne Water*, *Red Hand* and *Cavehill*. The prices ranged from 12 to 40 guineas. In hope that one day the school would re-open, horses with good long term international competition prospects were retained at grass. Among that group, which were to return to the arena after six long years of war, were *Owen Roe*, *Duhallow*, *Tramore Bay*, *Lough Neagh* and *Ireland's Own*. But heroic mounts like *Limerick Lace*, *Blarney Castle* and *Red Hugh*, while retained in honoured retirement, were never to carry the Irish colours again. The sadness of all this is difficult to embrace fully, but it was both the result and the necessity arising from war.

For the riders this was a time of dramatic change. In addition to being international sportsmen, they were also fulltime soldiers, and this is what they were called upon to be for the uncertain years ahead. Men who had become household names and whose pictures had adorned the front pages of newspapers at home and abroad, now all but disappeared into the underbelly of a much beefed-up army that had to cater for the very real national needs of the time. Back then, in the bleak winter of 1939, none of these riders had any idea when, if ever, the school would re-open or if any of them would ever again have the opportunity to carry the tricolour on their saddle cloths in peaceful international competition.

## THE RIDERS IN WARTIME

GED O'DWYER became Commanding Officer of the 18th Infantry Battalion based at the Royal Hibernian school in the Phoenix Park. This author can remember offering homemade bread to his troops as they passed our farm one day during their Border manoeuvres on their way to 'capture' the town of

Kingscourt (in a mock battle this was their objective). Serving under him were former army grooms Finlay, Doyle and Fitzgerald. Also in his unit was a future army rider, Comdt. J J O'Neill. Having successfully served three years in this role, Ged resigned from the army in October 1943. For the rest of his life he farmed back home in his beloved Limerick.

COMMANDANT FRED AHERNE became Officer Commanding the Second Infantry Battalion and in the post-war years would return to command the Equitation School.

CAPTAIN DAN LEONARD served with the Coastal Defence Artillery.

CAPTAIN JACK LEWIS was appointed Director of Signals and Transport and also led the 19th Battalion. He too would become an OC of the school.

CAPTAIN JAMES NEYLON moved to a different kind of horsepower with the 4th Motor Squadron. After the war he was first a trainer in the school and then its OC from the late fifties into the sixties.

CAPTAIN JACK STACK served with Jack Lewis in Signals and Transport. He was to play a major role in the re-enactment of the Battle of Benburb during the 1945 Military Tattoo in the RDS. He returned to jump with the team for a number of years after the war.

COMMANDANT DAN CORRY was with the 16th Infantry Battalion in Kilkenny and Waterford as Administrative Officer. Near the war's end, Dan was in charge of the Waterford barracks. Always the jovial horseman, he was once heard to declare that he was 'prepared to defend the position until the last race on the card at Mallow, Clonmel, Limerick Junction and Gowran Park'. Dan again successfully rode on teams right into the fifties.

# REOPENING TO A
# CHANGING WORLD

## 1946 to 1953

*'When Peace comes tottering feebly*
*To the tattered remnants of civilisation*
*The little things of life will matter most'*[1]
*Stanislaus Lynch*

Long before World War II ended, Ireland's love of equestrian sport had blossomed into life again at shows all over the country. Even at the RDS, despite having a large part of its grounds occupied by the military in the Emergency, curtailed versions of the Horse Show were run between 1942 and 1945. A full-blown international show joyfully returned in 1946. At all of these many events, in Dublin and in at least a hundred venues in other counties, civilian rider talent matured and became ready to claim places alongside the military in post-war international competition. There were other important horse-sport developments as well during the war years, such as the founding of showjumping associations north and south of the Border.

## THE SHOWJUMPING ASSOCIATIONS

Up until the war years, while the Army Equitation School and the RDS looked after the international side of showjumping, it was largely up to individual shows around the country to supervise their own competitions. However, as competitor numbers grew, the frequency of disputes over rules and the judging of results also increased. This led to a demand for an overall governing body to oversee the running of national events. It was during one of the shows run in the immediate aftermath of the outbreak of war in September 1939 that

## THE SHOW JUMPING ASSOCIATION OF IRELAND

### National Jumping Rules

the first feeble steps in this direction were taken. Interestingly enough, this happened at the very show in Ballinasloe at which the army riders were unable to fulfil their entries due to the imminent closure of the Equitation School. To deal with these issues within the sport, a meeting took place in Hayden's Hotel and was attended by representatives from both north and south of the Border. However, it was to be five years after that Ballinasloe meeting before the next moves on organisation were made. In the south, a Horse Jumping and Riding Encouragement Association (HJ&REA) came into being in August 1944. Its first president was former OC of the Equitation School, Major General Liam Hayes, while among its vice-presidents was Major Ged O'Dwyer.

That same year, The Northern Ireland Showjumping and Riding Association (NISJ&RA) was also formed. A full ten years later, after protracted negotiations, these two groups, the HJ&REA and the NISJ&RA, were amalgamated into the Show Jumping Association of Ireland (SJAI) in April 1954. More recently, this has become known as Show Jumping Ireland (SJI). The SJAI's first chairman in 1954 was former British team member Colonel Joe Hume-Dudgeon. Colonel Jack Lewis took over that role in 1966 and was also the Association's first Secretary General. Although the overwhelming input to the organisation has, down the years, come from the civilian sector, former and current army riders have always played a part in its development. They have also contributed to the organisation of Irish horse trials and to the overall governing body of equestrian sport in Ireland, first the Equestrian Federation of Ireland (EFI) and now Horse Sport Ireland (HSI).

It is interesting that one of the first public calls for the restoration of the Army Equitation School came from the Horse Jumping and Riding Encouragement Association. In March 1945, a full two months prior to the Nazi surrender, HJ&REA issued the following statement: 'This Association comprised of those interested in Show Jumping request the Government to proceed with the formation of an Army Jumping Team to succeed the Team which so brilliantly represented this country throughout the world up to 1939.'[2] The press followed up on this and an *Irish Independent* editorial of 12 May stated: 'Seeing particulars of a draft of surplus horses sold recently by the Army makes me wonder if any steps are being taken to ensure that an Army Jumping Team will be available when hostilities have finally ceased.'[3] Unknown to that writer, steps were already being taken within the Government towards the school's reopening. A Department of Defence Conference, held in January 1945 and attended by officials from both the Department of Defence and Department of Agriculture, considered the pros and cons of such a move. They postponed a conclusion until 'the prospects of international shows being held could be more clearly determined'.[4] A detailed memorandum on that meeting was forwarded to the Cabinet and a decision was reached on 24 April. In a letter dated that same day to the Department of Defence, it was instructed that 'the Army School of Equitation should be re-established and that the necessary steps to that end should be taken without delay'.[5] Echoing general public assent to the team's revival, a writer to the *Independent* said, 'It will bring pride and joy to the hearts of Irish men and women to know that this, one of our greatest national glories is to start again, to raise the flag "on far foreign fields" and to win applause from admiring crowds of every tongue and clime.'[6]

The team was operationally re-formed in November of that year. Back in the saddle again were pre-war heroes like Commandants Dan Corry and Fred Aherne, along with Captains Jack Stack and James Neylon. Now ranked a Lieutenant Colonel, Jack Lewis was put in charge of the school as riding Officer-in-Command. And there were new recruits as well, in Lieutenants Bill Mullins from Kilkenny, and Meath man Louis Magee. Also joining was well known County Clare athlete and GAA star, Michael Tubridy, who in a very short time was to become a showjumping household name. This author can remember cheering Tubridy on at the post-war RDS shows. To us he was an Irish Tom Mix or Roy Rogers, riding out to take on the opponents in strange foreign uniforms. I recently met a young grandnephew of his named Harry Tubridy, from Wexford, who would dearly love to follow in his footprints.

Bill Mullins came from a farming family and has always been credited with being a good judge of a performance horse. He admits to having the dream of riding for Ireland at the back of his mind when he first joined the army during the war years. That ambition came to fruition when he was selected for further training out of the first post-war cadet class. Although he retired from international showjumping in 1954, he continued to have a long association with the school after that in his role as OC of the Transport Corps. He also later served on the school's Horse Purchase Board and was part of negotiations to buy some great horses like *Rockbarton* during the seventies. After his retirement from international showjumping, he became very much involved in the sport of eventing and represented Ireland at Olympic level. In the late sixties, he also used his considerable influence in encouraging the school to broaden its programme to include the eventing aspect of equestrian sport, which, over three days of competition, included dressage, showjumping and cross-country riding.

Louis Magee also joined the school at this time. He was from a very sport-oriented Dunboyne, County Meath, family. His father was a vet, but had also played international rugby for Ireland. Louis joined the army during the war and was a participant in the great post-war military exhibition at the RDS, the Tattoo, prior to taking up training along with Mullins and Tubridy.

And what were these men to ride? Some good pre-war performers like *Duhallow*, *Tramore Bay*, *Lough Neagh* and *Owen Roe* were back again. The great *Limerick Lace* still lived at McKee, but like his principle rider, Ged O'Dwyer, he did not return to competition. Young horses bought during the latter part of 1945 and early 1946 included *Antrim Glens*, *Kilkenny*, *Ardmore*, *Galteemore*, *Roscarbery*, *Clontibret*, *Bruree* and *Aherlow*. The *Tiger Hill*-sired mare *Kilkenny*, bought from Colonel Hume-Dudgeon, and *Bruree*, by the thoroughbred stallion *Dick Turpin*, that came from Jack White of Dublin, became the best known of this latter group.

The first major public outing of the post-war team was at the RDS Spring Show in May 1946. An *Irish Field* report on the restored military jumping competition there noted: 'After many years' absence from the arena, the army got a hearty welcome from the spectators. There were 20 horses entered ... The point that impressed most was that a majority of the horses were only recently broken.'[7] The writer also forecast that both *Kilkenny* and *Clontibret* had the quality to make winners.

In July of that year, *The Irish Times* ran a lead article headed, 'Army Jumping Team Prepares for Horse Show' in which it was noted that thirty-three horses from McKee were entered for a variety of classes at Ballsbridge. In almost poetic terms, the text describes a group of eleven jumpers being brought out for exercise: 'Out into the sun-drenched glory they came: out into the sylvan beauty of the Phoenix Park, 11 lovely horses, stepping as daintily as ballet dancers in an idyllic setting. Everything seemed dancing this morning: the immaculately groomed horses, the foliage on the lordly elms, the ever-changing shadows on the grass.'[8]

But there is one 'shadow' not mentioned in that article – the shadow of a much-changed sport of showjumping that riders and horses from the Army Equitation School would soon face into during the post-war years. In the immediate aftermath of the war, from 1946 to 1948, as they competed against familiar re-formed military sides, matters did remain much as they had been for the heroes of the thirties. But from then on, it is no exaggeration to say that the difficulties they soon encountered were on a par with those faced by the men and horses of the very first school cohort back in 1926.

It has to be remembered, that while the war was on, the sport of showjumping had in no way stood still. Young riders the world over were honing their talents. Then, just about two years after war's end, the governing body of the sport, Federation Equestre Internationale (FEI), issued a directive which, for the first time, allowed both civilian and military riders to represent their countries in Nations Cup competition. As elsewhere around the globe, Ireland saw a hugely increased level of civilian participation in the sport. When the Horse Jumping and Riding Encouragement Association and the Northern Ireland Show Jumping and Riding Association were formed in 1944, they had a combined membership of about two hundred, north and south of the border. By the time the Show Jumping Association of Ireland came into being ten years later, in

1954, the number of registered riders had more than trebled. Rising out of this increased group of enthusiasts were names like Seamus Hayes, Iris Kellett, Billy McCully, Dick McElligott and many more who could hold their own in any international competition. This fact was to have a profound influence on the Army Equitation School's story from that time onwards.

In addition to all of this, the new mounts purchased by the school in the post-war years came from a dramatically changing horse market in Ireland. Prior to the war, there were over half a million horses of various kinds on Irish farms, from which a selection could be made. In the post-war era, that number dropped steeply and by the end of the fifties it was more than halved to 235,000.

Another factor in the post-war years was the very make-up of that Buying Commission. It was still dominated by Judge Wylie of the RDS, along with representatives from the Department of Agriculture, whose primary focus was the Irish hunter-type horse. This was bred in the traditional hit-or-miss crossing of Irish Draught and three-quarter bred mares with thoroughbred stallions. This process, combined with a horse-friendly land and climate, produced brave, cool-tempered horses that had plenty of stamina, and which continued to serve us well. But their numbers were declining and they were beginning to come up against a new type of Continental purpose-bred showjumper. The Dutch, Germans and French were already taking the first steps toward developing sophisticated breeding programmes based on jumping performance pedigree in both mares and stallions.

Ireland continued to produce good jumpers. But smaller numbers, combined with a massive increase in civilian riders, both at home and abroad, meant that competition for any promising youngster that came on the market grew ever keener. The Irish army riders were totally committed to using only Irish bred horses. But the teams they competed against had no such restraints on the source of their mounts, so these opponents were competitors not only in the jumping arenas but in the Irish horse market as well.

Another important change to face the school during this period came from within the sport itself. This was the accelerated technical development in course-building, led internationally by the genius of pre-war German rider Hans Heinrich Brinckmann. To

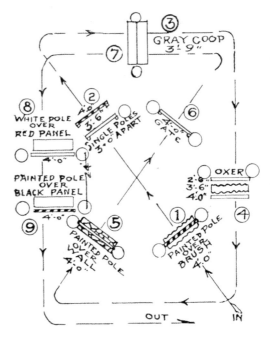

The lay-out of the jumping course for the Inaugural competition at Madison Square, New York last November.

*Above:*
*One of the more complicated courses jumped during the post-World War II years at New York.*
*(Margaret Lynch).*

suit the newer type of Continental horse coming into showjumping, fence materials began gradually to become lighter, cups for holding poles got shallower, and the variety of obstacles multiplied. Following this trend, the RDS introduced new fences in 1949. Automatic timing came to be used at Ballsbridge for the first time in 1951. Instead of leisurely rounds over heavy rustic-type fences, riders were now forced to hurry on over more synthetic-type jumps within a specific time. A report in the *Irish Field* of this period noted, 'Few of us in Ireland would relish tackling the fences that these Army men encounter at Continental shows. Most of them are timber, but the structure of the timber takes almost every conceivable shape and form ... The Continental fences are much bigger and their presentation is nothing short of alarming.'[9]

Following the 1947 FEI directive, teams taking part in Nations Cup events, like Dublin's Aga Khan competition, would no longer be confined to military riders. It is impossible to exaggerate the importance to the Army Equitation School of this change. For one thing, it meant that a whole new cohort of world-class stars emerged. It has to be remembered that many of the new civilians were, in a real sense, professionals, whose livelihoods depended on both riding and selling horses. The army riders were, indeed, professional soldiers, but the riding part of their lives was in the amateur mode and was recognised as such by the still amateur world of the Olympics.

All of this meant that the men from McKee were going out to compete in national and international shows against opponents that were not only trained in the art of showjumping but were also practiced to a degree that never previously existed. These riders annually attended many more shows than ever before and a whole new series of events, both indoor and outdoor were brought into existence to accommodate them. Rotterdam, Harrisburg, Madrid, Wiesbaden, Dortmund, Blackpool, Le Zoute, Ostend, and many more, came on stream at this time. This, then, was the changed world into

*Below*:
*The 1946 Irish winning team in the first post-war Aga Khan Cup: Captains Jack Lewis on* Clontibret, *Dan Corry on* Antrim Glens, *Jack Stack on* Tramore Bay.
*(Margaret Lynch)*

which the reconstituted Army jumping team emerged.

It was utterly fitting that at war's end the 1946 revival of Nations Cup competition should happen at the recognised birthplace of world showjumping – Dublin. The RDS had dearly hoped to have at least six teams taking part. Sadly, owing to continued difficulty in travelling across Europe, Switzerland, Spain and Portugal had to withdraw. Just the cup holders, France, along with Sweden made the trip for a three-way Aga Khan battle with the home side. Selected to carry the Irish flag were pre-war campaigners, Lieutenant Colonel Jack Lewis, Commandant Dan Corry and Commandant James Neylon. Commandant Jack Stack and new recruit Lieutenant Michael Tubridy were listed as reserves. From a total Army entry of 33, their team horses were to be *Antrim Glens*, *Tramore Bay* and *Clontibret*. Despite the paper's overall support of the Army team, an *Irish Field* preview of the show registered regret at a lack of 'new blood' on the Irish side.[10]

At that 1946 Dublin Horse Show, Ireland rode out winners in the Aga Khan. Hero of that outcome was the redoubtable Dan Corry, who had just a single fault over two rounds on *Antrim Glens*. The following day there was elation as well when the new man in town, Michael Tubridy rode the mare *Kilkenny* to a popular win in the Grand Prix.

Having won both the Aga Khan and the Grand Prix, the army team could be forgiven for assuming that the good old days were here again. As if in celebration, they ran a hugely entertaining Sunday afternoon military gymkhana at McKee Barracks in September of that year. With performances by the masse army bands interspersed with seven jumping competitions, this proved to be a superb family day out. It also paved the way for the much-needed creation of a new schooling ground, aimed at better preparing teams for competition abroad. Work on the new facility at the back of Áras an Uachtaráin began in August of the following year.

Early in 1947, Col. Jack Lewis took the brave decision of testing his forces against the re-formed teams of the world by contesting seven Nations Cups – Nice, Rome, Lucerne, London, Dublin, New York and Toronto. His gamble came close to paying off since, in a unique result, the Irish placed second in all of them. That same year, Ireland's first ever civilian team of Jim Bryson from Loughbrickland, Joan Uprichard of Portadown, and Noel Hayes from Banbridge, along with young Dubliner Iris Kellett went out to compete at an official Federation Equestre International (FEI) approved Nations Cup at Blackpool in England. This was the beginning of something that would not fully mature until the sixties and would cause a good deal of controversy along the way.

Commenting on the army squad's runner-up performances at their first four 1947 outings, an *Irish Field* report somewhat ominously commented, 'It would seem that, in spite of the effects of war, the other nations have teams of horses and riders of an extremely high standard, who are capable of testing to the utmost our high prowess in

*Above*:
*Post-war hero of the Army team Capt. Michael Tubridy, who won the Dublin Grand Prix in both 1946 and 1953.*
*(Army Equitation School)*

*Below:*
*Last public outing of*
*the Hussars at the*
*RDS, escorting*
*President Sean T*
*O'Kelly in 1948.*
*(RDS Library Archive)*

any future jumping contests at home and abroad.'[11]

That prediction was certainly proven true as the Irish faced an entry of five visiting nations hungry for a win in the 1947 Aga Khan at Dublin. The OC Jack Lewis got the Irish off to an encouraging start with a win on opening day. But over the next two days the home side struggled to keep in touch. When it came to Friday's Nations Cup, the Army trio of Lewis, Corry and Aherne put up a good fight but had to settle for second again behind Britain. They added two more seconds at New York and Toronto before Christmas. By now, the message must have sunk home fully at McKee that post-war competition was to be the toughest they had ever faced.

Nonetheless, determined to accomplish what his great pre-war compatriots had been so cruelly prevented from doing at Berlin, Lieutenant Colonel Lewis set the highest possible target for 1948 – an Olympic medal at the renewed Games in London. In a bid to save the likes of *Lough Neagh*, *Clontibret* and *Tramore Bay* for London, Lewis entered *Kinsale*, *Rostrevor*, *Aherlow* and *Baldoyle* for the Dublin Cup. This was the first year at Ballsbridge that each team consisted of four riders. So, when both *Aherlow* and *Baldoyle* were injured in heavy going early in the week, *Lough Neagh* and *Tramore Bay* had to be called up. But in the end, it was of no avail and the Irish placed a disappointing last, on 60 faults. Bringing some real joy to the Irish fans at the RDS that year was Iris Kellett,

who with *Rusty* was the first woman to win the Grand Prix there.

Colourfully winning the 1948 Aga Khan for the very first time was the USA with a military team based in Germany. Leading their charge was Colonel FF Wing on the brilliant *Democrat*. Also on their side was the former French team horse *Honduras* (now named *Nipper*) that had been captured by the Germans at the start of the war and then recaptured by the Americans (see Chapter 5). This was the last time that an official American Army team would jump at the RDS. After the Olympics of that year the army team was disbanded and replaced by a civilian side that has been a dominant force in world showjumping ever since.

Also ordered to be disbanded at the end of that year was Ireland's mounted escort troop, the Blue Hussars. The process of Blue Hussar disbandonment was completed early in 1949. Their last outing was to Áras an Uachtaráin in early 1949.

Immediately after Dublin 1948, the three-member Army team of Lieutenant Colonel Jack Lewis, Commandant Fred Aherne and Commandant Dan Corry set out for Roehampton in the heart of London, their Olympic preparation base. The selected horses were *Lough Neagh*, *Tramore Bay* and *Clontibret*. When *Clontibret* lost form, *Aherlow* had to be brought in at the last moment for Aherne to ride. The competition was held over a single round of 19 big fences that counted for both the team and individual medals.

The official result lists Ireland as one of the eleven nations eliminated, but that does not tell the whole story. In fact, the Irish trio came close to winning the very-much desired medal. With the OC left to jump, Ireland was still in contention for a medal. Over the first half of the course Jack and *Lough Neagh* were described as 'taking the jumps coolly'. But at the third last fence, it all fell apart. There, *Lough Neagh* gave a first refusal, then a second. But that was not the worst of it. For some still unexplained reason, Jack did not make a third attempt. Instead, he opted to bypass the fence altogether and jump the last two. This was put down as 'taking the wrong course' and hence incurred elimination, not only for himself but for the whole Irish team. Perhaps Jack knew in his

*Above:*
*Numbered armband worn by Captain Dan Corry at the London Olympics 1948 where the Irish team came within reach of the much-desired medal.*
*(Donal Corry)*

heart that there was no way that *Lough Neagh* was ever going to jump the fence on a third attempt and felt that it was better to go out in style. We will never know. Anyway, the Mexicans took gold on 34.25 faults and their great rider, Humberto Mariles Cortes on *Arete*, was individual champion. (A plaque commemorating Cortes' superb horse *Arete* was later presented to the Army Equitation school). Spain got the silver medal with 56 faults and Britain the bronze on 67. Some 21 or less faults from *Lough Neagh* would have given Ireland the bronze, but it was not to be. This was the last international round jumped for Ireland by Lieutenant Colonel Jack Lewis, whose career with the school spanned sixteen eventful years. In June of the following year he retired as Officer Commanding and went on to play a major role in the development of the Show Jumping Association of Ireland.

The words of WB Yeats, in his poem on 1916 'all changed, changed utterly' could be applied to the challenges that faced the school during the following decade, 1949 to 1959.[12] Among the more important changes were the appointments of a new Officer Commanding and of a new international trainer in 1949. Also came the addition of new riders and mounts. Star of the pre-war team on great horses like *Blarney Castle*, Colonel Fred Aherne was named as Officer Commanding in June 1949 and he was to hold the post for almost ten years. Coming in as resident trainer under Colonel Aherne in 1949 was the Polish pre-war rider, Major Severyn Kulesza, who had been on winning sides for his country during the thirties. When Poland fell to the Germans, he went on to serve with General Anders' resistance force in Italy and was later taken prisoner by the Nazis. Among his first students at McKee was Dublin man Lieutenant Jimmy O'Neill, who later described him as a 'Beautiful horseman, whose methods with young horses and riders were excellent.'[13] This positive view of him was not altogether shared by some within Army administration, particularly Colonel PA Mulcahy, who at that time was Quartermaster General. In a 1952 report to the Minister for Defence, he referred to Kulesza's employment as 'a mistake', and went on to note: 'He was a Cavalry officer, not a Show Jumping Instructor. The principles on which he taught have proved false in the jumping arena. It will take time to eradicate the effects of his teaching.'[14]

Facing into this new situation in 1949 was a mix of riders: from pre-war times, Dan Corry and Jack Stack; immediate post-war additions were Michael Tubridy, Colm

O'Shea, Louis Magee and Bill Mullins, along with newer recruits Jimmy O'Neill, Kevin Barry from Charleville, Co Cork, and another Dubliner, Brendan Cullinane. In contrast with the long serving teams of pre-war years, personnel in the Equitation School began to change more frequently. While during the thirties just ten riders in total carried the flag, from 1949 to 1959 double that number are listed. It has to be remembered that most of the new recruits still had little or no experience in the art of showjumping prior to entering the school. They were drawn from those who showed potential during the riding phase of the cadetship course and had to learn their skills from scratch. This could be one reason for the rapid change-over. But another had to be the shortage of replacement horses for them to ride. Each international rider was usually assigned a team of three horses, and when one or more of his top horses lost form, it was difficult for that rider to continue. Hence competition for mounts was intense. An insight into this problem is given in the previously quoted Colonel PA Mulcahy report: 'the general atmosphere in the Equitation School is not harmonious ... mainly from undue anxiety on the part of each riding officer to outshine his colleagues.' Lieutenant Jimmy O'Neill recalls of this period: 'the early post-war years were difficult not only for the Equitation School, but for the Army as a whole. It was only natural that there should be a reaction after the end of the war and in the special case of the School, the difficult task of developing new international horses and riders had to be undertaken.'[15]

Brendan Cullinane jumped internationally for just four seasons during which he scored some impressive wins. After leaving the school, Brendan studied law and went on to be Chief Justice in both Zambia and Lesotho. Tall Dublinman, Colm O'Shea, had his first team outing on the winning Aga Khan side of 1949. He retired in 1954, emigrated to Canada where he married, and worked in TV. Sadly he died while still a young man. Charleville man Kevin Barry, whom fellow rider Bill Mullins described as a 'most energetic rider, who kept on no matter what', jumped on the team from 1950 until 1956. Carrying a very familiar name from revolutionary times and scoring some well publicised Grand Prix wins in London, Dublin and Rotterdam, Barry soon became a household name, like O'Dwyer, Aherne and Lewis. He would win the King's Cup at London in 1951 with *Ballyneety*.

Nations Cup results from this decade bear out the difficulties faced by the school. By way of comparison, in the decade between 1929 and 1939 the Equitation School team entered a total of 71 Cup events and won 21 of them, an average unsurpassed by any other nation. From 1949 to 1959 the team contested 64 Cups, but managed just seven wins. However, against the odds, the school survived the fifties and along the way produced some great morale-boosting performances just when they were needed most.

Colonel Fred Aherne's term as Office Commanding actually began very well as Ireland won the 1949 Aga Khan trophy. By this time, a wonderful new horse, *Bruree*, had come to top form. The previous month he won the Country Life Cup for Captain Mick Tubridy at White City in London, and then at Dublin contributed mightily to the Aga Khan win by delivering a clear round for Captain Bill Mullins. Mick Tubridy was switched to *Lough Neagh*, and they showed good form by winning the Military Competition on the second day of the show. Giving a further morale-boost to the team, Captain Colm O'Shea brought out a recent purchase named *Ormand* to win the Minister for Defence's Trophy on the Thursday. For the Nations Cup itself, in addition to Bill Mullins on *Bruree*, Michael Tubridy rode *Lough Neagh*, Colm O'Shea was on *Rostrevor* and veteran of the side Lieutenant Colonel Dan Corry coaxed a first clear round from the mare *Clonakilty* to help Ireland emerge as winners, ahead of France, Britain and USA. The Grand Prix at 1949 Dublin was won by young lady rider Peggy St John Nolan on Sally Hall's *Outdoor Girl* – a combination that had been on one of the first Irish civilian teams to go abroad after the war.

The successful Dublin team of Tubridy, Mullins, Corry and O'Shea remained intact for that autumn's North American tour. And they had immediate success as they powered to a win at the new show in Harrisburg ahead of

*Below*:
*President Sean T O'Kelly presents the Aga Khan cup to the captain of the winning 1949 team at Dublin, Captain Dan Corry on* Clonakilty. *Also on the side were Captain Bill Mullins on* Bruree, *Captain Michael Tubridy on* Lough Neagh *and Captain Colm O'Shea on* Rostrevor.
(Bill Mullins)

Chile, Mexico and Canada. At New York, the Irish sustained a narrow three-quarter of a fault defeat by Mexico, while in Toronto just one fence divided the two sides. And so ended what was a very encouraging first year for new OC Aherne.

The promising good form of 1949 continued into the early part of 1950 as the team of Captains Tubridy, Magee, O'Shea and Mullins swept to victory at Nice. Mick was again on *Bruree*, Louis Magee rode *Clontibret*, O'Shea was on the grey *Ormond* and Bill Mullins had *Lough Neagh*. Their combined score of 41.75 placed them ahead of Spain, France, Holland, Switzerland and Italy. At Rome, where Ireland has never won the Cuppa di Nazione, they were fourth, but then climbed back to third in Lucerne, where Captain Kevin Barry made his international debut.

*Above:*
*Captain Colm O'Shea taking the high jump with* Ormond *at the Rome show in Piazza di Siena.* (Army Equitation School)

But very soon after that, disaster struck with the sudden death of their most promising young horse, *Bruree*. Having been brought on carefully and slowly, in the patient hands of National rider Captain Pat Needham, *Bruree* had just begun to demonstrate his superb ability when he fell victim to a heart attack. The post mortem revealed the fact that he had what must be the heaviest heart for a horse of his type on record. It weighed 14lb 3oz, thus being three ounces heavier than that of *Eclipse*.[16] Up to that point the known record of heart size in a horse was accorded to the British race horse *Eclipse*.

Within a short time the school also suffered the loss of two other young horses, *Rineanna* and *Glanmire*, through injury. Then a promising horse called *Enniskerry* was killed when hit by a car while out exercising during the 1950 New York show. But at this time they had a bit of luck in acquiring a former carriage horse whose yard name was simply *Trooper 1001*. When ridden by J J O'Neill, Colm O'Shea and Bill Mullins, he was known as *Glandore*. He was on the winning Irish team at Toronto and also scored a first for O'Shea at Madison Square Garden.

Although short on horse power, the team put up a good fight at 1950 London, being

*Below*:
*Capt. Kevin Barry*
*jumping to win the*
*King's Cup on*
Ballynonty *at*
*London, 1951.*
*(Army Equitation School)*

placed second to an increasingly strong British civilian side. But the loss of fresh mounts well and truly showed where it mattered most – on home ground at Dublin. They were fifth behind a red-jacketed British team that included Peter Robson on the great *Craven A* and Harry Llewellyn on the legendary Olympic team gold medalist and three times winner of the Kings Cup, *Foxhunter*. The Italian team that came fourth on this occasion had another star of the fifties and sixties, the brilliant rider Raimondo d'Inzeo, who was making the first of many visits to Dublin. A cryptic note at the end of a lengthy report on the 1950 Dublin Horse Show in *The Field* noted, 'the Irish Army horses, except for *Glengariff* and *Lough Neagh*, were rather disappointing.'[17]

Disappointing too was that year's North American tour, as the school came fourth at all three shows there in Washington, New York and Toronto.

In a bid to revitalise his team's hopes in the dramatically changing world of showjumping, OC Fred Aherne decided to try some of the old medicine that had worked so well twenty years earlier. Following the departure of Major Kulesya, he brought back Colonel Paul Rodzianko in March of 1951 for a sixteen-month tour as trainer. Since at this time serious questions were being asked about the team's then current form, just as at the time of his first arrival there in 1927, the Russian needed to

produce some good results.[18] There can be no doubt that matters did improve during the 1951 season as the school achieved some very impressive individual wins in Switzerland, Britain and Dublin. London has to be seen as the high point of that year when the diminutive Kevin Barry on the sizeable and very brave *Ballyneety* scored Ireland's first winning of the King's Cup since Ged O'Dwyer took it in 1936.

It is interesting that Ged had a

hand in this victory too, since he discovered *Ballyneety* and had him sold to the army. Making it an Irish double that year at the Royal International, Iris Kellett won the Queen's Cup for the second time. Her horse, *Rusty*, also had an O'Dwyer connection since he came from Ged's brother, Nicholas. Kevin Barry further demonstrated how well he suited *Ballyneety* by steering him to two victories at Dublin, where they also helped Ireland into second in the Aga Khan behind the, by now, all powerful British.

Aiming at giving wider experience to some of the younger riders, Colonel Aherne and Rodzianko decided to field two teams during the autumn of that year – one to North America and the other to a new show in Geneva. Dan Corry led the Swiss campaign, along with Captains J J O'Neill, Colm O'Shea and Brendan Cullinane, who sustained injury on the very first day. They came last of seven in the Cup, and their best result was from Colm O'Shea on *Glenarm* who took the Longines Trophy.

*Above:*
*Young Princess Elizabeth presenting the King's Cup to Kevin Barry at White City, London 1951.*
*(Army Equitation School).*

There was better luck in North America where the side of Captains Tubridy, Magee and Barry were a very close second to Mexico at New York, and then, with former carriage horse *Glandore*, and *Red Castle* and *Ballyneety*, they came up with six clear rounds to win the Toronto Nations Cup ahead of the USA, Mexico, Brazil and Canada.

Thus they faced into what was to be a controversial 1952 season during which a total of thirteen individual wins had to compensate for a complete shut-out in Nations Cup competition. Controversy arose over the school's decision not to send a team to the Olympics in Helsinki. For the first time, a civilian Irish eventing side was going to the XV Olympiad and the question was asked: Why not an Army jumping team? Due to a clash of dates with the Olympics, the Aga Khan Trophy was cancelled that year, and it was suggested that the Army team was kept at home in order to maintain interest in the jumping at Ballsbridge.[19] The criticism was somewhat off the mark and the real reason appears to be that they just did not have the horse power to challenge for a medal, and thus could not justify the substantial outlay of perhaps £5,000 in sending a squad to the Olympics. From a team point of view, this reasoning was certainly borne out as the season progressed when they failed to win any of nine Nations Cups contested. However, along the way they did pick up some good individual wins. On his farewell North American tour as a rider, the ever young Dan Corry won the Whitney Stone Trophy in Madison Square Garden. At the same event, *Glandore* had a win for Colm O'Shea. O'Shea went on to score five more wins on *Ballyneety* during the tour, including the Arete Trophy in Mexico. This trophy, named after the great horse that Humberto Mariles Cortes rode to the Olympic Gold medal for Mexico at London in 1948, was later presented to the Irish Government and still has a pride of place at McKee Barracks.

At the end of that season Colonel P A Mulcahy issued a critical report on the school to the Minister. He concluded: 'I propose to pay special attention to the Equitation School for a period and should the situation not show improvement, I will be recommending other employment for some of the officers.'[20]

In a bid to save their limited resources, the team did not reappear on the international circuit until July of the following year, when they made a determined bid to win back the King's Cup. Mick Tubridy and Colm O'Shea both got through to the jump-off, but in the end they had to give best to the great Harry Llewellyn on *Foxhunter*. Tubridy was second on *Red Castle* and also joint third with *Ballynonty* along with O'Shea on *Kilcarne*. The Irish were third behind the all but unbeatable British in the Prince of Wales Cup.

Named on the Aga Khan side for 1953 Dublin were Captains Kevin Barry, Colm O'Shea and Louis Magee, along with Colonel Dan Corry, who was making his last of many Aga Khan appearances at Ballsbridge. Over almost thirty years of consistent riding, he had helped Ireland to seven home wins there with horses like *Fingin*, *Red Hugh*, *Clonakilty*, *Duhallow*, *Antrim Glens* and *Miss Ireland*. This time, on *Kilkenny*, *Kilcarne*, *Ballycotton* and *Ormonde*, Barry, O'Shea, Corry and Magee had a superb first round. At the break they held a fractional lead over France and Britain. However, the British added only three and a half faults in the second round to win for their third time in a row and take possession of the third Aga Khan Trophy. Ireland dropped back to third place. The Army men finished on a high note, however, as Mick Tubridy on *Ballynonty* scored his second winning of the Grand Prix. This was the Clareman's last appearance at Dublin, and he certainly went out with his usual flourish. Following this good win, he joined Colm O'Shea and Kevin Barry for the North American circuit on a team that had former international, Colonel James Neylon, as Chef d'Equipe. O'Shea had a win on *Kilcarne* in Harrisburg. The trio then went on to take the New York Nation's Cup. O'Shea on *Clonsilla*, Barry on *Kilcarne,* and Tubridy on *Ballynonty* put up a score of 28.75 to beat the British side of Pat Smyth, William Hanson and Harry Llewellyn. The British got their own back in Toronto, where they won ahead of the USA, Canada and Ireland.

With the 1953 campaign ended, another era in the history of the Army team came to a close. By Christmas of that year, Colm O'Shea, Michael Tubridy, Louis Magee and Bill Mullins all retired from the Equitation School and were replaced by what was termed the third generation of riders there. Colm O'Shea went on to compete as a civilian in Canada; Bill Mullins continued his competitive career in the sport of eventing; Louis Magee rode horses on the national circuit for private owners like Lady Dorothy Mack; and Michael Tubridy took a job with the McGrath racing stables, but sadly, early in 1954, he died in a fall while riding a young horse at Trimblestown stud in Meath. With the threat of constant review by Colonel Mulcahy hanging over them, a new wave of officers would have to carry on the tradition from there.

*Below*:
*Members of the army team in a group of riders received by Pope Pius XII during a visit to the Rome show in 1952. Included are Dan Corry, Colm O'Shea, Michael Tubridy and Kevin Barry.*
*(Donal Corry)*

# 7

# NEEDING A STAR

# 1954 to 1963

*'A horse! A horse! my kingdom for a horse.'*[1]
*William Shakespeare, King Richard II*

With the beginning of 1954, the waiting began – but waiting for what? Waiting for the star horse-and-rider combinations that could make the Army Equitation School truly competitive again at the very top level of the sport. That was a very demanding order indeed, since the top level was quickly becoming more and more proficient and professional. What might be called the 'civilianisation' of showjumping was by this time in full gear and some of the greatest riders of all time were appearing on the scene.

There was one true difference between these great new stars and the then current group of international riders at the Irish Army Equitation School: just about all of the new opposition were, in a very real sense, born to the saddle and trained to the highest level of riding from a very early age. For example, Germany's Fritz Thiedemann had won Olympic medals in both dressage and showjumping. Britain's Pat Smyth began her competitive career in ponies and was taught by her mother, an accomplished horsewoman. French star Pierre Jonquères d'Oriola, who won individual Olympic gold in both Helsinki (1952) and Tokyo (1964) had his equestrian expert father as tutor.

In contrast to these stars, our army riders came to the school with little or no riding experience. Their route to the international arena was something of a hit-and-miss affair that grew out of the need for careers in the job-starved Ireland of the fifties. Young men who were lucky enough to have completed their Leaving Certificate applied for army cadetships. Some of them might have worked horses on their home farms, but most would never have sat in a saddle until their two-year cadet training course at the Military College on the Curragh of Kildare.

Commissioned as Second Lieutenants, they would then take up positions within the regular army. At different stages circulars were sent around the various barracks inviting applications for the Army Equitation School. Those who might have shown some talent during their Cadet school days would apply and then join a group of perhaps ten for a six-month training course at the school. Out of that class, two to four might be chosen to compete at national level for some two years before proving themselves good enough for the international circuit. This was clearly a very different route to the big arenas of the world that was unique to Ireland and which depended for its success on the natural horsemanship of the Irish and the innate ability of the Irish horse.

Commenting on the Irish recruitment methods of the fifties, British equestrian author Pamela Macgregor-Morris had this to say:

> The policy of the Department of Defence in Dublin altered radically as the older generation of riders became superannuated. Hitherto a man had been commissioned and put on the team very largely on the strength of his riding ability – a system that is followed in army teams all over the world, and is surely logical. Now however, a new type of young man began to be trained in the riding school by Colonel Rodzianko. For the first time the pupil had to comply with a certain educational standard – including an ability to speak Irish. In the majority of cases, though they may have exhibited marked athletic prowess in other sporting spheres, they had never previously had a leg over a horse.[2]

That same criticism was echoed in an *Irish Times* article written by knowledgeable commentator Stanislaus Lynch:

> In the field of international showjumping, the Irish Army Team has been having a somewhat lean period … What most people do not seem to realise is that modern showjumping, like most other competitive sports has become highly specialised and no detail in training or execution can afford to be overlooked. My personal opinion is that the officers learn riding too late in life … Change the recruiting system and induct into the army some of the scores of superb youngsters that are seen riding at shows and the Irish tricolour will soon be hoisted victoriously in the arenas of the world.[3]

Despite the authority of these two well informed authors, it appears that their analysis of the situation does not go deep enough. In the Ireland of the mid to late fifties, jobs were very scarce. Thousands of young men in the age bracket of the army jumpers were emigrating. The army did not have the luxury of selecting a few talented riders from what was still a relatively small cohort of well trained youngsters in the twenty-six counties. According to SJAI records, in 1954 it had just about four hundred registered members south of the Border. A small percentage of those would have been in the Army Cadet age group, but it is certain that many of them came from a financial bracket that was not without job prospects. No! In the Ireland of that time giving young men an option of gaining a cadetship and perhaps then progressing into the Army Equitation School was the only way it could be done.

For good or ill, this is indeed how it was for Lieutenants Billy Ringrose, Patsy Kiernan and Tommy Moroney as they came onto the team in early 1954 as replacements for the retiring Michael Tubridy, Colm O'Shea, Louis Magee and Bill Mullins. Remaining on the side to make up six international riders for the 1954–1955 seasons were Kevin Barry and Brendan Cullinane. Dan Corry still continued to ride on occasion right up until 1958.

Billy Ringrose, from Limerick, was an excellent athlete, but his only contact with horses was in working them on a relative's farm in Limerick during summer holidays. Following his commissioning in 1950, he did service in Cork and Clonmel before being accepted in 1952 for training under Colonel Rodzianko at McKee. His first international test came in 1954. Patsy Kiernan was Dublin-born and came with no riding experience. Before joining the school, he did regular active service. On retirement from the army in 1958, he went on to run a successful retail business in Rathfarnham. Limerickman Tommy Moroney excelled in Gaelic games and played at senior level for Galway prior to his riding career. All three of these men had the benefit of instruction under Colonel Rodzianko during his second term at the school, which lasted until August 1952. They then continued their training under pre-war rider, Commandant Jim Neylon.

In late January 1954 it was intended that Colonel Aherne would lead a combined new-recruit and older-hand team to Berlin on the twentieth anniversary of the school's last visit there back in 1934. However, due to the temporary illness of Captain Barry and complications with travel, the trip was called off. It was unfortunate that the new riders missed out on a valuable opportunity of testing their skills against the kind of opposition they would face in the big internationals to come. Among those events would be the very important matter of participation in the 1956 Olympics. The school had taken severe criticism for not jumping in Helsinki (see Chapter 6); they were not about to have that happen again. The 1956

*Above*:
Lt. Billy Ringrose on Flower Hill, *one of the first horses he rode after joining the army team in 1954.*
(*Army Equitation School*)

games were set to take place in Melbourne, but due to stringent Australian quarantine restrictions on horses being brought into their country, Stockholm, which had hosted the very first Olympic horse competitions back in 1912, was awarded the honour. From that point on, the Army Equitation School had the Swedish city in its sights as it geared towards winning the prized medal that had so cruelly eluded them since their foundation.

For Lieutenant Billy Ringrose, the 1954 competition year began on a good note when, on one of McKee's newer horses, *Flower Hill*, he scored a win at Dublin Spring Show. One week later, the side of Dan Corry, Brendan Cullinane, Kevin Barry and Patsy Kiernan headed out for the more serious challenge of the Swiss Nations Cup at Lucerne, followed by the team's first-ever visit to Lisbon. Included in the group of horses travelling were two new ones that were soon to prove their value – *Glenamaddy* and *Hollyford*. Commenting on the new-look team's chances, the *Irish Field* noted: 'It would be a mistake to expect sensational results right away but with training, they could develop into a pre-war team.'[4]

By the time of departure for Lucerne and Lisbon, a decision had not been made as to whether the largely new squad would take in the newly created World Show Jumping

*Opposite:*
*Army horses being*
*shipped out for the 1956*
*Olympics. The shipping*
*of horses was a*
*complicated matter. They*
*were brought to the*
*docks in army trucks and*
*then carefully loaded on*
*board. Sometimes they*
*were stabled on deck, but*
*at other times they were*
*below deck.*
*(Margaret Lynch)*

Championships at Madrid on 12 June. In the end, discretion prevailed. Their new young team did not yet have the experience to compete at that level of competition. As a matter of fact, it would be a further twenty years before an army rider took part in this important new competition (held at Hickstead in 1974).

At Lucerne, the Irish placed second by 8.75 faults to a very strong German team led by the Hans Gunther Winkler on *Halla*. This great combination went on to win the first of two consecutive world titles a few weeks later in Madrid. The Irish were a disappointing fourth in Lisbon.

Soon after his return home from Lisbon, Patsy Kiernan had a win on *Kilcarne* at a new An Tóstal show held in Cork. At Dublin that year, the side of Kevin Barry on *Ballycotton*, Billy Ringrose on *Liffey Vale*, Patsy Kiernan on *Ballynonty* and Brendan Cullinane on *Glanmire* were again fourth behind Britain, Germany and Portugal. However, there were a couple of bright moments for them at Ballsbridge. On opening day, Brendan Cullinane had a win with *Glanmire*, and on the Thursday, Patsy Kiernan on *Glenamaddy* scored his first international victory when beating no less than Hans Gunther Winkler on *Halla*. It has to be remembered that just four years earlier Patsy was a raw recruit with no riding experience. Now he was powering home ahead of the reigning world champion.

Despite these two wins at Dublin, the new team was still very much in need of a morale boost.

That came six weeks later at Rotterdam. That autumn, it had been decided not to contest the North American circuit but instead to take in the new Dutch international. It proved to be a good choice since, in a very close contest, the squad of Kevin Barry on *Ballycotton*, Brendan Cullinane on *Ballynonty*, Billy Ringrose on *Liffey Vale*, and Patsy Kiernan on *Glenamaddy* won the Nations Cup. Adding to the Irish joy was a win in the Grand Prix by Kevin Barry on *Hollyford*. It would be another ten years before an Irish rider would repeat that Grand Prix feat when, in 1964, the great civilian competitor Seamus Hayes won it with his star horse *Goodbye*.

After fifths in both Nice and Rome, third in London and Dublin, the army team went on to score well on the North American tour. But along the way they had some superb individual wins that kept morale high. At Nice, Patsy Kiernan emulated the achievements of Fred Aherne in 1935, John Lewis in 1939 and Dan Corry in 1952 by winning the

Grand Prix on the army's most consistent horse at this point, *Ballynonty*. In a main jump-off event at Dublin, Kevin Barry took up the ride on this superb jumper and got the better of Aachen World Champion Captain Raimondo d'Inzeo on Irish-bred *The Quiet Man*. And on final day at Ballsbridge, it was again the turn of Patsy Kiernan as he won the Grand Prix on *Glenamaddy*. This was the

school's eighth time to take this prestige event that down the years has had all of the world's greats as its victors. Another thirty-two years would pass before an army rider would again claim this trophy when Captain Gerry Mullins took it with the mighty *Rockbarton*.

In the autumn of 1955, the team of Kevin Barry on *Ballyneety*, Patsy Kiernan on *Ballynonty* and Billy Ringrose on *Hollyford* had a great run on the North American circuit. They began brilliantly in Harrisburg by winning the Nations Cup there ahead of main rivals, Mexico. At New York these same two teams were tied on 12 faults after two rounds. It was decided in a jump-off, which the Mexicans won. But at Toronto the Irish were back on top. This time they tied with USA on eight faults after two rounds. In the jump-off, they won by seven faults. This good North American tour was certainly the encouragement needed as the school faced into the Olympic year of 1956. In order to save horse power, Colonel Aherne passed up invitations to the earlier shows at Nice and Rome. Instead, the side of Lieutenants Billy Ringrose, Kevin Barry, Patsy Kiernan and Tommy Moroney began Olympic warm-up at Lucerne on 10 May. Moroney opened well when, on the first day, he

won the Prix St George on *Greenore*. But as a seven-day downpour descended on the Swiss venue, matters did not go well for the Irish after that as both *Glencree* and one of their main Olympic hopefuls, *Ballynonty*, were injured. After Lucerne the Irish took in an event at Ludwigsburg in Germany. There, young Lieutenant Ringrose scored his first individual international win on *Flower Hill* ahead of soon-to-be-crowned Olympic champions Hans Gunther Winkler on *Halla*.

Heading for Stockholm, Fred Aherne talked up their chances of putting in a good performance. 'The horses are in magnificent shape. All we need is a wee bit of luck,' he said.[5] But with nineteen other countries taking part and the stiffest 14-fence course that they had ever faced, this was a big ask for the less-than-experienced young Irish team. At the last moment, Patsy Kiernan's preferred ride, Dublin Grand Prix winner *Glenamaddy*, was injured in practice and replaced by the recently recovered *Ballynonty*. So the final three-man squad was Captain Kevin Barry on the fourteen-year-old bay gelding, *Ballyneety*, Kiernan on the still-young nine-year-old bay gelding, *Ballynonty*, and Lieutenant Billy Ringrose on the twelve-year-old chestnut gelding, *Liffey Vale*.

To their credit, the side was holding fifth place after the first round on a total of 66

faults. After a tough second round, the Irish were eventually pushed down into seventh place out of the twenty teams taking part. The two rounds of the team event also counted for the individual medals and emerging as hero of the contest was the magnificent Hans Gunther Winkler, who, although severely injured, still finished his round to help win team gold for his country and individual gold for himself. It still is seen as one of the most heroic moments in the history of international showjumping. Ireland's individual best out of the fifty-two riders taking part was eighteenth for the more experienced Kevin Barry.

Also taking part at Stockholm that year was a three-member Irish eventing team that included former army rider Bill Mullins, Ian Dudgeon, who was the son of former mentor of the army team Lieutenant Colonel Hume Dudgeon, along with prominent showjumper, Harry Freeman Jackson. They were in contention for the bronze medal when, sadly, a mistake on the cross-country led to team elimination. Bill Mullins ended up a very creditable tenth out of fifty-seven individually. It is an interesting statistic that a quarter of the horses taking part in this event were Irish-bred. Our exports were thriving, but competing in the market was becoming ever more difficult for our own teams.

Taking Olympic showjumping bronze at Stockholm was a powerful British side mounted on Irish horses. They continued their success with Nations Cup wins at both London and Dublin. In London, the Irish Olympic squad, plus Tommy Moroney, came fourth out of eighth in the Prince of Wales Cup.

Brazilian legend Nelson Pessoa paid his first visit to Dublin in 1956 and he made an impressive entry by winning the opening international class. In the Aga Khan, the Irish four of Kevin Barry, Patsy Kiernan, Billy Ringrose and Tommy Moroney were third by one fence behind Turkey, who, on this their first visit to Ballsbridge, were runners-up to Britain. Lieutenant Moroney on *Ballynonty* had one of only two clear rounds in the contest.

Taking beatings from a mighty British civilian side had become unpleasantly common for the Irish at this point. So, it appeared to be good news when Colonel Aherne announced in October 1956 that he had negotiated a contract with Seamus Hayes to come as trainer to the school. During an eleven-year sojourn in England, this genius horseman had beaten the best that Britain had to offer in the main events on the British

*Above:*
*International star and later trainer of the Army Equitation School, Seamus Hayes, with his son, Lieutenant William Hayes, who rode with the school in the 1980s and 1990s.*
*(Mary Rose Hayes)*

circuit. The OC hoped that with some of his personal training the army lads could do the same.

From a team point of view, there was no joy for the school on the 1956 North American tour. While placing a close second to Mexico by just 4.25 faults at New York, they were pushed down to third in both Harrisburg and Toronto. However, they had plenty to celebrate in the big individual contests. Lieutenant Billy Ringrose struck top form on *Ballynonty* to win the Grand Prix events at both Madison Square and at the Great Winter Fair of Toronto. Ringrose was a most focused individual, whose dedication to his own fitness translated into superb riding technique. While *Ballynonty* was a good and trustworthy mount, Billy was still in waiting for a horse that could match his talent. The same would apply to a new recruit of the following year, Galway-born and Meath-based Lieutenant Sean Daly. Also a focused and determined rider, Daly would make the most of horses like *Glenamaddy*, but he too was awaiting a special mount that could match his winning potential. That waiting was to continue for another two long seasons during which the school had to make do with some horses that were either past their prime or just that bit short on the quality needed for winning at the top end of international competition.

Along with Sean Daly, two more riders joined the international squad in 1957 as replacements for Kevin Barry, Colm O'Shea, Brendan Cullinane and Patsy Kiernan, who were all retiring. Sean Daly was joined in the new group by Desmond Ringrose (brother to Billy) along with Dublin man Roger Moloney. All three had completed at least two years of national competition before being selected along with the now more experienced Billy Ringrose and Patsy Kiernan for the 1957 spring continental tour. It was a learning tour with few good results.

For the 1957 Aga Khan, Colonel Aherne fielded the two Ringrose brothers – Billy on

*Ballynonty* and Desmond on *Flower Hill*, along with Sean Daly on *Glencree* and Roger Moloney on *Ballycotton*. Against strong sides from France, Germany, Italy and Britain, the Irish had a disastrous outing as they again finished last.

Previewing things to come, there was one interesting result in the military/civilian competition on the second day of that 1957 Dublin show. It was won by Piero d'Inzeo, the Italian Stockholm Olympic bronze medalist. But second to him was young Cashel man, Tommy Wade, on a former cart-horse named *Dundrum*. This brilliant little Connemara/thoroughbred cross was just a six-year-old then, but in the years to come, he and his ingenious rider were to make winning headlines. Over the next six seasons, Tommy would also lead the battle for a combined army/civilian team in the Aga Khan. Despite the FEI directive of 1947 that had opened Nations Cup competitions to civilian riders, the Irish teams for the Aga Khan still remained confined to army riders. Tommy, along with other potential team riders, aimed at changing that.

Except for Billy Ringrose, whose expertise was growing stronger, the 1957 North American tour did not bring any better results for the army men. They came fourth in Harrisburg and third at both New York and Toronto. Billy keep the flag flying on *Ballynonty* as he scored three individual wins – the Biddeo Trophy in Harrisburg, the Pennsylvania National Trophy in New York and the Winter Fair Cup in Toronto.

Sadly, at the beginning of 1958, Colonel Fred Aherne, who had been ailing for some time, retired as OC. This great campaigner with the team during the thirties and leader during the fifties died soon afterward. He had tried just about everything during a decade of change to improve the team's fortunes. But the odds had been against him. He was replaced by another pre-war rider, Lieutenant Colonel Jim Neylon, who held the post for the next decade.

The magnitude of the task facing Neylon was clearly illustrated by the results from 1958. Except for an encouraging win by newcomer Lieutenant Sean Daly on *Glenamaddy* in the Horse Show Committee Cup at Dublin, the whole season might well be termed a disaster. So, once more, the Army Equitation School was at the knife-edge of extinction. With all of the difficulties facing it in terms of acquiring the horse/rider combinations needed to remain competitive, no easy solution was in sight.

Yet as Sir John Pentland Mahaffy said when made Provost of Trinity College late in his life, in Irish affairs we should never look for the inevitable but rather the unexpected. Well, for the army team both the inevitable and the unexpected happened at the same time in February of that difficult year when they were supremely lucky to a find a future star then called *Frenchman*. This attractive and athletic four-year-old gelding had been bred by John Delahunty in Mullinavat, County Kilkenny. He was the nineteenth foal out of a *Marshal Ney* dam and was by the thoroughbred sire, *Knight's Crusader*. His early working life was spent as a hunter and farm horse. Sold to the Lawlor family of Bishopslough, County Kilkenny, Vincent Lawlor rode him, until he went to the army for the then substantial price of £1,500. His new name was *Loch an Easpaig* (Irish for his former home of Bishopslough). This was the horse the army had been waiting for. But was it enough to have the team continue in the independent vein to which it was accustomed? This was the question facing the school and its new OC as they entered the final year of the fifties.

At the very beginning of 1959 an extra element of pressure was placed upon the army with the creation of a fully-fledged civilian team by the Show Jumping Association of Ireland. This now-expanding association was, in effect, saying to the army, 'If you cannot do it, we can.' That may have been a vain boast, but it certainly made good press. With

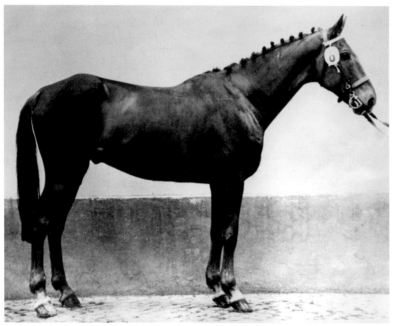

the likes of Tommy Wade, Leslie Fitzpatrick, Tommy Brennan and Diana Conolly-Carew making headlines for wins both at Dublin and abroad, the argument began to ring true. When in August 1959 the army side placed last in the Prince of Wales Cup at London and then a disappointing third behind a new young British team in the Aga Khan, the *Irish Field* baldly voiced the previously whispered theory that 'One could pick three [civilian] teams at the last Dublin Horse Show, which would have been hard to beat in any Prix de Nations competition.'[6] In hindsight, that was an overstatement, but it did represent growing sentiment of the time.

Much happened on the Irish showjumping scene in that year of 1959 which helped set in motion a series of events that would eventually culminate in the development of a new army/civilian axis that survives down to this day. Firstly, in April 1959 Seamus Hayes finished his term as trainer at the Equitation School and resumed his professional career in the employ of Dublin stud owner, Omar van Landeghem. There he was mounted on a team of good jumpers that included *Kilrush*, on which he won the following August's Dublin Grand Prix. Seamus's availability added enormously to the potential strength of any civilian team.

Then in April of his final year at the head of matters in the RDS, Judge William Wylie initiated an Equestrian Team Travel Fund which was to be used to defray the expenses of civilian riders travelling abroad. Through it, the RDS pledged to match private contributions pound-for-pound. Over the next twenty years, this proved to be a most generous legacy from this great leader of the sport, who died in 1964. In its very first year of operation, the fund raised over £3,000. By the time it was wound up in 1979, the sum contributed and used totalled almost £80,000. In effect, this initiative opened the door to international competition for enthusiastic young riders from north and south of the Border who otherwise would never have got their chance in the great arenas of the world.

But perhaps the most dramatic development in this year of change came just one month after the establishment of the travel fund when the first SJAI selected team was sent to compete in England. The announcement of this selection was expressed in the following very precise press statement: 'On the initiative of the Federation Equestre Internationale of Ireland [the RDS] the SJAI has selected a team to compete at Manchester and Oxford shows.'[7] Included on the squad were Leslie Fitzpatrick, Tommy Wade, Seamus Hayes and Ian Dudgeon.

That year, the RDS also announced that the famous banks in the main arena would no longer be used for international team competitions. These obstacles had been very popular features for the home crowd ever since they were installed away back in 1884. They also gave something of an advantage to the Irish team whose horses were adept at

negotiating natural obstacles, but they were anathema to some of the visiting sides from the continent, whose power-jumping horses found them very difficult indeed.

While all of these developments were taking place, the army team was by no means standing still. In addition to their new Officer Commanding, they also added two new international riders for the 1959 season in Lieutenants Pat Griffin from County Clare and Galway man Eamonn O'Donohue. Reflecting the sparse resources at the school in those years, Pat Griffin lightheartedly recalls that the first horse he was given to ride 'was of uncertain origin and made a snail seem like a jet'.

The school attended no early shows abroad in 1959. Instead, Colonel Neylon concentrated on getting some good results at the Dublin Spring Show. Despite having to share the spoils with the likes of Tommy Brennan, Tommy Wade and Leslie Fitzpatrick, the new-look army team did garner a good deal of praise for a spirited performance. Newly promoted Captain Billy Ringrose had his first major outing there with *Loch an Easpaig*. Pat Griffin had wins on both *Glencree* and *Garryowen* while Lieutenant Sean Daly again demonstrated how he was blending with *Glenamaddy* when winning the overall show championship.

Making his first public appearance with the team at that spring show was Lieutenant Ned Campion from Laois. A good all-round athlete, who had senior medals to his credit for both his home county and Kildare, Ned was one of those young men who, without any previous riding experience, immediately demonstrated superb natural talent when given the chance during his cadetship course. 'Ned stood out from the first day of our course at McKee and we knew he was something special,' comments his classmate General Paddy Nowlan, who later served as the army's Quartermaster General. Lieutenant Campion went directly from his Cadetship into the Equitation School but he did not get his first international outing until 1961. From then on he was to be a central figure in Irish showjumping for more than thirty-six years – first as rider, later as OC to the school and then as Chef d'Equipe to Irish teams right up to Olympic level.

It is interesting that despite the absence of any notable results from their first international appearance of 1959 at London, the army side of Captain Billy Ringrose, along with Lieutenants Sean Daly, Pat Griffin and Eamonn O'Donohue did receive some fulsome, if somewhat pointed, praise in the *Irish Field*. Its reporter noted: 'For the first time in 10 years they are beginning to show a vivacity that was associated with the men and horses of the early years of the team. They really rode like horsemen. It was a delight to see the change.'[8]

The same report referred specifically to *Loch an Easpaig* as 'being full of latent ability'. The team remained unchanged for the 1959 Aga Khan – Ringrose for the first time on *Loch an Easpaig*, Daly on *Glenamaddy*, Griffin on *Ballynonty* and O'Donohue on *Liffey Vale*. There can be no doubt that over the previous twelve months since the superb *Loch an Easpaig* had joined the school there was hot competition among the officers as to who would ride him. This was always the case with a new horse that showed exceptional talent and it was particularly so with this one. But, in the end, the cool determination of Billy Ringrose tipped the balance. Over the coming seasons this partnership became key to the army team efforts. It began at the 1959 Dublin Horse Show as they opened with an encouraging win in the Sandymount Stakes and then jumped clear in the Nations Cup. Despite this, Ireland still placed third behind Britain and Spain. But lifting Irish spirits on the final day was Seamus Hayes as he won the Grand Prix on Omar van Landeghem's *Kilrush*.

The army's efforts in the autumn of that year (last at Le Zoute and third in Rotterdam) were overshadowed by Tommy Wade's sparkling live television performance on *Dundrum* at the Horse of the Year indoor show in Wembley. For the first time in decades, Irish showjumping got front-page coverage in reports of his five clear rounds that had him share first place in the Victor Ludorum competition with Robert Greyston of South Africa.

This same overshadowing of army riders by SJAI stars continued in 1960. Temporarily wearing red jackets with green collars, a side composed of Seamus Hayes, Leslie Fitzpatrick and North of Ireland rider John Brooke (son of Sir Basil Brooke) had wins at Wiesbaden and Ludwigsburg on the first continental tour undertaken by the civilians. They finished with a flourish as, live on Eurovision, they won the Nations Cup at Enschede in Holland. On their return, they received a hero's welcome and were fêted at the new SJAI fundraising show in Dundrum, County Dublin.

Thus, this season of 1960 marked a difficult and somewhat painful period of adjustment for the men from McKee Barracks. Instead of being Ireland's sole showjumping team, they now had to share that distinction with civilian sides drawn from both north and south of the Border. For over thirty years, in their distinctive green uniforms, they had become the equestrian image of Ireland abroad. They wore the tricolour on their saddle cloths. They snapped a smart salute when 'The Soldier's Song' rang out over arenas around the world. Now a totally new phenomenon had entered Irish showjumping – a team that wore red coats trimmed with green, had a flag of the four provinces of Ireland on their saddles and a tune called 'St Patrick's Day' as their anthem. It has to be remembered that the people who brought this civilian team to fruition, like Leslie Fitzpatrick's dad, Bernard, and Iris Kellett's dad, Harry, had been the same people who just six years earlier had painstakingly brought about the compromises that allowed Irish showjumping north and south of the Border to unite into a single All-Ireland body. A team growing out of that body was bound to reflect those same compromises that would allow Northern Ireland riders of the Unionist tradition to take part. Hence the red coats, four provinces saddle cloths and strange anthem.

Despite these challenging changes, relations between the army and the civilian organisation, the SJAI, grew closer. In 1960, the Equitation School, for the first time, accepted a new rule that army horses must register if they were to jump at SJAI-affiliated shows. Later that year, Minister for Defence Kevin Boland was given an honorary SJAI membership.

But politics aside, the 1960 season got off to a good start for the army as Lieutenant Sean Daly on *Loch Gorman* had a win at Pau in France, and Billy Ringrose on *Loch an Easpaig* shared first with Captain Grappela of Holland in the Marseilles show championship. In its build-up to the Rome

*Above*:
*Irish side for the 1960 Aga Khan Cup: Captain Billy Ringrose, along with new team members Lieutenants Eamonn O'Donohue, Pat Griffin and Roger Moloney.*
*(Pat Griffin)*

Olympics, the team came third at both London and Dublin, where Argentina had its first Aga Khan victory and young British star David Broome took his first Grand Prix on the Irish-bred *Sunsalve*. Billy Ringrose won the Puissance on *Loch an Easpaig*, while Tommy Wade and *Dundrum* scored a treble of wins.

Selected for one more bid by the school to gain an Olympic showjumping medal were Captain Billy Ringrose, Lieutenant Sean Daly and Lieutenant Eamonn O'Donohue. Lieutenant Roger Moloney travelled as reserve. A civilian eventing team, made up of Ian Dudgeon, Captain Harry Freeman-Jackson, Eddie Harty (son of Cyril Harty) and Tony Cameron also made the trip to Rome. The eventers were in contention for a medal until the end. But when Freeman-Jackson took the wrong course in the showjumping phase, their hopes died and Ireland's Olympic jinx remained alive.

That jinx continued for the army showjumpers. *Loch an Easpaig* was their best performer in the team event, with a total of 40 faults over two rounds. Sean Daly on *Loch Gorman* totalled 66.50. Eamonn O'Donohue on *Cluain Meala* was eliminated in both rounds, and thus the team suffered one more humiliating elimination. This result surely added fuel to the argument that a combined army/civilian team was the answer.

Matters improved for the squad when they travelled to North America that autumn. They collected a total of forty-six place rosettes at the three shows. While disappointingly fourth and fifth in the team events of Harrisburg and New York, they improved to come a close second to Canada in Toronto. Win or lose on this circuit, in particular, the army men on their Irish horses represented the home country to Irish emigrants there in a way

*Above*:
*Princess Grace of Monaco presenting the trophy to Captain Billy Ringrose on* Loch an Easpaig *after they had won the 1961 Grand Prix at Nice.*
(*Army Equitation School*)

*Below*:
*Billy Ringrose jumping to win the Grand Prix of Rome on Loch an Easpaig.*
(*Army Equitation School*)

that no other group of individuals could.

With Ned Campion joining the international squad for his first time, the school had a blazing start to the 1961 season. And with the army's public relations apparatus making a strong effort to match that of the civilian side, they got well-deserved publicity for their efforts. Colonel Neylon had set them a very ambitious task for the year, with nine Nations Cups on their schedule. It all began in the sunny south of France at Marseilles. And it began well as Billy Ringrose won the Grand Prix there on *Ceanannus Mor*. With this morale boost under belts, it was on to Nice where the icon of the time, Princess Grace, was on hand to present the prizes. Ringrose again rose to the occasion by winning the Prix de Monaco on *Loch an Easpaig*. But topping even that superb result was the winning of the French Nations Cup by the side of Lieutenants Ned Campion on *Cluain Meala*, Sean Daly on *Loch Gorman*, Eamonn O'Donohue on *Cill an Fhail*, along with Ringrose, who had a double clear on the brilliantly on-form *Loch an Easpaig*. This was the first team win by the school in seven long years and a convincing one it was. In the end, they had seven faults to spare over Spain and a further five ahead of the Italians, whose four included Olympic gold and silver medalists Raimondo and Piero d'Inzeo.

Rome Show 1961 was televised live on Eurovision and attended by Queen Elizabeth II as guest of honour. In this superb setting, Captain Ringrose had one of the true crowning moments of his eighteen-year international career. He first powered home as winner of the

Grand Prix with *Loch an Easpaig*, and for good measure placed second as well on *Cloyne*. Then on the final day, he repeated the victory, by taking the Premio Aventino, on *Cloyne*.

In the Rome Nations Cup, the Irish side had to be content with third behind Italy and Britain, but over the whole three-show tour they had won a total of thirty-eight prizes. Included among them were six firsts, seven seconds and four thirds by star of the trip Captain Ringrose, who was also Leading Rider at Rome. The side was welcomed home at Dublin Airport by Minister for Defence Kevin Boland, along with a large crowd of supporters. Among them was Captain Ringrose's mother, who was quoted in the *Irish Times* as saying, 'This is one of the greatest moments of my life.'

Billy Ringrose and *Loch an Easpaig* retained their good form during the rest of that season, winning the Manifestation Stakes in London, the Pembroke Stakes at Dublin, the Martin Trophy in Washington, the Democrat Trophy in New York and the Goodwill Trophy in Toronto. An *Irish Independent* lead editorial of 27 November had high praise for the team: 'There is a new spirit at work and a heartening number of brilliant faultless rounds were achieved to put Ireland back in her proper place as a serious rival to the best the Continent can produce.'[9] Even more important from the point of view of the school's future, the *Weekly Bulletin* of the Department of External Affairs, which was distributed widely around the world, devoted almost its whole 15 May issue to the team's success and its promotion of the Irish horse.

In the meantime, there were some exciting developments in the civilian camp. Seamus Hayes moved on from Skidoo stud to ride a truly talented team of horses for Joe McGrath's Sandyford stables. Coming in to take his place as lead rider of Omar Van Landeghem's string, was another star of the sixties, Kilkenny man Tommy Brennan. He was selected to join Leslie Fitzpatrick and

*Below:*
*The victorious Irish team welcomed home at Dublin airport by Minister for Defence Kevin Boland.*
*(Army Equitation School)*

another young rider, Brian McNicholl, to contest the Nations Cup meeting at Enschede, Holland. The Irish trio won six of the seven competitions on offer – including the Nations Cup, which they took on a zero score ahead of Germany and South Africa. Their triumphant homecoming at Dublin airport was again a well-publicised affair.

Despite the successes of both the army and civilian sides during the first half of the season, their results were totally eclipsed by the individual exploits of Tommy Wade and Seamus Hayes during the second half. At the first ever Hickstead Derby run in July 1961,

*Above:*
*Star of the fifties and sixties, Tommy Wade, on the magnificent little Connemara-thoroughbred cross, Dundrum.*
*(Margaret Lynch)*

Seamus emerged the popular winner on *Goodbye*. Wade then dominated the headlines as he and *Dundrum* uniquely won five events, including the Grand Prix, at Dublin Horse Show. He went on to take the Victor Ludorum (the traditional final championship competition at the show) live on television at London's Horse of the Year Show. This sparkling win under the lights by the enthusiastic twenty-three-year-old came ahead of David Broome on his recently crowned European Champion *Sunsalve* and Brazil's Nelson Pessoa on *Beau Geste*. Illustrating the public interest in this Irish first, it was the front-page lead story in the following day's *Sunday Press*. On his return to Ireland, Tommy was paraded into his home town of Dundrum, Tipperary, like the folk hero that he had become.

The pattern of good individual performances both by the army and the civilians continued into 1962. But that season brought none of the much longed-for Nations Cup wins. And as the year progressed there were more and more calls for what was seen as the only solution to this problem – a combined army/civilian team. But that development was still slow in coming. So the two sides still went their separate ways.

In February it was announced that young twenty-one-year-old Dublin man Lieutenant Ronnie MacMahon had joined the school. He had been a winner with Irish junior teams during the previous two years and was a seasoned rider with the South County Dublin hunt. Later in his career he would spearhead the army's expansion into the sport of eventing.

The school's best result at their opening 1962 show in Lucerne once again came from Captain Ringrose as he won the Grand Prix Militaire on *Loch an Easpaig*. Lieutenant Ned Campion had a good placing with *Kilenaule*. Ringrose was a winner again in Barcelona, taking the speed championship on *Cloyne* and the Puissance on *Loch an Easpaig*, who sustained a slight injury prior to London and was unable to compete there. But he was fit again for Dublin. Along with Ringrose on *Loch an Easpaig*, the side for the Aga Khan included the new combination of Ned Campion on *Sliabh na gCrot*, Lieutenant Sean Daly on *Glenamaddy* and Lieutenant Eamonn O'Donohue on *Cill an Fhaill*. More than justifying his inclusion, Ned jumped a clear and a four but the Irish were pushed down to fourth behind Italy, the USA and Britain. Matters did not improve much on their next Nations Cup outings. They were fourth again in both New York and Toronto, but did manage a second behind the USA in Harrisburg. Lieutenant Campion scored his first international win at Madison Square Garden.

Retiring from international competition at the end of that season were Captains Pat Griffin and Sean Daly. Both remained in the army. Sean went on to be Aide de Camp for Taoiseach Liam Cosgrave and would later become OC of the Equitation School in 1975. Pat did United Nations service in Cyprus with the Third Infantry Group and became Company Commander, Fourth Battalian, Collins Barracks, Cork.

In the meantime, Tommy Wade and *Dundrum* continued on their winning ways. They took major prizes in Belfast, Brussels and Newcastle-upon-Tyne, scored two more wins at Dublin and finished the season once again in a blaze of publicity as, live on the BBC, they jumped the wall at 6ft11in to share first place in the Puissance with the great Harvey Smith. BBC commentator Dorian Williams described the event as the most exciting he had witnessed during his career in broadcasting.

After each of his triumphs, twenty-three-year-old Tommy was not slow to emphasise the inequality of civilians not being allowed to jump on the Irish team for the Aga Khan Cup. The logic of his argument had, by this time, become irrefutable. So, during the winter of 1962 discussions were already in progress between the Army Equitation School and the RDS about a dramatic change in policy. OC Colonel James Neylon later put on record how this much-needed development came about.

> During this time civilian jumping under the SJAI and in particular its chairman, Jack Lewis was making considerable progress as was the BSJA in Great Britain. Horses had considerably decreased in European armies and mixed army-civilian teams were now the order of the day. In the spring of 1963 the Department of Defence approached the National Equestrian Federation with the proposition that mixed army-civilians should be the National Teams in future. The chairman, Judge Wylie, readily acquiesced. The Officer Commanding Army Equitation School was appointed Chef d'Equipe.[10]

Not only at home, but abroad as well, this was a newsworthy happening. *The Chronicle of the Horse* in the USA referred to the decision as 'The biggest news in the history of show jumping in Ireland since the formation of the Army team in 1926.'[11]

Thus, like so many other Irish long-standing controversies, this one had finally evaporated. It was now up to the combined force of the army and the SJAI to keep Ireland competitive on the international showjumping circuit. Even for a combined side, this was not an easy task. To be sure, there was no shortage of riders with international potential, but what were they going to ride? At this time the number of home-bred jumpers was getting smaller. Between 1945 and 1970 overall horse numbers in Ireland fell by some 300,000. Just like the army teams, the civilian teams going abroad were potent adverts for the Irish horse. But there was an added difference with the civilians – a number of them were also agents who aided in the sale of showjumpers out of Ireland. In 1963 the Swiss, British and Italian teams all largely jumped on Irish-bred horses. Even the Germans at this time were buying Irish. In that very year, at least ten of their team mounts came from Ireland. The result, of course, was a huge increase in the price being asked for what was a scarce product. So while Ireland had plenty of riders, both civilian and military, with world class talent, getting the horses for them to ride had become an almost impossible task.

But as the year of change, 1963, began, there were hopes that the available horsepower was sufficient to mount a strong combined army/civilian side to take on the main challenges at London and Dublin. For the army, it was a matter of aiming at having at least two of their best combinations on the Aga Khan team. Captain Ringrose remained their top contender, followed by Lieutenant Ned Campion.

The civilian riders were also laying claim to selection for what was going to be a most exciting watershed moment for them at Ballsbridge. Tommy Brennan won the Grand Prix in Wiesbaden on *Kilbrack* and was leading rider in Enschade; Diana Conolly-Carew on *Barrymore* took the Enschade Grand Prix and came fourth in the Ladies European Championships at Hickstead; Tommy Wade on *Dundrum* all but dominated the Spring Show in Dublin and went on to score Ireland's first win in the King's Cup at London since Kevin Barry had taken it back in 1951. Also at that Royal International Show in White City, Seamus Hayes on *Goodbye* won the Imperial Cup, which was presented by none other than former army trainer, Colonel Paul Rodzianko. For the Prince of Wales Nations Cup, Ireland fielded a full civilian side for the first time. Seamus Hayes and his wife, Mary Rose, joined Diana Conolly-Carew and Tommy Wade to place second behind a crack British side that had already won the Rome Cup earlier that year.

Hence, it was with good justification that the press previews for Dublin spoke of 'good hopes for Irish success'. Due to the degree of publicity that had built up about the long-awaited creation of a combined army/civilian team, the anticipation surrounding this year's Aga Khan Cup could only be compared to what had prevailed when Ireland fielded its first army team back in 1926. Attendance for the four days of the show climbed by 10,000 to 123,627.

The Irish side eventually named by Chef d'Equipe Colonel James Neylon for that historic 1963 event were Tommy Wade on *Dundrum*, Captain Billy Ringrose on *Loch an Easpaig*, Diana Conolly-Carew on *Barrymore* and Seamus Hayes on *Goodbye* to contest the cup against strong sides from Italy, Switzerland, Germany, along with Rome and London winners, Britain. Among the team riders taking part were newly crowned European Champion and future Olympic Champion Graziano Mancinelli for Italy, European silver medallist Alwin Schockemöhle and the great Hans Günther Winkler of Germany, along with Max Hauri of Switzerland, who rode an Irish-bred horse from the Hughes family in Kilkenny, named *Millview*.

Winning against this kind of opposition was going to be no easy task. As Tommy Wade put it, 'We had a hill to climb and everyone had to pull their weight.' Tommy had complained for years about sitting on his backside in the stand while the Irish Army side was being beaten. His time had now come. A new game was on for army and civilian alike as on that Friday, 9 August 1963, one more dramatic chapter was written in the history of Irish equestrianism. There had been worries that a change like this would spell the end of the Equitation School. But that simply was not the case. So strong was the image presented both at home and abroad by the army riders, their value to both the state and the Irish horse still outweighed any other consideration.

As the new-look team paraded before the packed stands, the acclamation received spoke volumes about how positively the public received the decision of opening the Aga Khan to civilian and army alike. And what a picture the side presented: the young, feminine beauty of Diana on the superb grey *Barrymore*; the folk hero Tommy on the diminutive *Dundrum*; the ultimate horseman Seamus on great Hickstead winner *Goodbye* and the long-lionised army man, Captain Billy Ringrose, with the superb *Loch an Easpaig*. This was a team that could win the hearts of any Irish crowd. But what they had to do now was combine their experience and their horsemanship to win the most coveted Irish trophy, the Aga Khan Cup.

Dramatically. they were drawn first of the five teams to go, and Seamus Hayes brought the stands alive with an opening clear. Faults by Germany and Britain raised hopes. But a clear from Switzerland put the pressure on. Ireland's second out Diana – and *Barrymore* had the bogey coral-coloured upright fence down. Switzerland got a clear with just quarter of a time fault from Max Hauri to put them in the lead. Ireland was in need of a clear, but did not get it this time when Billy came back with eight. Switzerland and Germany got clears from their third riders, so Ireland had to come up with something special. To a rousing reception, Tommy Wade did what he had long promised. He went brilliantly clear to keep Ireland well in touch at the break. The script was written for a nail-biting second round, with Switzerland on quarter of a fault, Ireland on four and Germany with eight.

There was a groan from the stands when first out for Ireland – Seamus on *Goodbye* – had one fence down. But matters evened up when the Swiss also knocked one and the Germans got a clear. It was a battle to the finish. Both Diana and Billy got huge applause as they both came up with vital clears. When the third Swiss rider knocked three, the door opened for Ireland. One more clear from them would be the winner. Once again, it was all down Tommy Wade and *Dundrum*. And once again they fulfilled their promise. After a circuit that had some hair-raising moments, when they jumped the final wall clear, the old arena erupted into a thunder of elation. After a wait of fourteen long years, Ireland had again won the Aga Khan Cup. An old Irish saying '*Ní neart go cur le chéile*' (there's no strength without pulling together) applies here. This was indeed a new beginning. But was it, like 1926, a false dawn? This had yet to be seen.

*Below:*
*The first combined army/civilian side to win the Aga Khan trophy at Dublin in 1963: Captain Billy Ringrose, Diana Conolly-Carew, Seamus Hayes and Tommy Wade.*
*(RDS Library Archive)*

# NEW DIRECTIONS

## 1964 to 1975

*'We wanted to see Ireland's strongest teams fielded for major events like the Aga Khan …
we were happy to be an important part of that effort.'*
*Lieutenant Colonel Ronnie MacMahon[1]*

Where to now for the Army Equitation School? Having made the crucial move of linking up on a joint army/civilian team in 1963, it was adjustment time for the men from McKee Barracks. The totally changed situation in which they were unable to provide enough horse power for an Aga Khan team would surely have been viewed by earlier riders as a bitter blow to former pride. But for the current batch of riders at the school during the 1963-64 season, the response seems to have been more philosophical. A young cadet of the time, later international event rider and a future OC of the school, Lieutenant Colonel Ronnie MacMahon recalls the mood in this way: 'We wanted to see Ireland's strongest teams fielded for major events like the Aga Khan. We would have very much liked that to be a full army side, but when that was not possible we were happy to be an important part of that effort.'

In the autumn of 1963 the first combined army/civilian side went on the North American tour. Captains Billy Ringrose and Ned Campion were joined by Diana Conolly-Carew on a three-member squad. Billy won two events in Harrisburg but they had no team firsts.

One issue arising out of the decision to form a combined army/civilian team involved the flag, anthem and emblems to be used. This matter had been discussed at length within the Show Jumping Association when civilian sides were first being formed and an effort was made to accommodate riders from a Unionist tradition. However, when the army joined in, a solution had to be found that would suit their ethos as well. Instead of the first rather complicated solutions, they ended up with the tricolour and 'The Soldier's

Song'. From the seventies onwards, there has been unanimity in using the national flag and anthem at all events.[2]

As the 1963 season ended and a very much changed era began, two far-reaching events happened that should be noted. Firstly, there was the sale by the Equitation School of future champion three-day-eventing horse, *Durlas Eile*. Secondly, just months prior to his death, stalwart school supporter Judge William E Wylie put into words his vision of the school's future role.

The sale of *Durlas Eile* at the end of 1963 has to be seen as a golden opportunity missed. Neither in terms of finance or overall Department of Defence policy had the point yet arrived when eventing could seriously be included in the school's programme. So *Durlas Eile* was sold into the civilian hands of Eddie Boylan, who rode him to many wins. This missed opportunity must have had an influence on a gradual change of thinking within the Equitation School. By 1968 riders from the school began to take part in the exciting sport of three-day-eventing for the first time.

The second seminal happening of that time took place during a presentation to the victorious 1963 civilian/army Aga Khan team (Captain Billy Ringrose, Diana Conolly-Carew, Tommy Wade and Seamus Hayes) at the annual Show Jumping Association of Ireland ball in January 1964. In the presence of Army Chief-of-Staff Lieutenant General Sean McKeown and Equitation School OC Colonel James Neylon, the man at whose behest the school was first formed back in 1926, Judge William Wylie, outlined his vision of the unit's future. He noted that with the international sport of equestrianism becoming more and more professional and year-round in nature, Ireland's greatest need was for the establishment of a top-class national equestrian training centre. He suggested that the Show Jumping Association of Ireland, the Irish Olympic Committee and the Army Equitation School should unite their efforts to provide for this.[3]

It is interesting to note that later in 1964 the then Minister for Finance, Charles J Haughey, officiated at the opening of a large indoor school attached to the Grand Hotel in Malahide, which became central to competition development in the Dublin area during the years ahead. But it still was not the national centre envisaged by Judge Wylie.

Having moved to his new home in Abbeyville, Kinsealy, Haughey at this time was becoming more and more involved in horse sport of every kind – racing, hunting and showjumping. He was one of those taking part with some of Ireland's business leaders in the 'breakfast sessions' at Iris Kellett's riding school on Mespil Road. His sons Sean and Conor, along with daughter Eimear, were all competing in showjumping. Eimear on *Feltrim* went on to win a team bronze medal at the European Junior Championships of 1972. Hence, Haughey was familiar with both the possibilities and the problems within the Irish horse world. Thus, soon after becoming Minister for Agriculture in the mid-sixties, he set about taking an active role in the development of that disparate world. For the rest of the sixties and on into the seventies, this was to have a profound impact on the Equitation School.

In 1965 Haughey appointed a 'survey team' to do an in-depth study of the horse-breeding industry. In his initial address to the five-member group,[4] he included this reference to the Equitation School: 'The Minister for Defence is agreeable that you should examine the role of the Army Equitation School at McKee Barracks and make recommendations.'[5]

In its lengthy 1966 report, the team recommended the establishment of an Irish Horse Board and the creation of a National Training Centre. On this latter item it concluded, 'The Team, therefore, consider that given the maximum of goodwill on all sides, it would be possible to convert the Army Equitation School at McKee Barracks into a National Training Centre.'[6]

Over the next ten difficult years, from the moment that report was released, the school's future role was thrown into some confusion and doubt. But more of that later.

As the plateau year of 1963 ended and the 1964 season progressed, any hopes that the combining of army and civilian teams would bring about a dramatic resurgence of Ireland's Nations Cup fortunes were quickly dimmed. Nations Cup success eluded the Irish civilians at events contested in Madrid (where they placed 4th), Lisbon (3rd), Ostend (3rd) and Rotterdam (6th). The army joined in for London, as Captain Ned Campion teamed up with Diana Conolly-Carew, Seamus Hayes and Ada Matheson in a bid for the Prince of Wales Cup. Despite a double clear by Seamus on *Goodbye*, they still ended up fourth. The army man was at this point coming to terms with his new horse *Inis Teague*, and they had a good consolation London win in a qualifier for the Imperial Cup. Two weeks later, he continued on that same note in Dublin, scoring two firsts, including the Simmonscourt Stakes.

Captain Billy Ringrose and *Loch an Easpaig* represented the army in the home team's bid to retain the Aga Khan Cup along with Ada Matheson on *Fru*, Diana Conolly-Carew on *Barrymore* and Tommy Wade on *Dundrum*. In the end, the result mirrored the reality of no quick fix for Ireland's flagging cup results. On a total of 24.25 faults, they finished last.

Before the year 1964 was out, Irish equestrianism mourned the death of Judge William Wylie and, with that, an era in the sport well and truly ended. His full story has yet to be written, but his high place in the history of Irish equestrianism is beyond doubt.

Back in 1964 there was no North American Tour. Neither was a showjumping team sent to the Tokyo Olympics, though an eventing side did take part, at a cost of £20,000. The squad of Tommy Brennan, Harry Freeman-Jackson, Tony Cameron and Captain Cyril Harty's son, John Harty, came within 14 penalty points of a bronze medal (a very small margin in this sport). Such proximity to an Olympic medal may have stirred further thoughts within the Army Equitation School about eventing participation. But that move was still all of five years away.

At the beginning of 1965 the army's main international riders were Captains Ringrose, Campion and Ronnie MacMahon. Captain Eamonn O'Donohue was in his last year at the school. Coming in to replace retiring officers were Lieutenants Jimmy Quinn from Ennis, Larry Kiely from Thurles, along with Mayo's Captain Eoin Lavelle.

A nephew of thirties army rider Captain Tommy Quinn, Jimmy Quinn rode internationally from 1966 to 1971. He had a good win in Wiesbaden, and on the 1960 team in New York he jumped a clear and a four in the cup with *Duinin*. In civilian life he became a respected course builder and a driving force behind the development of his beloved County Clare Agricultural Show.

Larry Kiely was a top-class hurler with Tipperary and would like to have made this his prime sport after joining the army in 1961. However, during his cadet training, he showed sufficient talent in the saddle to be assigned to the Equitation School. He had his first international in 1966 and was a stalwart of the side right through the seventies. Of those years, he says: 'We were desperately short of horses, yet with all the new developments we were expected to be "all things to all men". But I loved my time there. We made the best of it and carried on until our horsepower improved.' After his retirement in 1978 Larry went on to do UN duty in both Croatia and Lebanon, where he was OC. He was OC of Clonmel Barracks for ten years and also served two terms as overall OC of McKee Barracks.

Eoin Lavelle had membership of the army jumping team as one of his earliest dreams. 'At fourteen I was asked to write a essay on what I wanted to be. I said I wanted to be a Lieutenant on the army international showjumping team.' He spent a number of years on the national circuit, but, sadly, when he did realise his international dream at Wiesbaden 1970, it was short-lived. On this, his first ever trip abroad, he took a severe fall on very hard ground from the young horse, *Duinin*. A shattered pelvis ended his international career before it had really begun. His story highlights the dangers that down the decades constantly lurk at the very next fence for all the school's riders. Since his retirement from the army in 1972, Eoin has had a most successful career in the world of engineering. His most recent project is in the very important area of wave energy. He still has a great pride in the army team. 'I am proud to have been a part of it. The school has not always had the horsepower it needed, but still, against the odds, always boxed well above its weight,' he says.

In 1965 Billy Ringrose and *Loch an Easpaig* struck top form and scored major wins at five of the venues attended – Grand Prix de Ville (Nice), Premio Piazza di Siena (Rome), Farewell Stakes (London), Grand Prix (Harrisburg) and National Trophy (New York). Team-wise, the Irish had their best results at London and Dublin. In the Prince of Wales Cup, Ringrose, Seamus Hayes, Ada Matheson and Diana Conolly-Carew came second by only quarter of a time fault to a strong British side. Ringrose, Hayes, Conolly-Carew and Ned Campion were second again behind Britain at Dublin.

The 1966 season was decimated through a severe outbreak of swamp fever in Europe. Horse travel to and from the continent was banned. The Nations Cups at both London and Dublin were cancelled. However, a special competition was arranged at Ballsbridge between Ireland and Britain. For Ireland, both an army and a civilian side were put forward and for the home crowd it became a fascinating head-to-head between these two well-known segments of Irish international showjumping. The British also sent over two teams, and one of them won the four-way challenge. But the real focus was on the army versus civilian battle for second place. The civilians fielded their strongest side, with Seamus Hayes, Tommy Brennan, Tommy Wade and Diana Conolly-Carew, who went on to win the Grand Prix with the very much in form *Barrymore*. For the army there were Captains Ringrose on *Loch an Easpaig* and Campion on *Liath Druim*, along with Lieutenants Ronnie MacMahon on *Sliabh na gCrot* and Larry Kiely on *Carn*, who were both having their first major Dublin call-up. There was little between the two Irish sides, but, for the record, the civilians came out ahead. Escaping Europe's swamp fever problems, the school sent the same team of four on the 1966 North American circuit. Billy Ringrose once more had the best results, with wins on *Loch an Easpaig* at Harrisburg and Toronto.

The men from McKee did not see international competition again until July 1967 when Ringrose and Campion joined Conolly-Carew and Hayes to place third in

*Above:*
*The 1967 winning
team of Captains Billy
Ringrose and Ned
Campion, along with
Tommy Wade and
Seamus Hayes.*
*(RDS Library Archive)*

London. But there were better things to come at Dublin, where the combined army/civilian side scored its second Aga Khan win.

The run-up to this success was not without drama as one of the most bizarre episodes in the history of Irish showjumping almost kept Tommy Wade and *Dundrum* off the team. It happened at Dungarvan show where Tommy, his brother Eddie and Clareman Gerry Costello had all jumped clear over four knock-out rounds in the main event. Having decided they had done enough, they asked the judges if they could divide the prizes. The judges refused their request and they were asked to jump again. What happened next is unique. All three riders went into the ring and either retired or jumped the wrong course, thus causing the divide they had requested in the first place. But that was not the end of it. All three riders were called before an SJAI disciplinary committee and suspended. Only after much argument was it decided, at the last moment, that the suspension applied only to national competition and did not prevent Tommy jumping on the Irish side at Dublin.

Perhaps as a result of all the controversy, Tommy had a totally disastrous first round. Following a refusal and a fall at the third-last fence, he returned with 22 faults. However, good rounds from Ned on *Liathdruim*, Billy on *Loch an Easpaig* and Seamus on *Goodbye* kept the Irish just ahead in the scoring, with 12.25 faults to Britain's 16. Tommy came powering back in the second round to go clear. Seamus did likewise. The Irish were able to count an eight from Ned and still win by the slender margin of quarter of a fault without Billy having to jump. Sadly, that was to be the last Irish Aga Khan win for another ten years.

No sooner had the army celebrated their 1967 Dublin success than disaster struck. During the Nations Cup meeting at Ostend later that month, *Loch an Easpaig* jumped a clear round but as he left the arena this brave, great horse dropped dead with a massive heart attack. 'This was a horse with the heart of a lion. I was devastated by his loss,' Billy recalls. In reality, that tragic moment in Ostend also brought an end to Captain Ringrose's fourteen-year international career, and it put a very severe dent in the horsepower available to the combined army/civilian teams. The star horses were all nearing the end of their careers and possible replacements were, at that time, selling for up to £15,000 to buyers from abroad. With international prize-money booming and professional sponsorship of riders growing in popularity, by the early seventies that figure had been

*Above:*
Loch an Easpaig *jumping his very last fence at Ostend in 1967. He died of a heart attack one minute later.*
(Colonel Billy Ringrose)

multiplied. Dublin Horse Show's classes were sponsored for the first time in 1968, and by 1972 it had a prize fund of £23,000. On the continental market, one jumper called *Beau Supreme*, which would be ridden for Britain by Derek Ricketts, was sold for a reported £80,000. Two others, called *Jagermeister* and *Askan*, went to the Schockemohle stables in Germany for over £40,000 each during 1971. Only the most dedicated of Irish owners could refuse offers of that nature. Among that small band of patriots was Iris Kellett, who spurned big sums and kept good horses in the country to help spearhead a revival of Irish fortunes during the seventies.

In 1967, out of an annual overall budget of £60,000, the Army Equitation School had a mere £10,000 for buying horses. Back in the early fifties it had had £3,000, but the price being paid for showjumpers had since multiplied one hundredfold. The army's budget had gone up by only a multiple of three. They could not keep pace, and it is a miracle that they survived at all. At that time they were paying fractions of the market average for horses on which they hoped to jump internationally. Larry Kiely's stalwart, *Inis Cara*, was bought at this time for a mere £1,500. *Duinin* cost £500. During the latter years of the sixties, and following on from the Survey Team Report of 1966, there was an understandable slow-down in the school's regular buying programme. With the prospect of a Horse Board buying team being set up, no doubt the army played a waiting game that had a cost in terms of horse shortages during the early seventies.

And so in 1967 began a decade of relative drought in the school's history during which wins became very rare indeed. In any given ten-year period, the team's horsepower strength can be gauged by the number of Grand Prix events won. For example, between 1929 and 1939 they scored 11 such wins; between 1979 and 1989 they had 8. But between 1967 and 1977 they recorded only one – Larry Kiely's first on *Inis Cara* at Wulfrath.

Early in 1968 came one more changing of the guard at McKee. After a ten-year stint in the post, Colonel James Neylon retired as OC and was replaced by Colonel Bill Rea, who served until 1971. His main contact with the equestrian world had been as National Chairman of the Olympic Horse Committee which was overseeing the sending of an eventing team to the 1968 Mexican Olympics. When he took up the post as OC, a determined effort was being mounted to also send a combined army/civilian showjumping team to Mexico. On the shortlist were Captain Ned Campion, Diana Conolly-Carew, Ada Matheson and Tommy Brennan, who was also named for an eventing team with a second horse. However, Tommy's hopes of wearing the green in both disciplines ended during the 1968 Aga Khan when his mount, *Tubbermac,* broke a leg at the water and had to be instantly put down. As the sharp sound of the vet's pistol faded from the arena, so too did the possibility of sending a full showjumping team to the Olympics. There was long debate as to whether they should withdraw, but in the end valour overcame discretion. 'It was an opportunity to represent the country at the highest level and so long as they were willing to go with a team of three, I would not

*Above:*
*Colonel Bill Rea, who took up the post of Officer Commanding in 1968, seen here in London with Prince Philip; Captain Billy Ringrose is in the background.*
*(The Rea Family)*

refuse,' Ned Campion recalls of his decision to take part. The trip proved to be a bridge too far for the Irish trio as they suffered elimination.

A stalwart in the school's administration at this period, during the late sixties and into the seventies, was Commandant Martin Dolan, who held the post of Adjutant. Beyond his normal duties of looking after the team's entries for shows both at home and abroad, Martin, on a number of occasions, also travelled as Chef d'Equipe. He was a familiar presence at home shows around the country as he looked after the needs of younger riders coming on to the team. Like Sergeant Major Steve Hickey and Captain Jack Stack, he had begun his army career in the Blue Hussars. On retirement from the army, Martin Dolan took up a post as inspector of riding schools with Bord na gCapall.

During the 1969 Dublin Horse Show, the great Iris Kellett finished her international career on a high note when winning the Ladies Senior European Championship on *Morning Light*. At that time, Iris was running one of the world's most respected training schools. Among her pupils were Paul Darragh and Eddie Macken, both of whom would become star performers on civilian/army teams of the following decade.

The following year's Dublin team included young Eddie Macken, who was getting his first cap with Iris's European champion, *Morning Light*. Also on that side was Tommy Brennan on Frank Kernan's big grey horse, *Ambassador*. This superb Irish-bred horse was soon to be sold to Italy for a reputed price of £30,000. Two years later, *Ambassador* went on to win the Olympic Gold medal for Italy's Graziano Mancinelli at Munich. Ireland was still producing the best showjumpers in the world only to have them ridden to glory under the flags of other nations. The army team was still advertising the Irish horse to these nations, but on its limited budget it could not afford to buy the best mounts for its own riders. In 1970 there were seventy Irish-breds competing on the top teams abroad. That same year a total of five thousand horses were exported out of Ireland.

As the sixties came to a close, one bright light on the horizon for the army team was from the sport of eventing. This came about through a rather fortuitous happening in faraway California. There, in Santa Barbara, one well-to-do Irishman, Sir John Galvin, had for some years been sponsoring jumpers and eventers for the USA Olympic and Pan American teams. Many of them were Irish-bred. Just prior to the Mexican Olympics, Galvin made the decision to bring thirteen of his horses over to Ireland – and he gave them to the army school. Among them was one called *San Carlos*. This horse became the mount of Lieutenant Ronnie MacMahon. 'I had my first outing on *San Carlos* at Punchestown in 1969 and I took to eventing like a duck to water.' Together they placed third at the home international that year, but they went on to win it in 1971. Meanwhile, they came a close second in the premier British event at Badminton in 1970. They competed at the Olympic Games of 1972.

In addition to branching into eventing, Colonel Bill Rea also brought in the British rider, Jock Ferrie, to be instructor at the school. Under his tutelage all of the riders in McKee at that time had a shot at the sport. But providing horses for them to ride in both disciplines only exacerbated the problems of shortages at McKee.

In 1970 another challenge to the school's future came when Minister for Agriculture Charles Haughey followed through on the 1966 Survey Team Report by introducing an Act in the Dáil for the establishment of Bord na gCapall (The Irish Horse Board). With annual Government funding of £200,000 to back it, the new organisation's purpose was: To establish a national centre for training in equitation, advise the Minister for Agriculture, and perform certain other functions in relation to the breeding, sale and export of horses and associated activities ...[7] Exactly how the Army Equitation School would fit within the plan envisaged in this Act was still unclear, but it was certain that they were once again being challenged to justify their existence as the best possible promotion arm for the Irish horse, and indeed for Ireland.

As the plan for the new Horse Board developed during 1971 and 1972, the board bought horses that were to be owned by the Minister for Agriculture and stabled at McKee. It also employed instructor Jock Ferrie to work with a group of civilian riders that he would train in the school. In other words, a roundabout bid was being made to convert the Army Equitation School into the envisaged National Training Centre. As time went on, there were further plans mooted to have the centre at the National Stud in Tully, County Kildare. Then it was announced that the National Centre would be at Punchestown. By 1973 there was so much confusion about the board's plans that then Minister for Agriculture Mark Clinton was asked in the Dáil if the Army Equitation School was to be disbanded in favour of the new National Training Centre at Tully. His answer was that no such thing was planned, but rather that the new National Equestrian Centre would be 'shared'.[8]

In the meantime, a number of Bord na gCapall horses had been bought and accommodated at McKee. Polish Colonel Wladislaw Zgorzelski was appointed trainer and coming in to study under him were the likes of Eddie Macken, Con McElroy, along with Northern Ireland riders George Stewart and David Mitchell. Paul Darragh joined the group in 1972. At first, Michael Hickey from Wexford was appointed as 'Full Time Rider for the Board'. He was later replaced by Kildare man Paddy Quinlan, and then Kevin Barry from Limerick. Christina Ledingham, sister to future army star Captain John Ledingham, took over in 1975 and was the last of the board's riders there. It appears that the whole set-up was a rather 'informal arrangement' in which army riders could also benefit from the instruction of the trainer and perhaps ride some of the board's horses as well. Colonel Zgorzelski's term came to an end in April 1973 and he was replaced for a short time by Eric Bubbel of Germany, who had formerly trained the USA team. However, even by June of that year the Bord na gCapall experiment in buying horses and training a civilian team had been declared a 'complete failure'.[9] Gradually the idea of trying to have McKee be a 'sort of' National Training Centre just petered out and by 1975 some of the board's horses were turned over to the army. The most useful of these were *Lough Sheelin* and *Water Lily*.

The year 1971 brought not only the introduction of Bord na gCapall, but also a change of OC at the school. With some newer mounts, like *Cluain Aodha* and the good mare *Garrai Eoin* reaching maturity, it was felt that the vast international experience of Lieutenant Colonel Billy Ringrose would have a role to play in reviving the school's fortunes. The former star replaced Colonel Bill Rea as the school's twelfth Officer Commanding in April of that year. Soon after, Larry Kiely broke his leg, and Billy got back in the saddle himself for the Military Nations Cup at Fontainbleau, France, where, together with Ronnie MacMahon and Ned Campion, they won the Nations Cup ahead of the Italians.

Larry recovered quickly enough to come out for Wulfrath, and on *Inis Cara* win the Grand Prix there. Ned on *Garrai Eoin*, and Larry on *Inis Cara*, both jumped well at Hickstead, but when teamed up with Tommy Brennan on *Ambassador* and Eddie Macken on *Oatfield Hills*, they came a disappointing seventh at Dublin. So the new OC had his work cut out for him.

The school got a huge morale boost at the end of that August in the Nations Cup at Ostend. Kiely and Campion again linked up with Eddie Macken, but this time everything went their way as they scored a superb Irish win ahead of Britain, France and Belgium. It should be noted that Britain fielded the likes of Derek Ricketts on the £80,000 horse *Beau Supreme* and Paddy McMahon on his 1973 European champion *Pennwood Forge Mill*. Larry Kiely marks this win as one of the most memorable in his ten-year international career. 'At that point it was only the second time in the history of the sport that a three-man team beat full sides of four,' he says. Further enhancing the Irish performance, Larry on *Inis Cara* divided first in the Puissance. Recalling that time, Ned Campion says, 'Our goal from then on was to provide at least two members of Ireland's Nations Cup teams.'

Carefully managing *Garrai Eoin* and *Inis Cara*, Ned and Larry Kiely admirably endeavoured to fulfil that role during the first half of the seventies. Bred by Lady Daresbury in County Limerick, *Garrai Eoin* was a wonderfully supple 1963 mare by *Candelabra*. *Inis Cara* was a 1961 Golden Years gelding out of a blue spec mare. A brave jumper, he became a star of the Puissance competitions and competed until he was fifteen.

Only Ned and *Garrai Eoin* made it onto the 1972 Dublin team that year, along with

the increasingly brilliant Eddie Macken on *Oatfield Hills*, Tommy Brennan on *Highland Lad*, and the coming-of-age Paul Darragh on the Bord na gCapall mare, *Water Lily*. This time they climbed to second place behind Germany and ahead of Italy and Switzerland. That winter, Captain Kiely joined Darragh and Michael Hickey to get his first taste of the growing European indoor circuit. He competed at Amsterdam, Zuidlaren and the new Christmas extravaganza in Olympia, London, where the army's first international encounter had happened back in 1927. There, he again made his presence felt when taking second in the Puissance on *Inis Cara*.

The year 1973 was one of fairly dramatic upheaval in Irish history as the Northern Troubles grew more deadly and Liam Cosgrave's coalition government took over from Fianna Fáil. This latter change was to have a very positive impact on the school. Son of the man who facilitated its establishment back in 1926, William T Cosgrave, the new Taoiseach was not about to have the school languish horse-poor as it approached its fiftieth anniversary. Neither was his Minister for Defence Paddy Donegan, whose family was deeply involved in the sport of showjumping. Very shortly after the new Government took power, the school's annual horse purchasing budget was trebled to £30,000. Within two years, it would be trebled again. Thus, for the first time in many years the army was able to make a serious bid for just about any good Irish horse that came on the market, and this was to bear rich fruit as time went on.

For the first half of 1973 Captain Ned Campion was on an instruction course with the Cadre Noir in France. Hence, while Ronnie Mac Mahon and newer recruits Lieutenant Con Power from Wexford and Galway men Jim Nicholson and Pat Phelan concentrated on eventing, Larry Kiely was left to carry the army's showjumping banner alone. He first joined Paul Darragh (on *Water Lily*) at Rome and, on *Inis Cara*, again took second in the Puissance.

Ned Campion returned to the Irish team for Dublin 1973 and won the second international on the thirteen-year-old gelding by *Bahia*, *Cluain Aodha*, beating Germany's Munich Olympic team gold medallist, Fritz Ligges. Larry again had his moment in the Puissance as he shared first with Germany's rising star, Paul Schockemohle, and Britain's David Broome. But the Irish side of the two army men, along with Macken and Ned Cash Jr, finished fourth behind Britain in the Aga Khan. Disappointment with the performance of the Irish team was raised at question time in the Dáil and Minister for Defence Paddy Donegan was asked if the army team would be disbanded. His answer was an emphatic No. Before the year ended, moments of Equitation School former glories were well recalled in the press as seventy-two-year-old Dan Corry was honoured with a Texaco Hall of Fame award.

Early in 1974 Minister Paddy Donegan told the Dáil that five horses had been purchased for the school at a cost of £35,000. Among them were the likes of *Coolronan*, that had been bred by the Dargan family in Meath and coming from Ned Cash was six-year-old *Castle Park*. Both horses would soon be heard of again. Also included in the group was an eventer named *Bothar Bui*, which in September of that year placed a good fifth for Captain Ronnie Mac Mahon in the World Championships at Burghley. At this time, as well, OC Ringrose was encouraging riders with former competition experience to apply for cadetships. Thus, names like Gerry Mullins, Brian McSweeney, John Ledingham, Ulick McEvaddy and future OC Gerry O'Gorman began trying out for the school.

In June of that year, a mighty talent began to emerge within the young ranks at McKee. Lieutenant Con Power, who had up to this point concentrated successfully on eventing, took up the ride on *Cluain Aodha* from Ned Campion. Con's eyes still light up as his practiced hands re-enact the moment when he and this fourteen-year-old really clicked. They won together at the Manresa show in Dublin, and then headed for Kill in County

Kildare, where the hot favourite to win the Grand Prix was the unbeatable star of the national circuit, Eddie Macken. Con and *Cluain Aodha* romped home ahead of him. Con relishes the moment still. Editor of the newly instituted column 'Irish Horse World' in the *Irish Field*, Avril Douglas later commented: 'Every so often, as though from behind a cloud a showjumping star emerges. One first catches a few glimpses and then the star appears.'[10] How right she was about the 'tall man riding' – Lieutenant Con Power.

Another beautiful moment from that year of recovery for Irish showjumping came at the Junior European Championships in Lucerne when the young James Kernan from Crossmaglen, County Armagh, won the individual gold medal on his father's mare, *Marcella*. This same mare would later breed him an Aga Khan team horse, *Touchdown*.

At that year's Dublin Horse Show, the team of Captain Ned Campion on *Garrai Eoin*, Ned Cash on *Dun Gleen*, Eddie Macken on *Pele* and Michael Hickey on *Lydican* came fourth once more in the Aga Khan. But in one stirring moment at that year's show, Captain Larry Kiely delighted the crowd when sharing first place on *Inis Cara* in the Puissance along with the great Raimondo d'Inzeo of Italy on the Irish-bred *Bellvue*.

At year's end, there was another glimpse of the future when the *Irish Field* presented its first ever Annual Equestrian Awards. Taking the three main trophies as senior, young and junior riders were Eddie Macken, James Kernan and Lieutenant Con Power. 'Irish show jumping has turned the corner' commented the paper afterwards. Not present on that occasion was another future star, Paul Darragh, who was away on a course with Britain's Harvey Smith. He would be home for a dramatic 1975 season and would soon be heard from.

## AMATEUR AND PROFESSIONAL

One of the talking points during the mid-seventies in world showjumping was the matter of professionalism. Riders had to declare whether they were amateurs, who participated in the sport as a hobby, or professionals who made their living from horses. This gave rise to odd situations at prize-givings in major shows. At some events the professionals got prize money while the amateurs were given feed for their horses or a new saddle. In Ireland, this issue was partly responsible for not sending teams to the Olympics, as riders like Tommy Brennan and Eddie Macken were classified as professionals. The matter also arose in a rather comical way in relation to army riders winning a car at Strokestown Show. In May 1975, live on RTÉ TV, Captain Larry Kiely, on *Lough Sheelin*, won a Hillman Hunter, but due to an agreement with the Department of Defence regarding the army riders' special position as amateurs, he was not allowed to accept the valued prize. A couple of years later, Captain Con Power won it, but this time the canny show organiser, Ado Kenny, found a way around the dilemma by presenting the car to Con's wife, Mags, as a wedding gift!

No sooner had 1975 begun than the shock news came that Eddie Macken had left Iris Kellett's school behind and headed off to ride at the top-class Schockemohle yard in Germany. Within months Eddie came upon the great Irish-bred *Boomerang* – and the rest is history. Paul Darragh took over the ride on Macken's horse, *Pele*, and before the year was out, would be hailed as Ireland's first winner of the great Hickstead Derby since Seamus Hayes took it back in 1964. Also before year's end Macken and *Boomerang* had won Grand Prix events in Wiesbaden, Aachen, St Gallen, The Royal International and the Horse of the Year Show in London.

All of this created stirrings at the Army Equitation School. With Ireland very much in need of heroic, peaceful, army heroes at this time during the Troubles, Taoiseach Cosgrave turned to the Equitation School. He and Minister Donegan visited there in February of that year to 'view the horses'. Acting as Unit Adjutant on that historic happening was Ulick McEvaddy, who would go on to be one of Ireland's leading businessmen in the years ahead. Soon afterwards the school's horse-buying budget was quietly boosted to £100,000 a year.

But there was a price on the increase – results, results, results. At Cosgrave's side on that occasion was former army rider Commandant Sean Daly as his aide-de-camp. Despite his new post, Sean was still very much involved in the world of showjumping. He was well up to date on the progress of rising stars like Macken, Kernan and Darragh. Somehow, it was felt that he could be the leader that would blend the rising army talent with that of the civilians. And so, without any great ceremony, Sean Daly replaced Billy

Ringrose at the end of June and became the thirteenth Officer Commanding at the school. Billy was promoted to full Colonel and made Director of Supply and Transport. But, like General McArthur, he would be back!

There can be no doubt that Sean Daly had the special kind of motivating leadership talents needed at just this time in Irish showjumping. An example of his style was once given to this author by Paul Darragh. In a class at Hickstead when an all-but-unbeatable pace was set, Paul was drawn last to go and neatly slotted into second. Very pleased with himself, he met Sean on the way out. 'Well, what did you think of that, Sean?' he asked. 'If you ever go for second again you will be off the team,' was the curt reply.

Anyway, back in 1975 it was at Hickstead that Sean Daly had his first test as Chef d'Equipe of a combined army/civilian team that included Captains Ned Campion and Larry Kiely, along with Eddie Macken and Michael Hickey. They threatened all the way in a tight contest, but were eventually pushed down to third by one fence. Britain won on a score of 8; Germany came second with 9 and Ireland third on 12. Dublin was next and Macken was selected again with *Boomerang*, Paul Darragh had *Pele*, Michael Hickey was on *Nordel* and Captain Ned Campion jumped *Garrai Eoin*. This time they moved up to second behind Britain and ahead of Germany. When it was over, the *Irish Field*, which had not been all that keen on Daly's appointment, was moved to comment that the team was riding with a 'new authority'.

Soon Captain Con Power and James Kernan would become part of this new 'authority' and that winning era is the subject of our next chapter.

*Above:*
*Colonel Sean Daly acting as aide-de-camp to Taoiseach Liam Cosgrave, with Mrs Cosgrave and Minister James Tully.*
(Robert Daly)

# THE RENAISSANCE OF IRISH SHOWJUMPING AND THE REIGN OF *ROCKBARTON*
## 1976 to 1988

'*True you ride the finest horse I have ever seen*
*Standing sixteen, one or two, with eyes so wild and green*'
*Ride On*
*(Jimmy MacCarthy)*

The school's fiftieth anniversary year began with a further increase in funding, but the tragic loss of *Garrai Eoin* who dropped dead while being exercised in the Phoenix Park. As one door closed, another opened however. Bord na gCapall's ailing finances led to the decision to sell off its string of horses stabled at McKee, and *Lough Sheelin*, already on lease and producing good results for Larry Kiely, was snapped up. The wisdom of the army purchase was quickly confirmed when the horse, and new rider Ned Campion, won at Rome in May where they also competed on the three-man team that finished third in the Nations Cup. Lieutenant Gerry Mullins, on the former showjumper *Cnoc an Aine*, won the final Olympic trial in Midleton Park in County Westmeath, and was shortlisted for the eventing squad at the Montreal Games while, despite having been retired to the showjumping ring after the Munich Games, Ronnie MacMahon's *San Carlos* was called back into eventing action when *Bothar Bui* sustained an injury. This decision would have unexpected consequences.

In an atmosphere of growing confidence, the jumping team was second in Lucerne despite being reduced to another three-man side when Paul Darragh on *Pele* had a nightmare crash in the combination, and a week later Con Power recorded his first international win at Wiesbaden, riding *Coolronan*.

At Hickstead in July, the Irish sensationally won seven of the eight classes on the card.

Macken on *Boomerang* scored a double, Power lifted four trophies, and Campion on *Lough Sheelin* won the Embassy Stakes. A little late in the day, everyone was now asking, 'Why are we not sending a team to the Olympics?'

Only the eventers travelled in the final analysis, however, and for the third Games in a row they got a mauling. Mullins didn't get the final call-up and when John Watson's *Cambridge Blue* was injured shortly after arrival, reserves Norman Van de Vater on *Blue Tom Tit* were drafted in. Meanwhile *San Carlos* had to be treated for a chill that threatened to develop into pneumonia and the medication, administered strictly in line with regulations, led to a positive dope test.

Gerry Sinnott on *Croghan* and Eric Horgan on *Pontoon* both went clear over the steeplechase course. As MacMahon was about to start, however, a German competitor missed the finish and in the ensuing confusion, the Irishman turned back. The cross-country course proved treacherous with 33 of the 49 starters falling, and 46 refusals racked up throughout the day. MacMahon had three falls and three refusals as he tried to make up for lost time, but, remarkably, came out to jump clear in the final showjumping phase. Sinnott finished a brilliant sixth and Horgan claimed fifteenth place, but Van de Vater withdrew, and in this Olympic year, when just earning a completion score was a considerable achievement, the team was denied even that when *San Carlos* was disqualified.

Back at home, Power's star was now truly in the ascendant. Born on the Hook Peninsula in Wexford to a family steeped in sporting tradition, his childhood ambition was to become a National Hunt jockey, but he grew too tall. So his father, who bred the 1947 Grand National winner *Caughoo*, bought Eddie Macken's experienced pony *Granard Boy* and sent his son showjumping. Shortly after taking over at McKee, new Commanding Officer Sean Daly gave the young Lieutenant a sharp tongue-lashing. 'He called me into his office and threw down a copy of my report about the horses I'd been riding over the previous few weeks onto his desk. He said "Read that out loud" and when I came to where I'd written "Four faults – horse jumped well" he slammed his fist on the table and roared, "Don't you ever tell me a horse jumped well when he came out of the ring with a fence down!" I got the message,' Con recalls.

At Dublin Horse Show he took the Leading Rider Trophy after sharing the honours in the Jameson Whiskey Stakes with Ned Campion, finishing second in the Wylie Trophy and producing a clear on *Coolronan* in the Nations Cup in which the Irish were runners-up behind Germany. And in celebration of fifty years of the Aga Khan trophy, the three surviving heroes of the 1926 contest – Dan Corry, Ged O'Dwyer and Belgium's Chevalier de Menten de Horne – were presented with commemorative plaques by the RDS.

At Hickstead in late August, Macken and *Boomerang* recorded the first of their historic four-in-a-row Derby wins and Power won the Embassy Stakes with *Coolronan* while Captain Larry Kiely scooped the Goodwill Stakes Trophy with his new ride *Look Out*. In Rotterdam they produced the most remarkable team result of the year when denied first place by none other than the newly-crowned Olympic champions from France by only the smallest of margins. In a cliff-hanger, Campion, Power, James Kernan and Macken forced the gold medallists into a jump-off and were beaten by just 1.75 faults in what was described as 'one of the great Cups of this or any other year'.[1] The German silver medallists had to settle for third. The Irish were back at the top of their game.

Kernan stepped in to join Kiely, Campion and Power who now had their sights firmly set on victory at Ostend in Belgium. The host country was confident that their Montreal bronze-medal-winning side would see off all comers, but the boys in green took control from the start and couldn't be caught. To cap this great victory, Power won the Grand Prix on *Coolronan* and claimed the Leading Rider prize. So as they headed for the North American fall circuit in October, Irish tails were up.

Newly-wed Power made a big impact in Washington, but the army string of horses faded fast at the end of a long season. Despite collecting 47 rosettes and almost £6,000 in prize money, it was a disappointing conclusion to one of the best international seasons for a very long time. One young horse who showed promise on this tour, however, was a seven-year-old bought from David Mitchell in Comber, County Down, a few months earlier. Originally called *Buccaneer*, he was now re-named *Rockbarton* and was learning his trade in the capable hands of Campion.

## THE BUYING OF *ROCKBARTON*

In the spring of 1969 a grand chestnut colt foal by a not too fashionable sire called *Come Fast* was born to a mare called *Golden Lily* on the farm of Leslie Leech at Clonroche near Enniscorthy, County Wexford. A lively fellow with a white star on his forehead, he was given the name *Buccaneer*. Tommy Wade bought him as a three-year-old for 1000 guineas at the Ballsbridge sales and sent him to David Mitchell of Cumber in County Down for his early learning. After an impressive outing at Dublin Horse Show as a six-year-old, he was put on the market and good offers came pouring in from abroad. The army's buying fund for the year was all but depleted, but the determined Sean Daly was not about to let this star escape, so he contacted former Taoiseach Liam Cosgrave, who explains: 'Sean, who had previously been my aide-de-camp, called and said, "There is this excellent horse on the market and we would like to buy him, but we don't have the money." I promised I would do what I could. So I rang Minister for Finance Richie Ryan and told him the story. "Sure, if you need money we will have to find it," he said. *Buccaneer* was bought for the then record price of £50,000 and was renamed *Rockbarton* after the home place of then Minister for Defence, Bobby Molloy, near Salthill. Over an eleven-year international career he won more than three times his purchase price. The list of his achievements in the Equitation School log book covers a massive twelve pages – more than any other horse owned by the army.

And as the final curtain came down on 1976, the international equestrian federation, the FEI, banned the non-steroidal anti-inflammatory, Phenylbutazone, or Bute, for the following year's championships. Ever more stringent drug-testing would become a feature of the sport over the next thirty years, but, as the governing body would be constantly reminded, the line between cheating and legitimate treatment is a thin one, and the headache that began in 1976 still rages today.

As 1977 dawned, the mood was upbeat. The export value of Irish horses was

*Opposite top*:
*The winning 1977 Aga Khan cup team: from left to right, Paul Darragh on* Heather Honey, *Captain Con Power on* Coolronan, *James Kernan with* Condy *and Eddie Macken on* Boomerang. *Chef d'Equipe Col Sean Daly proudly holds the trophy.*

*Opposite bottom*:
*President Hillery presents the Aga Khan cup to Colonel Sean Daly when, in 1977, Ireland claimed the trophy for the first time in a decade.*

continuing to rise and such was the popularity of showjumping in Ireland that Eddie Macken and Paul Darragh were signed up by the tobacco company, PJ Carroll, in a lucrative sponsorship deal. Sean Daly hoped McKee Barracks could produce 'a top team of four or five riders good enough to represent Ireland on their own' and 'a full international eventing team within two or three years.'[2] He had a budget of £100,000 to buy new horses.

There was an army hat-trick at Chepstow in April where Power recorded a double on *Castle Park* while Mullins was first and fourth on *Ashbourne*. Macken was coming to the zenith of his career now and won twice in Rome, where Power lined up second on both occasions and the team finished third in the Nations Cup won by Italy.

Campion, Kiely and Power were selected to join Macken for the Men's European Championships in Vienna. Power jumped a great clear on *Castle Park* on the opening day of the Austrian fixture but only Macken made it into the closing stages.

Ireland finished third at Hickstead in July, where Kiely on *Lough Sheelin* provided the only Irish clear. But come August, there was no holding the home boys back as they swept to victory in the Aga Khan Cup for the first time in ten years. The lead-in to this momentous occasion, however, was filled with the all-too-familiar drama surrounding team selection. Surprisingly, Larry Kiely had been nominated as an individual, but on the Sunday before the show began, Ronnie Smith was dropped and the army man promoted to team status. Then on Thursday, the day before the all-important event, Campion and *Sliabh na mBan* were de-selected and Smith restored to the side. Breeder and horse producer Eileen Parkhill became so frustrated with the entire affair that she resigned from the SJAI selection committee. The bickering didn't affect the team's focus, however, and Darragh, on the great little mare *Heather Honey*, returned with just four faults. When Kernan on *Condy* followed with a clear, the crowd erupted with excitement, and although Power faulted once on *Coolronan*, Macken's fault-free effort on *Boomerang* left the home side on level pegging with Germany at the halfway stage. And when the two sides were still neck-and-neck at the end of round two, now with eight faults apiece, a jump-off was guaranteed. 'A tense, nailbiting atmosphere gripped the stadium and for the next ten minutes nobody moved ... Now the best was really displayed by the Irish team, Paul Darragh and *Heather Honey*; James Kernan and *Condy* and Captain Con Power on

*Coolronan* all glided over every fence ... The Germans, however, could not reply with the same efficiency,' wrote Monty Tinsley.[3]

'I'll never forget the feeling at the end of that day,' Power recalls. 'There is no greater honour than winning the Aga Khan Cup.' The following morning the national newspapers were ablaze with excitement – 'Heroes all, and we're Proud of Them' said the *Irish Independent*.[4]

Still on a high, the riders moved on to the Hickstead August meeting where they won three of the four major classes and four of the minor competitions. Sensationally, Macken took the top two places in the world-famous Derby – *Boomerang* earning the red rosette and *Kerrygold* taking the blue. Power looked a contender on *Look Out* after winning the Derby trial, but they parted company at the bottom of the infamous bank, while Kiely also took a tumble from *Inis Cara*. Then, against all the odds, the three-man side of Power on *Look Out*, Kernan on *Condy* and Darragh on *Heather Honey* came out to win the Nations Cup at Rotterdam in convincing style a week later, finishing a full 12 faults ahead of the British and Dutch in joint second place. Power was also joint winner in the Hit-and-Hurry on *Look Out* and second on *Coolronan* in the Fault-and-Out. And as the relentless onslaught continued, the

*Opposite top*:
Sergeant Major Steve
Hickey, who suffered a
head injury, (left) and
the dazed Private
Donnelly (third from
left) at the scene of the
horrific crash at Dole,
France, in 1978.
The horses had to be cut
from the wreckage, but in
this snapshot of the
moment seem relatively
unperturbed by the
potentially fatal accident.

*Opposite bottom*:
The local fire brigade
had to cut the roof off
the horse transporter in
order to free the horses,
following the crash at
Dole in 1977.
Remarkably, the army's
top showjumpers all
survived relatively
unscathed. Sliabh na
mBan *kicked his way
out of the trailer on
his own!*

green brigade finished second of the three competing nations at Ostend in September, where Belgium won and Power on *Look Out* also recorded an individual victory.

Things could hardly have been going better for Daly, so the sudden announcement of his retirement and the re-appointment of Colonel Billy Ringrose as OC came as a complete surprise in September. Averil Douglas wrote that Daly was 'widely considered to have returned the Army School to the … former days when the Army team was considered one of the great showjumping teams in the world.'[5] Colonel Daly would, however, continue to wield considerable influence over team affairs for some years to come.

The ban which prevented Irish riders from competing on foreign-bred horses was a hot topic as 1978 began, and would eventually end up in court, with Eddie Macken fighting the case for those who felt they were being deprived of a livelihood as a result of the ruling. Others believed that the Irish breeding industry should be supported to the fullest extent, but these were changing times and many of the best mares in the national herd were being sold out of the country for good prices. As a result, instead of contributing to the Irish cause, they ended up refining the herds in France, Holland and Germany, which subsequently overwhelmed the Irish-bred in the showjumping market place.

For the army men, however, it was down to business in April, with a win for Mullins on *Moynalty* in Rome where the twenty-four-year-old rider also steered *Ashbourne* into fourth in the Grand Prix, won by Macken on *Boomerang*. The team finished second behind France in the Nations Cup in which John Roche made his debut. From Foulksmills in County Wexford where his father stood a number of stallions, Roche was a first cousin of Con Power.

In May, twenty-three-year-old Lieutenant David Foster from Rathcore in County Meath launched himself into the spotlight at the Punchestown Three-Day Event by winning the Gowran Grange Stakes. Riding *Gleann Eineach*, he led from the off, and also finished third with the eight-year-old *Inis Meain*, a former Dublin supreme hunter champion. Foster was on the way to becoming anchorman of not only the army's eventing campaign, but of Ireland's eventing team for many years to come.

Back at McKee, however, there were a lot of worried men and sore horses. A week earlier, a horse transporter went off the road near Dole in France during a storm, and its precious cargo of many of Ireland's top showjumping horses had to be cut from the wreckage. *Lough Sheelin*, *Sliabh na mBan*, *Castle Park*, *Inis Mor* and *Moynalty* were amongst those on board, but, amazingly, most walked away unscathed. Sergeant Major Steve

Hickey, who was injured along with traveling groom Private Donnelly, remembers the incident in detail and the unflappable character of one particular victim of that potentially-fatal incident.

> We were approaching traffic lights when they suddenly went red and as the driver braked, the vehicle spun out of control. We ended up in a field and I ran back onto the road to get help. The fire brigade had to cut the roof off the trailer which was lying on its side. While we were trying to free them, one horse somehow scrambled out and galloped off down the field. It was *Sliabh na mBan*. You'd think he'd be terrified after what he'd been through, but he had only one thing on his mind. We had landed in a field of lovely grass and he was going to make the best of it!

In June 1978 Macken claimed his fourth Hamburg Derby title, but this time on the German-bred *Boy*, after taking out an injunction against the Equestrian Federation of Ireland (EFI). Meanwhile Colonel Ringrose declared himself 'surprised and mystified' when informed that both *Sliabh na mBan* and *Heather Honey* tested positive for the local anaesthetic, Lignocaine, while competing in Nice – indeed, the allegation was withdrawn five months later when the FEI declared that the analysis had been faulty. By now Power had the ride on *Rockbarton* and was selected for Aachen in July along with Macken, Robert Splaine, and Mullins, while the winning

1977 team was recalled for the Aga Khan Cup.

The home event took place in a horrendous downpour, but nothing could dampen Irish spirits. The only alteration to the previous year's victorious side was the replacement of *Coolronan* by *Castle Park*. The British started favourites, but by the end of the first round found themselves sharing a zero score with both Ireland and France, and then faded as only the latter two went through to a jump-off. 'To say the atmosphere was electric is an over simplification' wrote Tinsley afterwards.[6]

It was nip-and-tuck all the way, with the opening French clear followed by an even faster round from Kernan and *Condy*, and a second French zero followed by four faults from Power on *Castle Park*. Another foot-perfect French performance really piled the pressure on the Irish and when Darragh on *Heather Honey* returned the quickest round so far and Hubert Parot left a fence on the floor for France, the result rested with Macken and the great *Boomerang*, who didn't let him down. The winning margin was a close-run thing and the following day's *Irish Independent* headline read: '4.3 Seconds Mean Irish Glory'.

Interest in showjumping in Ireland was now at fever pitch, boosted greatly by extensive television coverage. 'It was against this background of a nation of horse lovers, hungry for more success, that Macken, Darragh, Power and the young County Cork rider, Robert Splaine, headed for Aachen,' wrote Aengus Fanning.[7] The first day of the team competition at the World Championships went well, but it all fell apart on day two. *Heather Honey* was tested beyond her limits but, like her rider, demonstrated huge courage and determination, while Splaine retired and Power took a crashing fall from *Castle Park*. Visibly shaken, the army man remounted to complete the course. Only Macken survived to go into the closing stages but, for the second time in four years, it would be heartbreak as, having made it into the final four, he lost the title to Germany's Gerd Wiltfang by just one-quarter of a time fault.

Power quickly put the Aachen experience behind him by winning the Jockey Club Prize at Rotterdam in which Mullins finished second and third. By now the team had been withdrawn from the Eventing World Championships in Kentucky. Only John Watson was left to fly the flag with *Cambridge Blue* and he did it in style when taking individual silver.

The army jumping horses were again tiring after another busy year, but there was strong pressure to have an Irish presence on the late-season North American circuit, particularly in the light of a Government-sponsored trade promotion which, as it turned out, was extremely successful. So Power, Roche, Mullins and civilian rider Leonard Cave were packed off to do the business. They had hardly settled to their task, however, before Minister for Defence Bobby Molloy called them home to compete at the new Dublin Indoor International Horse Show 'which is' as Averil Douglas pointed out, 'being sponsored, amongst others, by his fellow Minister for Health, Mr Haughey'.[8] They did not cut the trip short, however, and it was during these few months that Power's partnership with *Rockbarton* was firmly cemented. 'We really clicked at last,' he recalls. 'He used to suffer badly from stage fright, but we jumped ten nights in a row in Washington, and in Madison Square Garden in New York we competed in front of twenty thousand people – he just had to get over it.' There was

**Over and ouch**

Capt. Con Power of Ireland looks like a cowboy instead of a jumping champion as his horse, Rockbarton, crashes through hurdle in the Grand Prix of New York last night, the final night of the National Horse Show at the Garden. With Rockbarton and three other Irish entrants failing to score in the event, the U.S. Equestrian Team came from behind to edge Ireland for the International Team Championship. Melanie Smith on Val De Loire and Dennis Murphy on Tuscaloose placed second and fifth, respectively, in the Grand Prix to give the U.S. 84 points to Ireland's 79. But Capt. Power
...ch points from the seven previous international events in the six-day...

one worrying moment however. America's Rodney Jenkins knew a good horse when he saw one and had his eye on *Rockbarton*. Con takes up the story: 'He was told our horses were not for sale, but he insisted that a telegram be sent home offering £1 million for the horse, and we had no choice but to do it for the sake of diplomacy – that was our job. We were sick waiting for the reply.' They had no need to worry, however, because the Minister for Defence's response, relayed in terse army-speak, was: 'Horse not for sale. Continue jumping.'

Power returned home as leading rider of the circuit and with fourteen World Cup points to his credit. He was lying third on the leader-board in the inaugural season of the Volvo-sponsored series as the New Year bells were ringing – and what a new year it would be...

*Above*:

*Con Power and* Rockbarton *established a world-class partnership, but in the early stages of their tour of the North American fall circuit in 1978 they were still only getting to know one another and, as this press cutting shows, it wasn't all smooth sailing.*

*Opposite top*:
*Paul Darragh (*Heather
Honey*), Captain Con
Power (*Rockbarton*),
Captain John Roche
(*Maigh Cuilinn*) and
Eddie Macken
(*Boomerang*) with
Chef d'Equipe *Colonel
Ned Campion *broke the
host nation's twelve-year
dominance on their home
turf to win the Nations
Cup at Aachen in
1979. This was only the
second Irish victory in
the history of the
prestigious German
show.*

*Opposite bottom*:
*Capt Con Power
and the legendary
Rockbarton in 1979.
(Maymes Ansell/RDS Archive)*

There were changes afoot as Campion retired from competition to become chief instructor following a course at the prestigious Cadre Noir training centre in Saumur, France. MacMahon began to divide his time between riding and teaching and, following a targeted recruitment drive, a group of five new young officers got their chance to show what they could do. Second Lieutenants Feargal Kavanagh and John Ledingham had both travelled to New York and Toronto as part of a junior showjumping team, while Brian MacSweeney, Pat Coleman and Pat McCartan were also experienced horsemen. During his nine-year army career, Kavanagh developed a passion for the law and took his first steps on the road to becoming one of Ireland's leading senior counsels. The army riding careers of McCartan and Coleman were equally short, but these two men became career soldiers. McCartan, whose Longford family sold both *Moynalty* and *Inis Oirr* to the Equitation School, reached the rank of Commandant and 2IC at the Equitation School following several deployments as a Company Commander in The Lebanon. Coleman spent much of his career based with the Southern Command in his native County Cork.

Ledingham, from Clashmore in Waterford, is one of fourteen children from a farming family. His father, James, was a showjumping course designer and judge, and his sister, Christina, was one of the elite group of riders which competed horses for Bord na gCapall. MacSweeney is son of Lieutenant Colonel Edward MacSweeney, who was Camp Adjutant at the Air Corps base in Baldonnell, Dublin, before moving to army HQ.

Macken and Power joined Roche and Darragh to take third in the Nations Cup at Geneva in March before competing at the first World Cup final in Gothenburg the following month. Power on *Lough Crew* was lying seventh after the opening speed leg and finished fifteenth overall, while Macken finished equal-third.

At Wiesbaden in June, Power on *Lough Crew* shared the Grand Prix spoils and Power also won a jump-off class on *Rockbarton*. Then at Aachen this partnership topped the first speed class and shared the honours in another, before playing a pivotal role as Ireland claimed the coveted Nations Cup for only the second time in the history of the German fixture.

Although victory was achieved by the narrowest of margins, it was a glorious triumph. Success at this venue is a significant achievement at any time and the Irish broke the host

country's twelve-year dominance on the winner's podium when coming out on top in a contest between twelve of the great showjumping nations of the world. Darragh on *Heather Honey*, Power on *Rockbarton*, Roche on *Maigh Cuillinn* and Macken on *Boomerang* shared the lead with Britain and France at the halfway point, eventually pipping the mighty Germans by just 0.75 faults, while the British had to settle for third. These truly were the glory days because the Irish were now rightly feared wherever they went.

The team arrived in Dublin with a glint in their eyes. A third Aga Khan success would see them win the trophy outright – something that had only happened twice before. Power was spoiled for choice with his great string of horses. *Castle Park* alone was a gem, winning speed classes all over the world, but still careful enough to rise to the occasion on Grand Prix day, and Power recalls David Broome saying to him that summer, 'You've a good team of horses when your speed horse is a Grand Prix horse and then you have

an even better one at home!' The 'better one' was, of course, *Rockbarton* which was Power's choice for the historic 1979 Aga Khan. 'That third win was the greatest moment of my career,' Power says. 'Eddie, Paul, James and myself were not just team-mates – we were four friends and we never wanted to let each other down. The team spirit and camaraderie was wonderful and we always wanted to make Ireland proud.' With *Rockbarton*, the 'Long Fella' also matched the Irish record of 7ft 2ins in the Puissance before joining Macken and *Boomerang* to share third in the Grand Prix. This series of results alone was testimony to the brilliance, courage and hardiness of the great Irish horse whose career would span another eight spectacular years.

Nothing seemed impossible now and few were surprised when the army played a major role in securing Ireland's first-ever European team medals when taking bronze in Rotterdam just a week later. And they did it with two relative 'rookies' on the side in the shape of Mullins riding *Ballinderry* and Roche on *Maigh Cuilinn*, while Power on *Rockbarton* and Macken on *Boomerang* provided the essential experience. They were only separated from the silver-medal-winning German side by just over four faults as the British reigned supreme.

The news of Power's sudden resignation, therefore, came as a huge shock. He had been unhappy for some time about the army system for distributing prize-money. It had long been policy that 50 percent of all winnings was divided equally between the riding officers, while the remainder went into the coffers of the

Department of Defence. Power challenged the ruling, arguing that the more successful riders should get a bigger cut of the takings, but his protest was in vain. 'There was a tradition to the old agreement, and Colonel Ringrose wasn't prepared to make a change – so I decided to go,' he says. He competed successfully in a civilian capacity over the following years and passed his undeniable riding skills on to both his son, Robbie, winner of the 2007 Grand National on *Silver Birch*, and his daughter, Elizabeth, who competes on Ireland's international eventing squad. Any question of disillusionment with his former boss is dispelled by his recollection of what happened following a near-fatal accident nine years later. Hit with full force by a runaway horse, he suffered a severe head injury and when, during his recovery, he turned to his old Commanding Officer for support, it wasn't found wanting. 'I needed a report about my riding career to complete some paperwork and I was overwhelmed by what he wrote about me – Colonel Ringrose always did what he thought was right, and I'll always be grateful to him,' Con says.

Meanwhile David Foster and *Inis Meain* were contributing towards Ireland's first-ever team gold at the European Eventing Championships in Luhmuehlen. The side, which also included Helen Cantillon on *Wing Forward*, John Watson on *Cambridge Blue* and Alan Lillingston on *Seven Up*, moved up from eighth to second place after the cross-country phase. Their situation was further enhanced when the best of the British horses, Lucinda Prior-Palmer's *Killaire*, was withdrawn, leaving them now in gold-medal position with seven fences in hand – although they almost threw it away in the showjumping ring. Last man in, Watson knew there was little room for error, but held his nerve to save the day and clinch the title.

Power's departure saw John Roche step out of the shadows. With *Lough Crew* he recorded a double victory at the Spruce Meadows Masters in Calgary, Canada, and with horses now re-distributed he also had the ride on *Coolronan* and *Castle Park* – the latter probably the greatest challenge because, as Averil Douglas wrote, 'It is difficult ... to maintain a high standard with this horse for it can be truly brilliant and knock nothing or be impossible to hold and knock everything!'[9]

The winning ways continued as the Irish topped the team contest at Wylye Horse Trials in England where Commandant Ronnie MacMahon and the seven-year-old

*Opposite top*:
President Hillery presents Chef d'Equipe Colonel Billy Ringrose with the Aga Khan trophy after Ireland's third consecutive win in 1979. The team – (left to right) Paul Darragh (Heather Honey), Captain Con Power (Rockbarton), James Kernan (Condy), Eddie Macken (Boomerang).

*Opposite middle*:
The 1979 European bronze medal-winning team – (left to right) Eddie Macken (Boomerang), Captain Gerry Mullins (Ballinderry), Captain John Roche (Maigh Cuilinn), Captain Con Power (Rockbarton).

*Opposite bottom*:
John Roche enjoyed a successful partnership with Lough Crew.

*Marwood* gelding *Parkhill* also finished second individually.

Plans were already afoot for the following Olympic year, with Mullins and Roche ear-marked for the jumping team while the Government agreed to provide army horses to civilians Power and Kernan in order to ensure a strong side. But that would all be blown away when, on Christmas Eve 1979, Russia invaded Afghanistan, leading to a major boycott of the Moscow Games. Foster, shortlisted for the eventing team along with MacMahon, was bitterly disappointed. '*Inis Meain* is ten now and at his peak, he simply will not have as good a chance in four years time,' he said.[10] It wasn't all just about world politics however. Ireland was fast approaching a deep recession, and once again money was becoming an issue.

Punchestown 1980 proved a happy hunting ground for the army men, however, as Foster secured his first major international victory on *Inis Meain* while Lieutenant Brian MacSweeney raised his profile when winning the novice championship on *Glenanaar*. Mullins, Kernan and Darragh acquitted themselves superbly on Ireland's first visit to the Festival of Sydney where, riding borrowed horses, they kept Australia's Olympic contenders at bay to win the Benson and Hedges International Team Trophy in January. And Mullins also collected World Cup points at the fixture before, riding *Inis Mor*, he joined Roche to win the Pairs Relay in Dortmund a few weeks later. But there was a different dynamic now. Money was drying up – and so were good results. *Boomerang* was out of action and the team was withdrawn from Paris. Roche won the opening competition at Lucerne, while Ledingham on *Sliabh na mBan* finished third in the Puissance, but the team finished ninth, and at Hickstead had to settle for tenth place.

Aachen and Dublin provided the only two remaining opportunities to relive the triumphs of 1979 and hopes were raised when Mullins on *Rockbarton* and Roche on *Lough Crew* scored a one–two in the first qualifier at the German fixture, but the team only scraped home in equal-seventh place. And in July, Irish hearts were deeply saddened by the news that the thirteen-year-old *Boomerang* would be retired after breaking a bone in his foot.

Mullins hit a purple patch when finishing second in the Grand Prix at La Baule, third in the French Derby and achieving good results at Deauville, but throughout the year there were consistent reports of a sharp fall in Irish horse exports. There was a poor attendance at Dublin Horse Show where, in terrible weather conditions, Macken, Kernan, Darragh and Mullins finished third in the Aga Khan Cup. Again riding *Rockbarton*, Mullins finished second to Macken on *Onward Bound* in the Wylie Trophy, while twenty-year-old Lieutenant John Ledingham gave a glimpse of his potential when winning the Boylan Trophy on *An Baile Nua*.

In late August the Irish eventing team finished fourth at the substitute Olympic Games in Fontainebleau, France, where, in a gruelling competition, the world champions from the USA were forced to retire, along with the British and Canadians. Foster had a bad fall from *Inis Meain* but remounted to complete the twenty-four-fence cross-country track. He was subsequently taken to hospital, where he was diagnosed with concussion and a fractured coccyx, but somehow persuaded the hospital staff to release him in time for the Sunday's showjumping phase. 'It was the toughest course I've ever come across,' he said afterwards.[11]

Calgary was a messy affair too that year. Macken borrowed the army's *Maigh Cuilinn* for the cup, only to take a tumble when the horse stopped and reared, and the sixth-place team result was a disappointment. But Ledingham was already attracting attention: 'The newcomer to the Irish team made a great impression when he finished second to Malcolm Pyrah in the Hi Tower Western Welcome Stakes and third in both the Krupp Relay [with Mullins] and the Cana Accumulator. Chef d'Equipe Bill Ringrose has high hopes for John and *Cill Chainnaig*.'[12]

Mullins came home to win a Texel Ewe as Leading Rider at the Dublin Indoor International, but the year-end statistics contrasted markedly to the previous season. Macken and Darragh had five wins apiece in 1980, while Roche was next-best with three wins, riding *Castle Park*. The previous year, however, Power challenged Macken for the Leading Irish Rider title with nine wins for *Rockbarton*, six with *Castle Park* and three with *Lough Crew*. The man who was now finding himself under increasing pressure was Gerry Mullins. He had inherited the ride on *Rockbarton*, and with the great horse came great expectations.

1981 began with the purchase of Alan Lillingston's *Seven Up* for Foster and a display by army riders and horses at the equestrian fair in Essen, Germany, where the Irish horses outshone all others. Mullins and *Rockbarton* hit early form in Vienna when second in the World Cup qualifier, won by world and European champion Gerd Wiltfang on *Roman*. who also pipped them in the Puissance. They shared the Puissance honours at Geneva in April when clearing 7ft 3ins and the team finished third in the Cup here. *Seven Up* was disappointing at Punchestown in May, not helped by some wild antics on the Curragh after escaping from his stable, while Roche got into gear in Paris. The show at Longchamp took place in scorching heat and on slippery ground, exacerbated by over-watering of the course, but the Wexford man clinched a win on *Lough Crew*, was second in the Puissance with 'big wall' rookie *Maigh Cuilinn*, and third with *Castle Park*, while the team finished sixth.

There was a dramatic improvement in Aachen where the team lined up second behind the British and Roche had two joint-third placings before Mullins on *Rockbarton* went on to win at La Baule. But the next few years would bring much leaner times.

Mullins claimed the Leading Rider title at the 1981 Dublin Horse Show in August where the team was fourth, but another army man would steal the limelight when writing his name into the history books a few weeks later. At one of the most controversial three-day events ever held – the European Championships at Horsens in Denmark – young Lieutenant Brian McSweeney scooped the individual bronze medal in the finest of style. The Irish side sent out to defend the team title won two years earlier included the experienced partnerships of Jessica Harrington (*Amoy*), Gerry

Sinnott (*The Prop*) and David Foster (*Cill Morain*, formerly *Seven Up*), but MacSweeney on *Inis Meain* was competing in only the second three-day-event of his entire career, which made the end result all the more remarkable. He produced a lovely test to slot into sixth place after dressage and the team was lying fourth going into cross-country day. But there was uproar about the thirty-fence cross-country track and before the competition began the *chefs d'equipe* jointly sent a letter to the Ground Jury President, Colonel Frank Weldon, requesting a meeting to discuss changes to the course – which underwent some minor alterations. One obstacle, known as Horsens Bridge, involved jumping across a wide stretch of river after galloping onto a platform and clearing a vertical fence, which was aptly adorned with a 'Road Closed' sign. This claimed a large number of victims – seven falls and two retirements – while in total there were 18 falls and many refusals around the track. From a 61-strong starting field, 21 failed to finish, leaving only 38 to

*Below*:
*Clearing the formidable Horsens Bridge – Lieutenant Brian MacSweeney shot to prominence when taking individual bronze at the European Eventing Championship at Horsens, Denmark, in 1981, riding the brilliant* Inis Meain.

*Below:*
*Last man standing!*
*Lieutenant Brian*
*MacSweeney was the*
*only member of the Irish*
*team still in action on*
*the final day of the*
*1981 European*
*Eventing*
*Championships at*
*Horsens, Denmark,*
*where he claimed the*
*individual bronze medal*
*with* Inis Meain.

line out on the final morning. Just six of the 13 participating teams survived to the last day and Ireland wasn't one of them, following falls for both Gerry Sinnott and *The Prop* and Jessica Harrington, whose great little mare *Amoy* was simply swallowed up by the scale of the course. Foster was airlifted to hospital after *Cill Morain* crashed into the bank on the landing side of the formidable Horsens Bridge. The 1979 team gold medal winning horse had been considered the better ride for the more experienced army man, but it would be the rookie, MacSweeney, who would come out best.

'I walked the course with Jessie and Gerry Sinnott – I was completely in awe of them as riders – and I could see that they didn't like the look of it. They kept stopping to examine the fences, and shaking their heads in disbelief. I had to pretend I realised it was all very difficult, but to be honest it didn't seem that hard to me and when *Inis Meain* set off, he just powered around that course like he was having a great old time!' MacSweeney recalls. 'He had such a big stride, a huge jump and a great gallop – he was

a class horse and an old pro, he loved his job, he was brilliant at it and he knew it. He gave me all the confidence I needed – I never had a worry in the world,' he adds. He modestly disregards his own input. The *Irish Field* pointed out that 'although *Inis Meain* is an old hand at this game, his jockey's experience could at best be described as limited. The pair had never tackled an entire course together, yet they flew around the toughest track in recent years with consummate ease to move into fourth place.' And when one of those ahead of him faltered, MacSweeney pounced on the bronze medal.

Things were looking promising for MacSweeney ahead of the following year's World Championships in Luhmuehlen now. 'He is a delightfully calm rider, yet has the dash to ride over a long and difficult cross-country track helping his horse every inch of the way. He is, undoubtedly, a young rider with enormous talent,' commented the *Irish Field*.[13]

The jumpers meanwhile headed for the European Championships in Munich where they finished sixth, but *Rockbarton* failed the first vet check and was withdrawn from the final day's competition, while Roche finished a creditable eighteenth individually on *Lough Crew*. Riding *Gortroe*, Mullins came out in November to jointly set a new world bareback high jump record at 6ft 7.5in at the Dublin Indoor International. But the weight of the expectations being piled upon *Rockbarton*'s newest rider would grow ever-heavier as the 1982 World Championships in Dublin loomed large on the horizon.

The event took place in a restive atmosphere as the recession had really begun to bite. Funding for foreign travel had all but dried up, Bord na gCapall was feeling the pinch and threatening staff cuts, and although Foster and MacSweeney made a successful raid on the British circuit in April there were no army contenders at Punchestown International Three-Day-Event in May due to injuries.

In May, *Lough Crew* fell ill in Rome where the showjumpers finished sixth, but recovered in time to produce a superb double-clear for Roche in the Nations Cup at Lucerne. The team result at the Swiss venue was poor, however, Ireland collecting 55 faults to slot into ninth place, and at Hickstead immediately afterwards they could only manage fifth. Prospects did not look hugely optimistic as the tenth World Championships got underway at the RDS on 8 June.

The home side of Roche on *Lough Crew*, Macken on *Spotlight*, Jack Doyle on *Hardly* and Mullins on *Rockbarton* finished a disappointing eighth behind medal winners France, Germany and Britain, but Mullins and *Rockbarton* truly rose to the occasion and attracted huge crowds to the RDS for the final day when the individual medals were decided. '*Rockbarton* was such a blood horse and he got better every time he jumped that week,' Mullins recalls. They made a modest start, but were lying eleventh going into Saturday's Grand Prix in which they beat the best in the world to make it through to Sunday's final showdown. 'The prayers of the crowd were answered, and *Rockbarton* sailed over the eight-fence second-round track to notch up one of only three double-clears and, with the best overall time, to win the class,' said the *Irish Field*.[14] It was career-defining result for both horse and rider.

The format for the world title is a cruel one, however, because the best four riders go

*Above*: Captain Gerry Mullins and Rockbarton *jumped their way to fourth place in the 1982 World Championships at the RDS.*

through to the last day when only three medals are awarded after this ultimate test in which each competitor must jump not only his own horse, but also those of his rivals. And it was Mullins who missed out this time around when finishing fourth while Germany's Norbert Koof (*Fire*) took gold ahead of Britain's Malcolm Pyrah (*Anglezarke*) in silver and Frenchman Michel Robert (*Ideal de la Hay*) in bronze. Mullins was a relative novice compared to these hardened professionals, but as *The Irish Field* pointed out the following weekend, 'he proved himself to be the fourth best rider in the world' and such was his consistency that he finished the week as leading money-winner, while *Rockbarton* was now a super-star – 'he has, effectively, proved himself as the best horse in the world, which is a sorely-needed boost for Irish breeding,' declared the *Irish Field*.

Looking back on it twenty-seven years later, Mullins says it was an amazing experience that taught him some valuable lessons. 'I over-rode the other horses in the final because I didn't trust their scope – that was a mistake, because they all had plenty of jump.' He didn't allow himself to dwell on 'what might have been' however, and growing in confidence with every ride, he brought *Rockbarton* out to win the Grand Prix at La Baule the following month. An injury sustained in the French Derby kept the horse off the team for Dublin, where Ledingham made his Aga Khan debut on *Lough Crew* as Ireland finished fourth. Ledingham was also second in the Wylie trophy while Roche finished fourth in the Puissance.

At Leeuwarden in October, Ledingham and *Lough Crew* racked up a win, in November *Rockbarton* finished third in the Grand Prix in Amsterdam, where Mullins also won the Take Your Own Line class, riding *Inis Mor*, the horse with which he contributed to Ireland's silver medal success at the World Military Championships in Rome. And with *Rockbarton* he took the Bordeaux World Cup qualifier by storm in December. Now lying second on the World Cup leaderboard, the Irish partnership were destined for the series final in Vienna the following April. But *Rockbarton* would be plagued by injury throughout 1983.

Mullins made it to the Viennese fixture where he won a class on *Inis Mor* but was forced to withdraw *Rockbarton* after the early stages. Ledingham was really finding his feet, however, and at Hickstead in May won a speed class on *Lough Crew* following the departure of Roche who, having transferred to the post of OC at the Curragh, left the army to ride in Switzerland the following year – in 1987 he took up a position at the headquarters of the international governing body for equestrian sport, the Federation Equestre Internationale, in Lausanne, where he now plays a major role as Jumping Director.

*Rockbarton* turned out for the Nations Cup at Hickstead in June where the team finished sixth and Mullins topped a class with *Mostrim*. However, he had to be withdrawn when unsound in Paris where Ledingham on *Lough Crew* contributed to Ireland's fourth-place finish and again at Aachen where the team repeated that result. People were beginning to wonder if the horse was coming to the end of his career, but Colonel Ringrose said it was 'only a slight problem which vets are having difficulty in identifying' and that the horse was '99 percent sound'. And he was right, for there was plenty more to come from the great one.

It didn't come right away, however. Mullins joined Ledingham, Jack Doyle and Macken at the European Championships in Hickstead the following month where he hit the deck when *Rockbarton* banked the notorious privet hedge oxer. And when Ireland finished eighth, the team withdrew to save their thunder for Dublin. This proved a good move, although a little frustrating when they were beaten in Dublin by only the tiniest margin – 0.25 time faults – by the new European Champions from Switzerland.

In September, Mullins took the Leading Rider trophy in Munich without *Rockbarton* who was now suffering from an over-reach injury, but this gave *Mostrim* a chance to shine. The eight-year-old was already a good speed horse, but showed he had a lot more to offer by taking third and then second in the two Grand Prix qualifiers, and then seventh in the Grand Prix itself. As the year wound to a close, *Rockbarton* returned to form again on the North American circuit, where he finished third in the Washington Grand Prix before winning the Whitney Stone Memorial Trophy in New York. And now the Equitation School had four more cadets, following a newly-devised recruitment campaign which opened the door to both male and female candidates. From a total of 350 applicants, the chosen ones were all young men, however. They were Walter Hunt from Claremorris in County Mayo (18), Edward Butler from the Curragh in Kildare (19), Gerald O'Grady from Sligo (20) and Will Hayes, the nineteen-year-old son of the legendary Seamus.

As the Olympic year of 1984 got underway Colonel Ringrose was confirmed as Chef d'Equipe for the jumping team in Los Angeles but, in the end, only Mullins and *Rockbarton* would travel. They made a great start to the season by beating Macken on *Carroll's El Paso* in the World Cup qualifier at Dortmund in March, and both Irishmen competed at the World Cup final in Gothenburg in April where the army partnership made it through to the top-twenty decider on the last day and, with a fence down in each round, finished joint-fourteenth.

The final decision about sending a team to LA would be made after the Rome show in May, and it was looking good when Ledingham recorded a win on *Gabhran* and a second place on *Inis Mor* at the Italian venue. But hopes were dashed when the team – MacSweeney on *Sliabh na mBan*, George Stewart on *Leapy Lad*, Trevor Monson on *Schnitzel* and Trevor Coyle on *Bank Strike* – finished last in the Nations Cup. Sean Daly, now chairman of SJAI selectors, believed that *Rockbarton* was Ireland's only true Olympic contender. 'The horse is in great form and undoubtedly has a chance,' he said, but he felt it was a pointless exercise to send anyone else. 'Unfortunately, we were honest enough to make all our top riders professional. And we are a nation of sellers. If the money is high enough, the horse is gone,' he pointed out.[15] There was no arguing with any of this. Professionals were still barred from Olympic participation, so Macken and Darragh were therefore non-starters, and the best Irish horses were indeed being snapped up by foreign buyers for big sums of money. Another poor team performance in Paris later that month really put the lid on it.

Ledingham had a win with *Ard na Croise* and a third-placing with *Gabhran* at the French fixture and, with *Lough Crew*, was selected for the Games along with Mullins and event rider Foster. However, great results at Hickstead in June, with a double for Ledingham on *Gabhran* and *Ard na Croise* and a win for Mullins on *Mostrim* were followed by the tragic news that *Lough Crew* had died of colic. 'I was totally devastated,' Ledingham recalls. 'He was a really nice horse. I got a big shot of reality and I learned an important lesson – that victory is sweet and short-lived, and that you need to have the same attitude to defeat.' It wasn't just his horse he lost that year, his father had passed away just a few months earlier.

'Now all we can do is prepare *Rockbarton* for the job in hand,' said Colonel Ringrose, who was very aware of the knock-on effect of this latest turn of events. 'All this is putting Gerry Mullins under enormous pressure. He has already lost the opportunity of a warm-up in the team event, and now he has lost the moral support of a team mate,' he pointed out.[16] As it turned out, Mullins and *Rockbarton* just failed to make it into the top twenty in LA.

The eventing team finished ninth, once again hampered by poor dressage results. New Zealand's Mark Todd took gold with the diminutive *Charisma*, and Foster finished twenty-seventh with *Aughatore* when adding only time penalties in both the cross-country and show jumping phases.

Meanwhile at home, Ledingham's mood was lifted when, riding *Gabhran*, he joined George Stewart (*Leapy Lad*), Jack Doyle (*Kerrygold Island*) and Eddie Macken (*Carroll's El Paso*) to keep the Aga Khan trophy at home for the first time in five years. It was a watershed in Irish showjumping history, as Macken had, at last, overturned the ban on foreign-bred horses competing on Irish teams a full six years after his battle with the Equestrian Federation of Ireland had begun. 'So the Irish team has regained some of the glory of the heady seventies,' wrote Grania Willis, who also commented on the lack of atmosphere at the RDS that summer.[17] In stark contrast, however, twenty thousand people flocked to the Derby at Millstreet two weeks later, where Mullins topped two speed classes with *Mostrim* and Lieutenant Nick Connors won on *Clais Dubh*.

Ledingham then truly made his mark by winning the Hickstead Derby on *Gabhran* at his very first attempt. In a drama-filled competition, German star Paul Schockemohle was unseated from *So Long* at the Derby Bank while Frenchman Pierre Durand's brilliant little *Jappeloup* slammed on the brakes. *Gabhran* made a single first-round mistake at the double of water ditches but, first to go in the four-horse jump-off, put in a copybook clear second time out to pip Britain's Nick Skelton and Michael Whitaker, while 1982

Hickstead Derby champion Schockemohle on *Deister* was forced to retire with a broken bridle. This was the eighth Irish victory in the twenty-four-year history of the Hickstead Derby and the first Irish win since Macken's great sequence with *Boomerang* ended in 1979. 'I felt I'd arrived,' Ledingham says. And indeed he had.

Mullins followed a win in Rotterdam, where the team finished fourth, with a double from *Mostrim* in Spruce Meadows, where the Irish side finished sixth as they struggled without both *Kerrygold Island* and *Carroll's El Paso*, who both suffered from travel sickness. Ledingham went to Chaudfontaine in Belgium, where he was second in the Grand Prix with *Gabhran*, and then in Tripoli he scored again with *Gabhran* while Mullins also notched up two more great wins with *Mostrim* as Ireland racked up five firsts, three second placings, a third, fourth and sixth finishing spot at the Libyan fixture. To top it all, Ledingham clinched victory in the Nations Cup and then travelled to Zaire where he was fourth in the Grand Prix, riding a borrowed horse.

To complete this more upbeat season, the men from McKee ran riot at the Military Show Jumping Championship in Mafra near Lisbon, Portugal, where Foster and *Cill Aine* won the individual title, MacSweeney scored a double with *Inis Mor* and *Cluain Mor* and Nick Connors was also in the ribbons. Ledingham ended 1984 as the leading money-winner with £23,000 to his credit and Sergeant Major Steve Hickey retired after forty-two years of sterling service. He would continue to work as one of Ireland's most sought-after course designers in the years to come.

While Japan's Crown Prince Akihito was being welcomed to the barracks by Colonel Ringrose and Quarter Master General Dermot Byrne in March of 1985, Ledingham was in Tokyo where he finished fourth in the Grand Prix. The Waterford rider then recorded the first Irish win of the year on *Gabhran* at Jerez in Spain, but the horse lost confidence after a fall there, and again in Madrid immediately afterwards, so Colonel Ringrose began to have doubts about his participation at the European Championships in Dinard later in the year. *Rockbarton*, however, was reported as 100 percent fit and with Mullins now back at the barracks after a six-month military course, they seemed likely candidates.

There were no sound horses for the Punchestown three-day event, and the absence of Foster and MacSweeney from the European eventing squad for Burghley was keenly felt. MacSweeney settled back to winning on the home circuit, which was thriving, and now included the new Show Jumping Festival at Salthill. The brainchild of Claregalway-man Paul Duffy, the event attracted unprecedented TV and general media coverage as well as vast crowds of spectators throughout the 1980s. With restored confidence, *Gabhran* bucked his way around the arena to take the Grand Prix while Mullins won the Fault-and-Out on *Cluain Mor*, and by July *Rockbarton* was also back in action, charming his fans with a great win in Clonmel. But Ringrose had grave reservations about sending any of his horses to Dinard. He said that '*Gabhran* is such a useful winner. He tries so hard that we could just ruin that by pushing him beyond his limit. He's just a shade short of really top scope and it seems the wisest course not to send him,' while as far as *Rockbarton* was concerned, he didn't want to expose his horse and rider to the situation they had faced in LA. 'It is very difficult to compete [in a championship] with no team back-up. The question to ask yourself is, can you see a sound prospect of winning a medal? If not, there is no point in going,' he pointed out.[18] And in the end they didn't compete.

*Above*:
*Captain John Ledingham and* Gabhran – *winners of the Hickstead Derby in 1984.*

This season, like many to follow, was overshadowed by a row over the appointment of a Chef d'Equipe for the senior team. The riders backed the appointment of Sean Daly, effectively disregarding the 'gentleman's agreement' that an army *chef* should be in control when there were two or more army riders on the side; and the argument spilled over into Dublin Horse Show week when the team riders boycotted the first day of competition. A compromise was reached when Ned Campion stepped into the breach and the team finished second behind the newly-crowned European Champions from Great Britain, but the acrimony would continue for years to come, fuelled to no small extent by governance issues within the SJAI. The year ended with wins for Mullins and Ledingham in Donaueschingen, Germany, and Norrkoping in Sweden.

Despite managing on a horse purchasing budget of just €90,000 there were plenty of promising heads hanging over the stable doors at McKee in early 1986 and included amongst them was the former *Super Steel*, a grey by *Arctic Que* bred by Mick Dwyer in

Nenagh, who campaigned successfully with MacSweeney at Navan show the previous year and who would soon begin a great partnership with Mullins under his new name, *Glendalough. Rockbarton* and *Gabhran* were still the stars, however, and were being aimed at the World Championships in Aachen.

A virus wiped out the army horses spring eventing campaign, but Foster won the Open Class at Templemartin on *Droichead Atha* and a novice section on *Tramore Strand* before heading to Britain for a six-venue tour. He was accompanied by MacSweeney, who won the open classes at both Tweseldown and Tidworth with the 1984 Dublin Supreme Hunter Champion, *Le Froy*, now re-named *Cairnhill*, and at Punchestown in May, Foster finished eleventh on *Aughatore* while MacSweeney slotted into twelfth on *Foyle River*. At Segovia in Spain the following month, Foster steered *Droichead Atha* into second place behind Olympic Champion Mark Todd.

Plans for the Show Jumping World Championships in Aachen were already descending into chaos, however. The civilian team for Lucerne fell apart and the side that travelled to Hickstead was withdrawn by Daly after collecting a disastrous 53.5 faults in the first round. He now didn't want to send a side to the championships at all, recommending that only Mullins with *Rockbarton* and Macken with *Carroll's Flight* should make the trip. Ringrose wanted *Gabhran* to join them to create a three-man team, but in the end the situation was resolved when Macken stepped down because he wasn't convinced his horse was ready for the challenge. When *Gabhran* was withdrawn after the first speed leg, *Rockbarton*, now in the twilight of his career, did what he always did best and rose to the occasion to finish seventh individually. The *Irish Field* commented that 'Mullins and the seventeen-year-old *Rockbarton* had more than justified the Army's and the nation's faith in them.' [19]

And the old boy wasn't finished yet. He didn't enjoy the ground at Dublin Horse Show where he put in an uncharacteristic stop during the Aga Khan Cup in which the team, with Campion again as *chef*, had to settle for third. But the following Sunday he crowned a triumphant week for the army and the host nation with a superb victory in the Grand Prix, the first in the twenty years that had elapsed since Diana Conolly-Carew held the trophy aloft. There were only five clears in the first round and *Rockbarton* escaped time penalties by the narrowest of margins when just 11 hundredths of a second inside the time allowed. Only Jay Land on *Leapy Lad*, Mullins, and Ireland's Kieran Rooney on *Hyland Serpent* stayed clear again next time out, and Land set the jump-off target when breaking the beam in 44.02. *Rockbarton* left a brick teetering on the wall, but raced home in 43.41 seconds to take the lead, and when Rooney retired, Mullins and *Rockbarton* took the honours. 'It's put the horse where he should be, in a class of his own – he really deserved it; in fact, the whole nation deserved it,' Mullins said. In one of the best-ever Dublin Horse Shows from an Irish perspective, Irish-bred horses filled five of the six top placings in the Grand Prix, while Mullins and Ledingham scored four of the six home wins – Ledingham including a joint-victory in the Puissance when clearing 7ft 5in with the eight-year-old *Kilcoltrim*.

On a roll now, the army went to Millstreet where Mullins scored with *Mostrim* and *Rockbarton*, Ledingham and *Ard na Croise* took a runner-up spot and Connors topped a class with *Cill Aine*.

Foster was flying the flag high too when he came second individually and was also a member of the winning Irish team at Hasselt CCI in Holland. John Watson on *Tullineasky* finished third behind Foster on *Foyle River* – the two Irish riders producing the only clear rounds within the time over the cross-country course.

The army was in good shape, but the horse industry was not. In a radio interview for RTÉ in September, Eileen Parkhill suggested that Bord na gCapall should be disbanded and her wish would soon come true. Show organisers, including the RDS, were in financial trouble, horse exports were down and breeding figures were at their lowest ebb, and by early 1987 the final nails were driven into the coffin of the once-proud semi-state organisation that had set out with strong ideals but which had fallen prey to a toxic mixture of party politics, lack of vision and leadership and dwindling financial support.

Ledingham and *Ard na Croise* started 1987 with a speed win at Warrington show in Kilkenny in May, and Mullins and *Mostrim* produced Ireland's only win at Hickstead the following month, where the team had to settle for seventh place in the Nations Cup. Ledingham on *Gabhran* and Mullins on his new ride *Glendalough* had just four faults in each round of the Nations Cup, however, and *Glendalough* also finished seventh in the Grand Prix and fourth in the Fault-and-Out. Still flying, Mullins won the Prix de la

Rose in Reims with his new mare *Limerick*, while *Glendalough* finished a creditable eighth in the Grand Prix.

At home, the sudden death of Sean Daly sent a shockwave through the equestrian community. The four members of his dream-team that had clinched those historic three-in-a-row Aga Khan victories – Con Power, Paul Darragh, James Kernan and Eddie Macken – joined Sean's eldest son, John, and jockey Ted Walsh to carry the coffin at his funeral.

Foster enjoyed a good year when following his fifth-place finish with *Kilmallock* in the National Championship at Punchestown with victory on *Killiney Bay* at La Granja in Spain, where he also came second with *Kinsale Harbour*. This was the army's first foreign international win since MacMahon and *San Carlos* topped the line-up in Fontainebleau. Brian MacSweeney slotted into fifth riding *Wexford* but later in July was seriously injured in a fall while schooling a young horse over a small bank at McKee. Knocked unconscious, he would take some considerable time to recover. In August, Foster competed at Zonhoven, Belgium, where the team had a disappointing result, but he was hailed a hero after preventing vets from destroying a horse which almost drowned in the water complex after hitting its head, but which eventually walked away after being calmed down by the Meath man and the horse's French rider. Foster's year was completed with a second place finish in the team competition at Waregem in Belgium riding *Killiney Bay*.

The jumpers meanwhile made no impression at Aachen where they finished thirteenth of the fourteen competing nations, but their year also ended with a flourish. At Franconville near Paris, Ledingham took fourth in the Grand Prix and second in the Puissance on *Kilcoltrim*, while at La Baule, Mullins scored on *Mostrim* and was second on *Limerick*.

Ledingham returned home to take the Speed King title at Salthill after a series of good results on *Ard na Croise*, and he was the hero of Ireland's fourteenth Aga Khan Cup victory. Riding *Gabhran*, he joined Mullins, Doyle and Macken in the quest to stop the British from winning the trophy outright after their dominance over the previous two years, and it was his fault-free performance that clinched it. *Rockbarton* also looked like returning a clean sheet for the day, but the final fence fell as he crossed the line. Crowning a great week, Ledingham and *Kilcoltrim,* whom the rider described as 'a special horse – one of the really brave ones' shared the Puissance honours for the second year in a row.

There was mayhem at Millstreet later in August where many of the best horses in the country were lucky to escape with their lives after a fire broke out. There were loose horses everywhere as stable doors were flung open, and one of those who galloped for miles down dark County Cork roads before being retrieved that night was a grey stallion called *Cruising,* who would play a hugely important role in Irish showjumping and breeding in later years. The chaos didn't stop Ledingham and *Gabhran* from winning the Derby Trial however, and they were unlucky not to take the Derby itself when a slip at the railway gates saw them having to settle for third behind his other ride, *Kilcoltrim,* which was runner-up to Britain's David Broome on *Lannegan.*

With no team at the European Championships at St Gallen in Switzerland, the Irish headed for Chaudfontaine and won the Nations Cup. Mullins, on the rejuvenated *Rockbarton,* Macken on the borrowed *Welfenkrone,* Ledingham on *Gabhran* and Darragh on *Trigger* were lying fourth of the eleven participating nations with 8.75 faults at the halfway stage, and when Ledingham and Darragh went clear second time out, they needed one more zero score to clinch it. Macken's horse hit the middle of the triple combination, but Mullins, in his new role as anchorman, was fault-free and they won by an impressive margin of more than eight faults over the French.

*Mostrim* also racked up another speed win at the French fixture, and on returning home Mullins won the Grand Prix with *Glendalough* at the Champions of the Year Show at Navan, which had replaced the now defunct Dublin Indoor International as the showcase end-of-season Irish fixture. Ledingham also claimed the Puissance title here with the bold and brave *Kilcoltrim,* and the men at McKee were in buoyant mood as the year was drawing to a close.

That wouldn't last long, however, because in October the spectre of closure suddenly returned once again with the news of a savage 50 percent cut in the 1988 budget. These were tough times, but Colonel Ringrose remained hopeful, despite his acceptance that participation in the following year's Olympic Games in Seoul was now seriously jeopardised. 'All we can do is hope the importance of the export industry is recognised and that we will be given sufficient funds to continue in our role as advertisers for the

Irish horse,' he said.[20] Mullins's answer to that was to go out and win the Grand Prix at Helsinki on *Glendalough*. In the three-way jump-off against Germany's Michael Ruping and Australia's Jeff McVean, the turn to the final wall was the deciding factor, and with his trademark do-or-die attitude Mullins asked the handsome grey horse a big question when attacking it at an acute angle and then had to 'sit and pray he would come up over it'. The super *Artic Que* gelding didn't let him down.

That result may well have contributed to the Government's change of heart as, in December, it was confirmed that an alternative source of funding had been found for army riders selected for Seoul. Ringrose was keen for Mullins to be there, and also felt that *Gabhran*'s great performances in Dublin and Chaudfontaine suggested that Ledingham, who also had *Kilcoltrim* and *Barrow River* in his string, should be in with a chance too. 'I think we could undoubtedly field two combinations well able to tackle the Nations Cup side of the Games,' he said. The question was, would the civilians be willing to back them up?

With the rules at last changed so that professional riders could now compete at the Olympics, and both Macken and Darragh expressing an interest in taking part, the SJAI came out in full support of a team for Seoul in early January 1988 and confirmed a long-list, including Mullins with both *Glendalough* and *Rockbarton*, and Ledingham with *Gabhran*, *Kilcoltrim* and *Barrow River*. *Rockbarton* was now nineteen years old, however, and in May his retirement was announced. The horse that had carried Ireland's hopes and dreams through an extraordinarily successful eleven-year career was to step down at last.

Preparation for Seoul included the Nations Cups at Hickstead, Aachen and Dublin, and the Irish Championships at Salthill that summer. But the funding situation took a dark turn when it was discovered that £165,000 would be needed to send the team to the Olympics.

The army men just got on with the job anyway, Ledingham and *Gabhran* winning the Spring Show Grand Prix and Mullins with *Glendalough* finishing fourth in the Eindhoven Derby. Mullins and *Limerick* won the first speed class at Wiesbaden before joining Ledingham on *Kilcoltrim* at Hickstead, where the team finished fifth. Stepping into *Rockbarton*'s shoes was never going to be an easy task, but *Glendalough* was rising to the challenge. *Kilcoltrim* was now shaping up as Ledingham's Olympic ride, even though he lacked experience, but fate would temporarily halt his learning curve when he had to be withdrawn from the Aachen side in July after being badly bitten by *Gabhran* while travelling.

When the 'talking horse' of its time, Trevor Coyle's *True Blue*, was sold by owner Helen Bond, the SJAI did an about-turn and announced it was not now sending a team to Seoul. Colonel Ringrose was disgusted, and an uninspiring joint-third in the Aga Khan Cup, despite strong performances from both *Glendalough*, who had just a single fence down, and *Gabhran*, who picked up 4.5 faults, didn't improve the situation. *Kilcoltrim* produced another spectacular Puissance victory – his third in succession at the RDS – when joining two others to clear a record 7ft 5in, while Mullins racked up a double on *Mostrim* and another win on *Limerick*. A glimmer of hope began to appear when Minister of State Joe Walsh suggested that the EFI should 'reconsider' its position on the Games. A week later, the Government suddenly announced that it would largely underwrite the cost of the Olympic effort.

At Salthill, Mullins was runner-up in both the National and Speed Championships, and at Millstreet, Ledingham and *Gabhran* won the £20,000 Dawn Milk Derby, while Mullins also scored with *Limerick*. Olympic fundraising was back on track, and things were looking up as Mullins with *Glendalough*, Ledingham with *Kilcoltrim*, Darragh with *For Sure* and Jack Doyle with *Hardly* arrived in Seoul. Mullins just missed out on the individual final by 0.5 time penalties and finished twenty-second individually. But *Kilcoltrim* was deeply disappointing. Ledingham blames himself now, even though his horse was a real novice at that level of the sport. 'I got "Games Fever",' he says. 'You try so hard that you over-try and over-train, and it comes against you. The horse was totally jarred because I did too much canter-work on the sand, and we were there for a month before the Games started. I know now that I should have looked at it like just another competition and should have blocked everything else out,' he adds. The team finished eleventh of the twelve competing nations, and Ireland's best finishers were Doyle on *Hardly* in twentieth place.

The ground conditions in Seoul didn't only affect the jumpers. David Foster's event horse, *Killiney Bay*, was badly jarred too after the cross-country phase, hardly surprising considering it included 17km of roads and tracks almost entirely on cement-covered

surfaces. He had opened his year with good results on the British circuit and a fifteenth-place finish at the Olympic qualifier at Saumur in May, by which time it was already clear that he and John Watson would be the sole Irish eventing Olympians. Watson took a horrible fall and broke his collarbone at Seoul when *Tullineasky* tried to bounce an oxer on the hilly course, which had a series of nasty drop-fences and proved a massive test. *Killiney Bay* completed the track, but vet Hugh Suffern, Chef d'Equipe Commandant Ronnie MacMahon, and groom Corporal Cowman spent that entire night treating the horse with ultrasound and massage. 'But for this, *Killney Bay* would not have passed the final vetting and I would not have completed another Olympics,' the rider wrote afterwards. He had been hoping for a top-ten finish, but eventually completed in sixteenth place – still a considerable achievement considering the severity of the competition.

Mullins and *Glendalough* came home to win both the Indoor Derby and the Grand Prix at Navan, where *Kilcoltrim* showed he was none-the-worse for his travels when equalling *Sliabh na mBan*'s Dublin indoor record by clearing 7ft 2in to win the Puissance. But in November it wasn't just the retired hero *Rockbarton* who found himself grounded. Funding had dried up yet again and there was uncertainty about the future.

Another special horse would soon grace the McKee stableyard to save the day, however. His name was *Kilbaha*, and he would allow Ledingham to show just how good he could be.

# 10

# A BURST OF BRILLIANCE, AND SOME FOND FAREWELLS

## 1989 to 1999

*'Cheers for the Irish Army School of Equitation*
*which can still produce fine and stylish riders, as well as winning ones'*
*Baron Alexis von Wrangel*

There were three key departures from the Equitation School as 1989 got underway. Brian MacSweeney moved to the Transport Corps at Clancy Barracks, and both David Foster and Colonel Ringrose retired.

During his forty-year career, Colonel Billy Ringrose did Ireland proud from the saddle before filling the role of Officer Commanding at the Equitation School for seventeen years. Already President of the Royal Dublin Society, he was appointed Main Arena Director for Dublin Horse Show which, in January 1989, sealed a £500,000 three-year sponsorship deal with Bord Bainne (The Irish Dairy Board). He continues to be closely involved in the world of Irish equestrianism today.

The 1989 army campaign kicked off at Hamburg in June where Ledingham was awarded the Most Stylish Rider prize in the Derby

*Above:*
*Colonel Billy Ringrose*
*retired in 1989 after*
*forty years of service.*

and shared the Puissance honours in a four-way tie over 2.20 metres, riding *Kilcoltrim*. At home, Longford-born Lieutenant Gerry Flynn was on the first rung of a ladder that would take him to the top as both event rider and showjumper.

But 1989 was a fairly dismal year from an international perspective, with little interest from most of the top riders in competing at the European Championship in Rotterdam and only one Nations Cup team lining out for the entire twelve-month period. This was at Dublin Horse Show, where they finished fourth. Ledingham's *Gabhran* had an uncharacteristic stop in the first round as did Eddie Macken's *Welfenkrone*, but *Gabhran* came back to jump a brilliant second-round clear while Mullins on *Glendalough* picked up just four faults both times out.

Ledingham had plenty to celebrate, however, when claiming his fourth successive Dublin Puissance title with *Kilcoltrim*. It takes a certain type of horse and rider to master the art of big-wall jumping, and this gelding's faith in his rider, and his amazing courage, were key elements of their record-breaking successes. And this time around they didn't have to share the spoils when they were the sole contenders to leave the wall intact at 7ft 1in. 'Puissance is all about confidence in knowing what you are doing and belief in your horse's ability to do it, but there is no room for doubt. Once the doubt creeps in, your horse knows it, and he will stop,' Ledingham says. And *Kilcoltrim* reminded his fans what a great all-rounder he was when pipping opening-day winners Mullins and *Mostrim* to win the Kerrygold Top Score.

At Millstreet a week later, *Kilcoltrim* and Ledingham looked set to win the Derby with a brilliant double-clear, only to be nudged into runner-up spot by British junior Nigel Coupe with the appropriately-named *Invincible Lad*. The following month it was Mullins who grabbed the headlines when flying the flag at Spruce Meadows, Canada, where he finished second on *Mostrim* in the Prudential Steel Cup. The Canadian fixture attracted the cream of the showjumping world, and Mullins's competitiveness throughout this big week, allied with his effervescent character, proved a big hit with the press corps. 'So taken was the Canadian press with him that … he merited full-page coverage … in two of the most important daily newspapers,' wrote Michael Slavin.[1]

He returned home to steer *Glendalough* to victory in the Furstenburg Indoor Derby for the second consecutive year at the Champions of the Year Show at Navan, which was a poignant fixture for young Lieutenant Will Hayes, who honoured the passing of his legendary father, Seamus, by sharing the honours in the Puissance, riding *Cluain Mor*. And Flynn announced his very definite arrival as an event rider when winning the Open Intermediate class at Kilcooley Abbey, County Tipperary, in October on only his second outing with Foster's Seoul Olympic ride *Killiney Bay*.

The year concluded with a notable trip in November to the two-nation tournament at North Fork Farm in Harare, Zimbabwe, where Mullins and Ledingham were joined by John Hall and Paul Darragh to win the Ged O'Dwyer Nations Cup. And as 1990 began, the heroes of the 1930s were recalled once more as Lieutenant Colonel Dan Corry died at the age of eighty-seven. In an appreciation, Thady Ryan, the great master of Limerick's world-famous Scarteen Hounds, said, 'Dan's name was synonymous, not only with the highest degree of sportsmanship in the world of horses, but also with an infectious spirit of fun, generosity and lasting friendship.'[2]

For many, however, competing for their country no longer seemed to have the same allure. Journalist Nick O'Hare commented that the thriving home circuit appeared to be providing a much more enticing alternative for Irish riders. 'They have been able to do well on the home circuit with booming prize-funds, whereas to capture the same amount of money at an international show calls for both outlay and tremendous performance,' he pointed out.[3]

The EFI recognised the problem and Secretary General Michael Stone set out a plan for the year with the Nations Cup in Rome high on the agenda. At a preparatory show at Firenze, Italy, in April, Mullins placed with *Glendalough*, *Mostrim* and new horses *Lismore* and *Rumbo*. *Glendalough* jumped clear in the first round of the Nations Cup in Rome in May, but the team finished eighth in the twelve-country competition. Ledingham on *Kilcoltrim* claimed third in a somewhat peculiar Puissance in which there was no big wall. Fears about safety had led to the decision to present a massive triple bar as the biggest obstacle, and the Irish partnership faulted when it went up to 2.10 metres. The Rome organisers subsequently relented, however, and the annual May fixture at the Piazza di Siena continues to present one of the few remaining opportunities to see horses take on the big red wall in all its glory.

Mullins and Ledingham were selected for Hickstead and the German shows at Aachen and Wolfsburg in June, but Irish results on the international circuit were so poor that the country was no longer ranked high enough to warrant an invitation to field a team in Aachen. Stung by that reality, the side that included Mullins and *Glendalough* produced a great second-place finish in the Nations Cup at Hickstead after a cliff-hanger of a jump-off against the victorious host country. British team manager Ronnie Massarella admitted afterwards, 'the Irish pressed us all the way − it's good to see them back.'

But he had his eye on another prize altogether. After a glorious twenty-one years as

*Opposite top*:
*Corporal Bridget Lawlor*
*checking that everything*
*is in order in the tack*
*room at McKee.*

British Chef d'Equipe he was about to retire. So the British Equestrian Federation promised him that, if he could win the Aga Khan cup outright by producing the final part of a consecutive hat-trick in Dublin this summer, then he could keep the trophy for his own mantelpiece. That idea didn't appeal to the Irish at all, however, so, having won the Speed Championship at the National Championships in Salthill a week earlier, Mullins joined Ledingham, Macken and Edward Doyle in an effort to keep it at home. And it very nearly worked.

Clears from the two army men and Doyle left Macken redundant and Ireland stood two fences ahead of Germany and three ahead of Britain at the end of the first round. It was looking pretty good. There wasn't such an easy passage next time out, however, and it fell to Macken to force a jump-off against the much-improved British, who added nothing to their twelve-fault first-round score. With typical cool, the genius from Granard did just that, but it wasn't over yet.

The Irish had managed to thwart their nearest neighbour's effort to win the cup outright in 1979, but the British had the scent of victory in their nostrils this time around. And despite another clear from Ledingham on *Gabhran*, Macken was only fighting for runner-up spot after eight and four-fault results for the remaining home runners. Clears from Nick Skelton, Peter Charles and Michael Whitaker had sealed the fate of the most desirable trophy in the world of Irish show jumping – or so it seemed.

But there was to be a nasty sting in the tail of this story. Three months later, David Broome, who had sat out the final round of the competition as his team-mates stormed to victory, was disqualified from the competition when his Irish-bred horse, *Lannegan*, tested positive for a banned substance. The international governing body, the FEI, stated that it wasn't an intentional breach of the rules by the revered Welsh wizard. But it would prove costly, as the win was forfeit, so His Royal Highness The Aga Khan would not be asked to replace the gold-plated cup, valued at the time at £16,000, but worth a great deal more than that in Irish hearts. 'It's nice to think that it isn't gone,' said Colonel Ned Campion, now Officer Commanding at the Equitation School and Irish Chef d'Equipe, 'but it would have been better to win it on the day rather than like this.'

In July, the twelfth World Championships and inaugural World Equestrian Games (WEG) in Stockholm was thrown into chaos following highly-publicised allegations of the abuse of horses in Germany. It didn't stop the German team from taking silver behind the all-conquering gold medallists from France, however. Neither Edward Doyle's *Love Me Do* nor Mullins's *Glendalough* showed their true colours, and Ireland finished a disappointing twelfth of the sixteen participating nations. It was very clear by now that Irish horses were losing their grip at the top end of the sport with only fifteen Irish-

*Above*:
*Some of the first girl grooms at McKee Barrackes enjoying a well-earned tea-break (L-R) Private Bernie Spain, Corporal Bridget Lawlor, Private Marianne O'Brien and Private Paula Kiely.*

breds listed from ninety-five starters at the WEG. But the good ones were still highly valued and the nine-year-old grey, *Love Me Do*, was snapped up shortly after the championships by Dutch rider Albert Voorn.

In August, Ledingham and *Kilcoltrim* were third in the Derby at Millstreet and the following month Mullins and *Glendalough* won the Grand Prix at the Champions of the Year show at Navan for the second year in a row, but the Irish circuit was beginning to feel the squeeze as PJ Carroll and Company had already pulled out of showjumping sponsorship, and the principal backers of the Navan fixture, Furstenberg, followed suit. In November the RDS announced payroll and general expenditure cuts totalling £500,000 for the following year as its financial situation continued in freefall. It had been operating with a deficit over thirteen of the previous fourteen years.

The arrival of the first female grooms brightened up the yard at McKee, however.

## FIRST FEMALE GROOMS

Breaking with the long-held all-male tradition, a ground-breaking recruitment campaign opened the doors to female grooms and lorry drivers for the very first time in January 1990. There were hundreds of applicants for the thirty places on offer and the successful candidates underwent specialised training with Sergeant Frank Dawson and Sergeant Major Michael Smyth.

The first group included Deirdre Keogh from Old Pallas in Limerick, Trish Hanlon from Cork, Marianne O'Brien from Westmeath, Niamh Sheridan from Clara in Offaly, Bridget Lawlor from Saggart in Dublin, Bernadette Spain from Birr in Offaly, Paula Kiely from Athlone in Westmeath and Lorraine Greene from Thurles in Tipperary. The female grooms are now one of the most valued assets to the operation at the Army Equitation School.[4]

The gloom of the previous year's sponsorship pull-outs was dispelled in the new year when Heineken announced it was increasing its support of the National Championships at Salthill to the tune of £400,000 in a new three-year contract. And Ledingham had a new spring to his step. In May he won the two-horse relay in Munich on *Meanus* and a newcomer called *Kilbaha*. The previous September he had taken a test-run on *Kilbaha* and the moment he sat on the big, striking chestnut gelding he knew this was a once-in-a-lifetime ride. Classically bred, by the thoroughbred stallion *Tudor Rocket* and out of a mare called *Scarlet O'Hara*, which was by the thoroughbred sire *Rhett Butler*, the rangy eight-year-old gelding, bred by Tim O'Sullivan in Newmarket in Cork, had been competing with David O'Regan under the name *Tied Cottage*. Ledingham couldn't sleep all night worrying about whether the horse would pass the obligatory veterinary inspection – which, of course, he did with flying colours. And also purchased on that same day was another chestnut gelding who would prove a faithful and hard-working army servant – *Castlepollard*.

In June, Ledingham and *Meanus* won at Babenhausen in Germany and Mullins won the Dairygold Grand Prix at Cork Show on *Lismore*. Team plans for the European Championships at La Baule unravelled, however, when both *Glendalough* and *Forsure* had to be withdrawn with hock injuries. Having missed three weeks' work, *Glendalough* was not considered fit enough to make the trip to France, so instead was aimed at the National Championships at Salthill in July, where he more than made amends when claiming the national title.

Mullins conjured up some superb jumping from the thirteen-year-old grey over the three evenings of competition at the Galway venue, reserving the very best for a nail-biting showdown against Macken on *Welfenkrone* on the final night. Just three points separated the top three going into the closing stages and Mullins and Macken were locked in combat right into the very last round. It took a jump-off to separate them, and Mullins afterwards described his winning tour of the track as a rider's dream: 'one of those rare, brilliant rounds where all the turns came off and we met every fence spot-on.' And he very nearly made it a back-to-back double of Speed Championship titles after winning the first speed leg with *River Shannon*, losing out to Harry Marshall only in the final leg. Remarkably, this was the only occasion on which his mother, Brid, ever saw her son compete. 'She couldn't bear to watch because she thought it was all far too dangerous!' Mullins recalls with a grin.

*Below*:
*Captain Gerry Mullins and* Glendalough *claimed the national title at Salthill in 1990, beating Eddie Macken and* Welfenkrone *in a thrilling two-way showdown.*

Dublin Horse Show would prove a big disappointment, however. Having won the opening class on *Foxfield*, which was on lease from Owen McElroy, Mullins had to retire with a very off-form *Glendalough* the following day, and his OC and Irish Chef d'Equipe, Colonel Campion, decided to drop him from the team. And Puissance specialist *Foxfield* also finished a reluctant third over the big wall.

For the first time in sixty-five years there was no army rider on the Aga Khan team, and as the British avenged the 1990 defeat, the home side limped home last. Even the Government was surprised at the level of public concern over the collapse of the Irish challenge, but the men at McKee were perfectly clear why they had not been in a position to ride to the rescue: there was a desperate need for a new intake of horses as the equine population at McKee was ageing rapidly. In a report compiled in the aftermath, the Department admitted that 'the present strength of top-class horses in the school is so depleted that the capacity … to compete at international level is in serious

Opposite top:
*Lieutenant Gerry Flynn and groom, Private Marianne O'Brien, featured in the 1993 Punchestown Horse Trials programme after* Lough Gur *finished best of the Irish at the 1992 fixture.*

Opposite middle:
*Captain Gerry Mullins and* Lismore *won the inaugural Millstreet Derby in 1991.*
(Tony Parkes)

Opposite bottom:
*Captain Gerry Flynn was Best Irish Competitor and claimed the Carew Silver Salver when finishing sixth with* Lough Gur *in the Heineken International at Punchestown in 1993.*

doubt.'[4] The horse-purchase budget had been cut by £40,000 to £82,000. It was enormously embarrassing that, in the year when the Aga Khan Cup got its biggest-ever TV audience – a massive 200 million households worldwide – Ireland had failed so dismally. 'A tremendous coup has been negated,' wrote Nick O'Hare.[5]

Mullins had the answer, however. He just picked up the reins again and galloped on regardless, winning the Grand Prix classes at both Waterford and Limerick in August, and then clinching the Derby title at the inaugural Millstreet Indoor International in November – all on *Lismore*. When he produced the only clear round of the Derby, earning an extra £500 bonus, the five thousand spectators went wild with excitement and course-builder Sergeant Major Steve Hickey and Millstreet's impresario Noel C Duggan hugged each other in the middle of the ring. It was the perfect end to a difficult twelve months. As Michael Slavin wrote, 'in typical back-to-the-wall style, the true high point of our international season was to happen right on our own doorstep.'[6]

The Olympic year of 1992 was a roller-coaster ride with its equal share of highs and lows. In May, British rider Peter Charles transferred his allegiance to Ireland. The thirty-two-year-old Liverpudlian, who had dual nationality as his parents hailed from Johnstown in Kilkenny, was immediately drafted onto the Olympic shortlist from which army representatives were noticeably absent.

*Kilbaha* showed his immense promise when fourth in the Derby at Eindhoven in June, where Ledingham also finished second in the Derby Trial on *Meanus*. And by the time *Kilbaha* won the Grand Prix at Hawthorn Farm in Kildare in July, the nine-year-old had already achieved Olympic qualification. Ledingham, however, didn't want him to go to the Barcelona Games. He had quickly forged a strong relationship with this horse of his dreams and believed he needed another year on the circuit before aiming at championship level. Mullins, meanwhile, finished a close second in the Grand Prix at Hickstead, where the Irish swept the boards to bring home eight winner's sashes and thirty-five rosettes, but the army man was not on the civilian team that claimed third in the Nations Cup. At Dublin Horse Show, however, he played a significant role as victory in the Aga Khan Cup boosted Irish confidence ahead of the Games. This was Mullins's tenth time to line out on the most important Friday of the Irish showjumping calendar and his third time to be part of a winning side. His two previous successes had been

with *Rockbarton* and *Glendalough*, and *Lismore* would now also rise to the challenge.

'One of the sweetest Aga Khan victories for many years' was how it was described by the *Irish Independent*.[7] The firm favourites from Britain fielded their full Olympic side and, just eight weeks after he had switched his allegiance to the green, Charles taunted his former team-mates with an opening clear on *Kruger*. When James Kernan followed suit on his stallion, *Touchdown*, and Mullins had just one fence down with *Lismore*, the Irish and their old rivals were inseparable at the halfway point. Charles's horse put a foot in the water next time out, while Kernan picked up eight faults, but Mullins kept Irish hopes alive with a great clear from *Lismore* – and then it was up to Macken to prevent another of those dreaded jump-offs against the battling British. A single fence down would lead to a third-round race against the clock, while any more than that would concede defeat. And it wasn't looking too promising after *Welfenkrone* kicked out two fences in round one.

When the Longford man rode through the start there was a huge intake of breath around the arena, but he was greeted by a wall of sound as he galloped past the finish without penalty – 'that was one of the most difficult rounds of my life' Macken said afterwards. It had been a true team performance, however, with each member of the side contributing one clear round to clinch it.

That great day was not reflected in the Olympic arena at the Real Club de Polo in Barcelona, however, where the team finished well down the order in fifteenth place, and it was a dark summer for Paul Darragh, whose mother, Terry, and star horse, *Killylea*, both died on the same day shortly after his return home.

*Glendalough*, though now retired to the national circuit, came out to win the Grand Prix at Ennis with

Mullins, but both *Kilbaha* and *Lismore* were withdrawn from the Derby at Hickstead in appalling weather conditions.

Despite continuing financial constraints, some new horses arrived in McKee in 1993 and Colonel Campion was in optimistic mood. 'We are out there trying our best with what is available to us. I am hopeful about this new group,' he said. And the role of the Equitation School was evolving too. 'We made a very conscious decision to become much more involved in the whole Irish scene – to take the lead where we could, to lend a hand and participate in the organisation of our sport so that we are in no way isolated from it,' he explained in an interview.[8] Mullins was already training up-and-coming young civilian riders and was a member of the RDS Equestrian Committee, while Ledingham had recently been elected to the Leinster Region of the SJAI whose Management Committee included Colonel Campion.

Ledingham and *Kilbaha* recorded the third international win of their career together in the opening class at the Hickstead Nations Cup show in May when producing the only clear round against the clock, and then followed through with the only Irish clear in the Nations Cup. At home, Captain Gerry Flynn was awarded the Carew Silver Salver as Best Irish Competitor when sixth on *Lough Gur* in the Heineken International Three-Day-Event at Punchestown. In this sport, any top-ten finishing place at international level is quite an achievement, and the army man was one of only three competitors to complete on his dressage score.

In June, Mullins won the Accumulator at St Gallen, Switzerland, with *Lismore*, but *Kilbaha* had to be withdrawn after over-reaching and, although Mullins's new ride, *Pallas Green*, had just four faults in each round of the Nations Cup, the Irish had to settle for eighth place here. *Kilbaha* was still out of action when they moved on to Gera in Germany where the team, including Mullins with *Pallas Green*, finished third.

*Kilbaha* recovered from his injury in time to line out in the Aga Khan Cup in which the Irish placed fourth as the Americans headed the field. There was disappointment in the aftermath and some head-scratching too. The competition was something of a 'hit-and-miss' affair from an Irish perspective, although *Kilbaha* was clearly maturing with every major outing. A single error in the first round was followed by a foot-perfect performance from the army duo next time out, and when Peter Charles also kept a clean

sheet in the second round, the Irish managed to claw their way back up from last place – 'but we just didn't get our act together in time,' said a frustrated Chef d'Equipe Colonel Campion. He believed there was an urgent need for some proper planning. 'We have to make a decision about whether we're going to go out on the international circuit or stay at the home shows. We can't do both,' he insisted. And Paul Duffy Senior, now Chairman of the SJAI's International Affairs Committee, agreed: 'We didn't go to the Europeans [at Gijon, Spain] because we put all our eggs in one basket for the Cup, and it didn't work. If we are serious about sending a team to the Olympics we have to finish in the top ten in next year's World Championships – and we're going to have to work on it,' he pointed out.[9]

For the men of McKee, *Kilbaha*'s third-place finish in the Grand Prix, however, brought just the right conclusion to Dublin week. And inside the main exhibition hall of the RDS throughout the show, huge crowds of well-wishers flocked to see *Rockbarton*. Still hail and hearty at the age of twenty-four, the horse who had quickened many an Irish heartbeat during his career was lounging in the spotlight, but unsure that he was enjoying it. The lush green meadows of Áras an Uachtaráin, where he had been grazing all summer, were probably calling him home…

Below:
Rockbarton *enjoyed a
long and happpy
retirement.*
(Tony Parkes)

Ledingham's second-place finish with *Castlepollard* in the Speed Stakes at Millstreet served as the perfect preparation for the first of their three consecutive Hickstead Speed Derby victories later in August. Huge crowds basked in wonderful sunshine at the Sussex venue as they witnessed an Irish whitewash in this competition, and a new track record from the winning partnership. The Waterford man's riding skills would win him high praise.

He set the target with a superbly flowing tour of the fifteen-fence track, riding the nine-year-old mare *Garraun*, who crossed the line in 98.54 seconds, but with *Castlepollard* he galloped flat out from the start, launching off the derby bank and barely touching down on the Irish bank. Their time of 92 seconds was a sensational new track record, and Baron Alexis Von Wrangel, husband of former Irish team member Diana Conolly-Carew and son of the last Commander in Chief of the White Russian Army, paid Ledingham – and the Army Equitation School – the greatest of compliments afterwards: 'We were privileged to see the impeccable rounds of Captain John Ledingham … The relaxed attitude of both horses, ridden forward in the correct seat of the rider, brought shades of Irish officers of the past … For those for whom just a clear round is not enough, but who also look for the aesthetic side of horsemanship, it has been a pleasant change from the sight of so many international riders sitting bolt upright on the back of their saddles on over-bent horses controlled by too short martingales. Cheers for the Irish Army School of Equitation which can still produce fine and stylish riders, as well as winning ones,' he wrote.[10]

In September, Mullins was third in the Grand Prix at Biarritz, where he was having his first international outing with the mare *Millstreet Ruby*, who was on temporary loan from owner and breeder Noel C Duggan. Ledingham won a speed class with *Garraun*, and in October the two army men were on the fourth-placed team in Linz, Austria. The Irish Horse

Board (IHB) was launched that same month at Millstreet Indoor International, where Mullins on *Lismore* won the Accumulator before slotting into third in the Derby.

At home Flynn won the Open Championship at Ballinlough in County Meath riding *Lough Gur* at the end of 1993 and made an impressive start to 1994 at Boro Hill in Wexford in April, where he claimed the top three places in the novice competition with *Night Fox*, *Caran* and *Meanus*. His luck deserted him at the international in Saumur in France a few weeks later, however, when *Lough Gur* knocked a splint bone and had to be withdrawn after the dressage phase.

A great fourth-place finish with *Meanus* in the Heineken International at Punchestown in May quickly restored his spirits. Lying in thirty-seventh position after dressage, they were clear and inside the time on cross-country day, to move up to tenth and clear again in the showjumping ring to improve another six places. This was a spectacular result for the eleven-year-old former jumping horse whose eventing career had only begun a year earlier. Adaptability, however, was always a prerequisite of entry into the McKee ranks for both horse and rider, and Flynn would show a similarly impressive level of flexibility over the years to come.

The McKee jumpers, meanwhile, kicked off their 1994 season with good results in Lucerne, where Ledingham on *Garraun* won the Speed Championship, and at Hickstead, where Mullins recorded his first big win with *Pallas Green* in the Grand Prix. There were ten in the jump-off here, and almost all the rest were quicker than the twelve-year-old mare, but none could leave all the fences up. The Hickstead Nations Cup was a controversial affair, however, with loud complaints about the height of the track on shockingly boggy ground. The Irish were lying equal-second at the halfway stage despite a shaky start, but it was a gutsy performance on terrible going and although they dropped to third, there was a determined streak re-emerging in the Irish camp.

At Aachen in June the team went all the way to a third-round tie-breaker before having to yield to the British – the best Irish result at the prestigious venue for fifteen years. Ledingham, Charles, Jessica Chesney and Macken were lying third behind Britain and Germany after round one, but as the Germans lost their grip the Irish drew level with the British and were beaten by only four seconds in the third-round jump-off. Topping that, Ledingham, Macken and Mullins won the Team Relay on *Garraun*, *Sky View* and

*Lismore.* Things were definitely looking up.

And at La Baule in July, just two weeks before the Word Equestrian Games at The Hague, *Kilbaha* was crowned Horse of the Show, and the team won the French Nations Cup for the first time since Sean Daly, Eamonn O'Donohue, Billy Ringrose and Ned Campion claimed the trophy in Nice in 1961. This was a special one to win. They led with eight faults after *Kilbaha* produced the only first round clear, and Chesney on *Diamond Exchange*, Charles on *La Ina* and Macken on *Schalkhaar* each had one fence down. They were being stalked by the Brazilians, only 0.25 faults behind, while the British were next in line, carrying 12, but second-round clears from both Charles and Ledingham, and just four faults from Chesney were enough to ensure the Irish had it in the bag. Macken, who was celebrating a quarter-century of team membership and who didn't have to go in round two, said afterwards that 'this is as good a side as I have ever jumped on.'

Despite the great build-up, however, the second WEG was another deep disappointment for the jumping team, which finished ninth. In the Nations Cup, Charles had two disastrous rounds and *Kilbaha* followed a first-round twelve-fault score with 18.75. Macken picked up twelve faults both times out and only Chesney shone under pressure, lowering just a single fence in each round and staying on gamely to slot into individual thirteenth place.

In eventing, however, Flynn produced an astonishing performance from *Meanus*, who finished twenty-fifth individually, to bolster the Irish team's solid fifth-place result. The hot and humid conditions took a heavy toll, but Flynn scorched around the cross-country track to keep Ireland in the hunt. He knew *Meanus* had given his all. 'It was asking a lot of a horse in only his second three-day-event,' he said, with typical understatement that also overlooked his own extraordinary effort.[11]

There was little time for the jumpers to recover from their

battering at The Hague because, two days after the WEG concluded, Dublin Horse Show began. The team finished fifth in the Aga Khan Cup, but Mullins had a great week, which concluded with fifth place in the Grand Prix on *Lismore*.

At Millstreet, Ledingham and *Kilbaha* were second in the Masters, while Mullins and *Millstreet Ruby* were runners-up in the Derby – and Ledingham was like a runaway train by the time he got to Hickstead where he scored a sensational double. He first took the Speed Derby title for the second consecutive year on *Castlepollard* and then, on the tenth anniversary of his victory with *Gabhran*, stamped his absolute authority on the Derby with a spectacular double-clear from *Kilbaha*, who might have been expected to be a little leg-weary after his long season. The *Tudor Rocket* gelding was in his element, however, as he eased his way over the big, natural obstacles. There was just one nervous moment. As *Kilbaha* approached the Derby bank, Ledingham patted him on the neck to reassure him, but the horse ground to a halt at the edge of the bank and stared down the

terrifying drop. 'He had a good look … I didn't want to kick him on or he would have jumped off and wouldn't have been able to jump the rails at the bottom,' Ledingham explained afterwards. So he gave *Kilbaha* time to take it all in before making his descent and, unpenalised for the hesitation, cruised home to go into a two-way jump-off with American Katie Monahan-Prudent and *Partly Cloudy*.

When the American rider's ten-year-old mare had two fences down second time out, that left the Irishman some leeway, but he didn't need it.

*Below:*
*Perfect harmony – Captain John Ledingham's beautifully balanced seat and harmony with his horse earned him numerous Most Stylish Rider awards, including at the Mecca of international showjumpng in Aachen. Here he is pictured with* Kilbaha *at full stretch but completely focused as he eases his way around another tough course of fences.*

Now he had his sights on the £5,000 bonus for a double-clear. 'Square up to that dyke and jump a clear,' advised Mullins, who abandoned the TV commentary position he had been manning – and Ledingham did just that to clinch the class. 'When I won in 1984 I didn't realise how important this was!' said the thirty-six-year-old rider who had experienced plenty of the ups and downs of the sport in the intervening years.[12] And he had entered the record books as the first rider to win both the Speed Derby and the Derby in the same year.

All this was the perfect response to the Price Waterhouse report that had been leaked to the *Irish Independent* during Dublin Horse Show week. Compiled by the Efficiency Auditing Group set up by the Taoiseach's office, amongst its recommendations was the closure of seventeen army barracks and the Army Equitation School. But the figures didn't stack up. They showed that the school was already operating on a shoestring and that Ledingham's two top rides had cost just £30,000 each when purchased on the same day in 1990. *Kilbaha* was reckoned by the Department of Defence to be worth in the region of £1m even before his first Hickstead Derby victory – and you couldn't put a price on the glory these two horses had just bestowed on Ireland.

And *Kilbaha* wasn't finished for the year yet. At Spruce Meadows in September, he was on the team, alongside Mullins and *Millstreet Ruby*, that took third in the Nations Cup, and in October *Kilbaha* brought his extraordinary season to a close when finishing second in the Grand Prix at Monterrey. Both Ledingham and Mullins were still buzzing at the Mexican fixture, earning $35,000 between them as they racked up a win, three second places, two thirds, two fourths and a fifth place from twelve classes. Mullins and *Lismore* topped the first day's $1.50m competition, pinning Canadian legend Ian Millar into second spot by more than three seconds, and on Saturday won the Viceroy Derby. With *Millstreet Ruby* he was second in the Goodwill jump-off and third in the World Cup qualifier, while Ledingham placed with *Castlepollard* and *Garraun* and was runner-up in the final day's $100,000 Grand Prix.

It was no surprise when Ledingham won both a Texaco Sports Star and *Irish Field* award for his 1994 exploits, but 1995 began with a team disaster in Rome in May, after Macken and Charles were late withdrawals, and the three-man side of Mullins, Ledingham and Trevor Coyle picked up twenty-four faults in the first round before retiring from the Nations Cup competition. Odd things happened, with *Kilbaha* throwing in a stop and *Millstreet Ruby* having three fences down.

At home, Lieutenant Tom Freyne and Lieutenant Derek McConnell underpinned the strength now present at McKee. Corkman Freyne was campaigning a string that included *Liscahane*, *Pallas Green* and *Castlepollard*, while twenty-seven-year-old McConnell, from Naas in County Kildare, had forged strong partnerships with *Togher* and *Carlingford Bay*. At the National Show Jumping Championships in Galway in June, Ledingham won with *Garraun* and *Kilbaha*, while Mullins and Freyne were also placed.

A week later the Irish team proved that what had happened in Rome was only a hiccup as they picked up where they had left off the previous season and stormed to victory in Aachen. And it was the perfect revenge for the 1994 result at the German venue because this time it was the British who had to settle for second place. Hartwell stud's stallion *Cruising* – by the Irish draught stallion *Sea Crest* and out of the army mare *Mullacrew* – was blossoming in the hands of Trevor Coyle and joined Charles's *La Ina* and Ledingham's *Kilbaha* to throw down the gauntlet when clear in the first round. *La Ina* and *Kilbaha* both faulted once in round two, but *Cruising* was error-free again, so it was up to Macken and his new ride – the eleven-year-old French-bred *Miss FAN*, for whom Macken's sponsor, Michael Nixdorf, was reputed to have paid £850,000 a few months earlier – to clinch it. Once again when the chips were down, Macken came up trumps, and Chef d'Equipe Campion could hardly contain his excitement as Ireland won by a margin of 3.75 faults. 'I knew we had four brilliant riders and four horses which could produce clear rounds under pressure, and I was in no doubt that we were in with a very strong chance,' he said afterwards. And the good stuff didn't finish there. The Irish also racked up three wins, a third, a fourth, three fifth placings and two sixth finishing spots. It was little short of a sensation. 'We certainly have a team to be reckoned with,' Campion added.[13]

Mullins wasn't going to be left out of the limelight either. With *Millstreet Ruby* in flying

Aachen '95

*Below*:
Captain John Ledingham celebrates Ireland's Aga Khan 1995 victory with Kilbaha, but his treatment of the trophy created a few anxious moments!

form, he was fourth in the Grand Prix at Wiesbaden before winning the Grand Prix at Falsterbo in Sweden, where they also lined up fourth in the Derby. They moved on to Germany, where they were fourth in the Spangenberg Grand Prix, before returning home to take second place in the Derby at Millstreet, pipped by Britain's John Whitaker on *Welham*.

The team meanwhile rolled on to La Baule, but couldn't re-live the glory of the previous season when finishing fifth. It all came right for them again in Dublin, however, where they claimed the Aga Khan trophy in a thrilling contest – the eighteenth Irish win in the sixty-nine-year history of the competition. And again, the British had to play second fiddle by the smallest of margins, beaten by just one-quarter of a time fault.

*Kilbaha* had four faults in the first round while Charles's *La Ina* and Macken's *Miss FAN* went clear, and *Cruising* collected eight. *La Ina* and *Kilbaha* each had a fence down in round two, and when *Cruising* left all the fences up this time out it was all over – Macken's magic wasn't required because Ireland's twelve faults could not be bettered by the British finishing score of 12.25. The home crowd was ecstatic.

Miriam Lord wrote: 'We stifled screams into little squeaks, then shushed all around us as the Irish horses negotiated the course. We jumped all the jumps from our ringside saddles,' and when it came to the victory gallop, the Irish didn't hold back, although Ledingham's antics as he galloped around with the precious cup led to some anxious moments. 'We had to conclude that somebody had taken the precaution of sticking on the lid with superglue!' she added. [14]

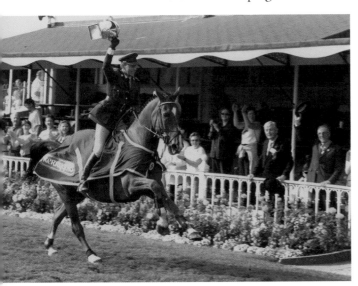

During this thrilling week, Ledingham and *Garraun* won the Accumulator and *Kilbaha* was fourth in the Grand Prix. But a terrible pall of sadness descended on the RDS arena on the closing afternoon after the tragic accident that claimed the life of Robert Splaine's lovely mare, *Heather Blaze*. The Cork man and the super-talented grey, whose bloodline represented all that is best in Irish breeding, had won the coveted King George V Gold Cup at Hickstead just a few weeks beforehand, but they missed their stride at the water jump, fourth fence out on the Grand Prix track, and as she struggled to her feet it was clear to every horseman's eye that she had broken her near-fore leg. Live on RTÉ Radio, commentator Michael Slavin couldn't hold back his tears as Splaine's long, lonely walk from the arena was followed by the news that she had to be put down shortly afterwards. She was just fourteen years old and should have had many years ahead of her as a valuable breeding mare. By comparison, *Rockbarton*'s final exit that summer, after suddenly falling ill at the ripe old age of twenty-six, was a timely passing.

There was no gloom about at the Hickstead Derby meeting, however, where Ledingham was untouchable once again. He was shattering all sorts of records during these years – no-one had ever achieved the whitewash of double Derbies before, and he now matched British rider David Bowen's consecutive hat-trick of Speed Derby wins. Adding further grist to the mill, *Millstreet Ruby* shone on her maiden Derby voyage with Mullins, to finish third when faulting only in the middle of the infamous Devil's Dyke. Hickstead was filled with Irish supporters following Ledingham's brilliant result the previous year, and amongst them was *Kilbaha*'s proud breeder, Tim O'Sullivan, keen to see for himself how the foal he had carefully nurtured had grown into a true champion.

It came down to a two-way second-round jump-off again, but this time Ledingham's opponent was Millstreet Derby winner John Whitaker, who sent *Welham* back to the stables after an early first-round clear. That may have been a mistake, however. *Welham* didn't come back with the same energy in round two, and was lucky to collect only four faults. The Yorkshireman admitted that the horse may have thought he was finished for the day. Ledingham was now left with the option of going for a slow clear, but his OC advised him to 'take out some insurance' by being fast enough to beat the Briton even with a fence down. There was no need for the insurance policy, however, as the Irish heroes raced through the finish in 83.79 seconds and with all the timber still in place. 'The biggest moment of my career,' was how Ledingham described it.

And just as remarkable was the fact that he had not sat on his triple Speed Derby champion *Castlepollard* during the previous twelve months, during which Freyne had the ride. Ledingham was only reunited with the gutsy gelding a week beforehand, but they clearly hadn't forgotten each other. As he set off, he was, once again, in complete

*Above*:
*Chef d'Equipe Colonel Ned Campion holds the trophy aloft after Ireland's historic first victory at Spruce Meadows in Calgary, Canada, in 1995.*

command as he was chasing his own target of 94.55 seconds set with *Garraun*. And when *Castlepollard* raced through the beam in 93.38 seconds to seize their fourth consecutive Speed Derby title, they set yet another new record time – two-tenths of a second faster than the one he had put in place in 1994.

The uniquely ambassadorial qualities of the army men were mentioned in the *Irish Independent* the following week where it was noted that Ledingham was so popular with the British showjumping fans that they were just as keen to see *Kilbaha* go clear in the Derby as their own man with *Welham*: 'It was a reminder of just how popular our army riders are abroad. Ledingham was besieged with autograph hunters and fans wishing him well.'[15]

At Spruce Meadows in September, he was second with *Garraun* in the Prudential Steel Cup and fourth in the Cana Cup with *Kilbaha*, who produced a brilliant first-round clear to help Ireland to her third glorious Nations Cup victory of the year, and the first-ever in the twenty-year history of the Canadian fixture. 'The Irish are the hottest showjumping team in the world right now,' wrote Canadian journalist Helen Dolik that day. And the Irish claimed one-tenth of the entire prize-fund of $1.1m at this fixture, despite having no luck in the final day's super-rich $700,000 Du Maurier Grand Prix. 'This has been a most historic year for Ireland and her horses,' said Campion. 'At the end of the seventies we had a good team, but we never had success like this before … I think we have a good chance now for the European Championship in St Gallen,' he pointed out.[16]

They gave it their best shot, but only Charles and *La Ina* would come home from Switzerland with a medal – individual gold, and the first since Iris Kellett in 1969. The Grundenmoos arena turned into a swamp after weeks of heavy rain. The first day's programme was cancelled, Friday's team championship was postponed to Saturday, and the Germans just packed their bags and went home, their Chef d'Equipe Herbert Meyer believing it was too risky for his horses ahead of the following year's Olympic Games in Atlanta. Campion also had his reservations – 'this situation is unprecedented in my experience' said the man who had plenty of it. But his team did make it into a jump-off for bronze in which they battled like lions, only to lose out to the French by four seconds. It was gut-wrenching stuff, because they could not have given more than they did, but such is the unforgiving element of sport – the roll of the dice had not fallen in their favour this time around.

In October, there was another historic moment when Freyne and McConnell were the first Irish army riders to compete at the Show Jumping Championships at Eglinton in Derry in Northern Ireland, and in December Ireland headed the annual international showjumping team rankings for the first time since they were first calculated in 1969.

*Castlepollard* was in for a bit of a surprise in the spring of 1996. Now aged thirteen, and in the autumn of his career, he would be asked to become an event horse in an effort to provide Flynn with a ride for the Atlanta Olympic Games, now just four months away. It was an audacious plan, even for a much younger horse, but McKee's eventing coach Second-in-Command, Commandant Ronnie MacMahon, wasn't going to allow the improbability of success get in the way, and of course the bold *Castlepollard* just got on with it. They made an inauspicious start at Boro Hill event in Wexford when falling at the water, and very nearly hit the deck again three fences later when *Castlepollard* put down in the middle of a triple bar. But they would make it all the way to the top international event at Saumur in France before calling it day. This would be a year of a good many 'almosts' for the army men and their horses.

*Below*:
*The brave and bold Castlepollard just took it in his stride when asked to transform himself from a top international showjumper to become an event horse in 1996. He didn't make it to the Atlanta Olympic Games with Captain Gerry Flynn, but as can be seen in this picture from the top-flight event in Saumur, France, he gave it his very best shot – as always!*

In March, Ged O'Dwyer passed away at the great age of ninety-seven, while in April the project to bring the 1998 World Equestrian Games to Ireland fell on its knees. In stark contrast, the Royal Dublin Society was in buoyant mood when, in April 1996, it announced a 47 percent rise in profits for the previous year as its financial reform programme began to pay dividends.

Mullins and *Millstreet Ruby* were on the team that finished second at Hickstead in May. The Irish were joint-leaders at half-way, and seemed likely to drop to third when only Francis Connors and *Spring Elegance* were clear second time out, but the French made one mistake too many. There was a joint-second place finish at St Gallen in June, but clouds were gathering on the Olympic horizon. *Miss FAN* damaged a suspensory ligament at the Swiss fixture and had to be withdrawn from the team. Mullins and *Millstreet Ruby* were an alternative choice, but the selectors opted for Macken's second ride *Schalkhaar* instead. Meanwhile, *Cruising*'s owners at Hartwell Stud didn't want to send their stallion to Atlanta for fear of the heat and humidity. Jessica Kuerten and *Diamond Exchange* were called up, but things were really not working out the way it had been expected.

Then things got even worse. The horses were scheduled to fly out well ahead of the Games in early July, but when *Kilbaha* arrived at Stansted airport he clearly wasn't well. His temperature had risen to 104 degrees, well above the norm, and it was decided that he should not be loaded onto the plane. A worried John Ledingham flew to London and by the time he got there the gelding, who had been taken to British rider Robert Smith's yard at nearby Quendon Park, had already been diagnosed with a lung infection. There were hopes that he might be well enough to travel out a week later, but Campion ruled against it because *Kilbaha*'s training programme had now been seriously disrupted. It was another bitter blow for Ledingham. But under the expert care of his devoted groom, Private Dessie O'Sullivan, *Kilbaha* made a great recovery, and Ledingham attributes the speed with which the horse bounced back to Private O'Sullivan's unique relationship with his charge. Ledingham recalls: 'As far as Dessie was concerned, he was his horse – he was totally dedicated to him. A lot of the success I had with *Kilbaha* was due to Dessie's care and attention.'

Mullins meanwhile went back to Falsterbo, Sweden, where he won the Derby with the eight-year-old *Killone Abbey*. They produced one of only three clear rounds from thirty-six starters and left the rest floundering in their wake in the jump-off. At Dublin Horse Show a month later, *Kilbaha* was back in business and picked up just 0.5 time faults in the Aga Khan Cup, in which Ireland finished second to the British by exactly that margin. The first-round time was very tight, with only seven of the twenty-four starters returning without penalty, and the British already had the whip hand with a zero score at the end of round one, while the Irish lay second with 0.5 after clears from *La Ina* and *Schalkhaar* and the discard 0.75 from *Cruising*. And despite clean sheets all the way for Charles, Coyle and Ledingham next time out, the Irish couldn't make up the deficit when the British refused to crumble.

Mullins won the Speed Championship with *Millstreet Ruby* on the final morning and *Kilbaha* was fifth in the Grand Prix in which, after twenty-seven previous attempts, Macken at last came out on top, riding *Schalkhaar*, who looked none-the-worse for the long trip back from Atlanta where the team had lined up eighth and Charles finished best individually in equal-eleventh place with *Benetton*.

Returning to his home-from-home, *Kilbaha*, still not back to full fitness, was second in the Hickstead Derby that August, where sixty-year-old Brazilian legend Nelson Pessoa won through with just four faults, riding the Irish-bred *Vivaldi*. Mullins had two Derby rides, but *Killone Abbey* gave him a heavy fall at the water and *Millstreet Ruby* stumbled on landing at the foot of the bank.

Ledingham was looking for his fourth consecutive win with *Castlepollard* in the Speed Derby, but it wasn't to be. The brave gelding had been whirled around from the unsuccessful attempt to qualify for the Games as an eventer with Flynn, and only had two spins at the RDS before Hickstead, where Ledingham subsequently found the horse, possibly suffering from an identity crisis, 'keener and hotter than ever'. Last to go, chasing the target of 98.21 seconds set by Frenchman Michel Robert on *Alligator Fontaine*, they did the time when crossing the line in 98.07 seconds, but the hard-pulling *Castlepollard* hit the fence after the bank for an additional five faults and had to settle for fifth spot, just ahead of Mullins and *Lismore* in sixth.

And to round up the season of frustrating second-place finishes, Mullins and *Millstreet Ruby* were second again behind John Whitaker and *Welham* in the Millstreet Derby. It was on to Calgary then, where the team that included Mullins and the mare and Ledingham with *Kilbaha* finished fourth before the final round-up in Monterrey, Mexico, where *Kilbaha* featured prominently.

In November, Mullins decided it was time to hang up his boots, and the winds of change began to gather momentum once again as the following July, Campion retired as Officer Commanding. Both men had dedicated their lives to the sport, and while Mullins would remain at McKee, becoming Second-In-Command to Lieutenant Colonel MacMahon in January 1998, Campion went on to fill the important role of Secretary General of the EFI for a five-year period, during which he helped to restore Ireland's credibility in the aftermath of the WEG '98 fiasco. His skills as Chef d'Equipe had been just as subtle as those he displayed in the saddle. They were crystallised in his description of the challenges of team management given in an interview some time later: 'The important thing is to know what not to say and how not to interfere. With experienced riders … it is very easy to upset their ethic. It's a question of trying to identify whatever brings them together as a team on the day, and to make the best of that,' he said.[17]

*Millstreet Ruby* was passed over to Ledingham, and they quickly gelled into a great partnership. Much smaller and more compact than *Kilbaha*, the mare was an explosive bundle of energy – 'great fun as well as a great jumper!' Ledingham recalls. On their first foray abroad in May 1997, they won the speed event at Oberhausen, Germany, the Accumulator in Eindhoven, Holland, and the Derby at Wiesbaden in Germany. In Hamburg, they were runners-up in the first Derby qualifier and tenth in the Grand Prix, but Ledingham teamed up with his old pal *Kilbaha* for the Derby proper to earn the Most Stylish Rider prize.

Kilbaha jumped a brilliant double-clear in the Nations Cup at St Gallen in June, but the team total of twenty-four points was only good enough for fifth place. At Aachen, where Ledingham again took the Most Stylish Rider award, he was second with *Millstreet Ruby* in the Speed Derby, and with *Kilbaha* was on the team that finished equal-third in the Nations Cup. Remarkably, three of the Irish team horses – *Kilbaha*, *Cruising* and *Schalkhaar* – all jumped double-clear in the gruelling Grand Prix and qualified for the seven-horse jump-off. In terrible conditions following heavy rain, *Cruising* and *Schalkhaar* both had a fence down against the clock, but *Kilbaha* looked on course for a clear until slipping after the third-last fence, and with the horse unable to regain his footing, Ledingham circled before coming down to the penultimate jump and the three faults accrued left him in third place. Then, at Rostock in Germany, *Millstreet Ruby* scored twice more and *Kilbaha* finished fourth in the Grand Prix. There were 152 starters in the first speed event in which *Ruby* kicked up a storm to win by a three-second margin.

Minister for Defence David Andrews visited the Equitation School that summer. Only Ledingham was considered to be adequately mounted at this stage, although some good young jumpers were coming along. The horse-purchase budget amounted to only £150,000, however, hardly enough to secure one horse with real potential at a time when good ones were costing at least £200,000. One of the up-and-coming prospects was the six-year-old mare, *Rincoola Abu*, owned by Harold McGahern from Longford and being campaigned by Flynn, who had now turned his attention to showjumping.

*Above*:
*Gerry Mullins pictured with his personal favourite, the bold and brave* Mostrim, *in action at Spruce Meadows, Calgary.*
(Bob Langrishe)

Ledingham was a member of Ireland's winning Aga Khan Cup team for the fifth time in his career that August. It was fifteen years since he first rode into that ring as part of an Irish side. He still talks about the experience as a vivid memory. 'There's nothing like the feeling … the expectation of the crowd is so huge – they want you to deliver. The roar from the stands – the noise is deafening – you can feel your horse shrink – he doesn't want to leave the pocket, but once you are in the middle of the arena he can see some space, and the fences, and he starts to breathe again … it takes two minutes for the noise of the crowd to die down … you don't hear the bell, you look for the person with the flag because you can't hear anything properly … you eventually learn to enjoy it, particularly that moment just before you start, that feeling of expectation coming from the crowd – it's fabulous – then you have to close it all off, because you know you've got a job to do…' he recalls in haunting detail.

This would be *Kilbaha*'s second Aga Khan triumph, and Tommy Wade's first as new Irish Chef d'Equipe. Paul Darragh was the hero when returning to the Aga Khan team for the first time in ten years to jump double-clear with the mare, *Scandal*, which belonged to his then pupil, Princess Haya of Jordan, who would go on to become President of the FEI nine years later.

*Cruising* and *Kilbaha* also jumped clear in the first round, so Macken's services were surplus to requirements – he only got to play around in the practice ring and had mixed

feelings about that: 'It was an anti-climax for me … but I don't mind missing out under the circumstances!' he said afterwards. It seemed that this time the Grand Prix title must belong to Ledingham and *Kilbaha* after they slashed 4.5 seconds off the target set by Holland's Jan Tops in the five-horse jump-off to the wild excitement of the crowd. But Britain's Robert Smith had been beaten by Macken the previous year and wasn't going to let it happen again, storming home with *Tees Hannauer* to wrest the trophy from the army man by an agonising 0.15 seconds.

*Kilbaha* had two fences down in the Hickstead Derby that summer, but *Millstreet Ruby* won the Silver Salver Speed and *Castlepollard* finished fourth in the speed Derby. At the European Championships in Mannheim, Germany, the team finished fifth – *Kilbaha* picking up eight faults in the first round and just four second time out in the Nations Cup – and the team was fifth again at Calgary in September, where *Kilbaha* produced the only clear in the first round and where Ledingham also won the Hurricane Cup with *Millstreet Ruby*. Then, following a move to introduce fresh faces to the pool of Irish team horses and riders, Flynn and *Carraig Dubh* and Ledingham and *Kilbaha* joined Cameron Hanley riding *Geometric* and Marion Hughes with *Flo Jo* to win the Nations Cup at Zagreb in Croatia – Flynn and Hanley producing two of the three double-clears in the competition. And *Millstreet Ruby* brought Ledingham's year to the perfect end when striking Mexican gold in the €100,000 Derby at Monterrey in November.

The men at McKee Barracks and the entire Irish equestrian world were shocked, and deeply saddened, by the tragic death of Captain David Foster in a competition fall in April 1998. There had been a number of fatalities in the sport of eventing over the previous years, and many more would follow, leading to a complete review of the sport. Rotational falls – where the horse somersaults on top of the rider, as happened to the Meath man – became the main focus of concern, and in subsequent years dramatic changes have been introduced, along with a brand new competition format. The reality is, however, that a sport in which horses jump solid obstacles at speed will always have a significant level of risk, and David Foster, who had retired from the Equitation School eight years earlier to pursue a successful career as a civilian, understood that very well indeed. One of the most popular and amiable competitors of his time, it wasn't just his riding prowess, but his great warmth and charm that would be sadly missed.

Ledingham and Flynn recorded good results at Schenefeld in Germany in June, and Ledingham took a red rosette with *Millstreet Ruby* at Hickstead, where *Kilbaha* was on the Nations Cup team that finished fifth. At Drammen in Norway in July, where the team finished fourth, Ledingham and *Kilbaha* won the Grand Prix.

Ireland was strongly fancied to win the Aga Khan Cup that summer while the British were also bullish about their chances. The Dublin honours fell to an inexperienced Italian side, however, with the Dutch lining up second ahead of the home runners. *Kilbaha* jumped a classic first-round clear and the team was lying second behind Italy at the halfway stage, but when Charles, Ledingham and new man Eric Holstein each collected four faults in round two, they dropped to third despite *Cruising*'s fault-free second effort. Ledingham on *Millstreet Ruby* and Flynn on his new ride, *Diamond Explosion*, which was acquired by the school in a lease agreement with American owner Dan Lufkin, which was brokered by horse agent Dermot Forde, also featured prominently.

Ledingham came dangerously close to winning his third Hickstead Derby trophy with *Kilbaha* this August, only to be foiled by the inimitable John Whitaker and the twenty-one-year-old *Gammon*. They were the only two riders to leave the course intact in the first round – *Kilbaha* putting in a copybook clear over the course he so enjoyed. Whitaker was first out against the clock and set the target at four faults in 82.36 seconds, so Ledingham had a fence in hand going into the ring. But heavy rain on hard ground had created a very slippery surface – *Millstreet Ruby* lost two shoes on her tour of the track and came in with 12 faults – and Ledingham's plans were thrown into disarray when *Kilbaha* slipped in front of the first fence and hit it. Now he could only chase Whitaker's time and *Kilbaha* responded by answering every question being thrown at him. Coming to the last, they were up on time, but then Ledingham made a split-second decision he would regret. 'As I jumped the second-last, I looked up at the clock, took a pull and he came back to me too much. I shouldn't have taken that pull,' he said, after breaking the beam in 83.38 seconds – fractionally over one second slower than his British rival.[18] For

*Above*:
*Kilbaha was retired at Dublin Horse Show 1999 after nine fine years of service to Captain John Ledingham. Pictured – (left to right) Main Arena Director Colonel Billy Ringrose, Captain Ledingham and Kilbaha, Kilbaha's lifetime caretaker Private Dessie O'Sullivan, and Corporal Gilligan.*

the second successive year, *Castlepollard* was fourth in the speed Derby.

*Kilbaha* was clearly off-form in Rotterdam later in August and again at the World Equestrian Games in Rome in September, where the team eventually finished eighth. The wonderful army horse's career was drawing to a close.

But at McKee there was a whole new dynamic as the recruits who had been commissioned over the previous few years, due to the support of Minister for Defence Sean Barrett, began to come onstream. And getting most attention of all was the first female riding officer: Lieutenant Danielle Quinlivan, from Kanturk in Cork, who was cutting quite a dash in her army uniform. On her senior international debut at Cavan in November, she was in the money twice, while her old rival from her pony-jumping days, Lieutenant Shane Carey from Crecora in Limerick, was also in the ribbons.

At Berlin in May of the following year, *Kilbaha* was seventh in the Grand Prix, but it was Flynn who was the on-form army rider as he steered *Carraig Dubh* into second place, only marginally beaten by German star Ludger Beerbaum on *It's Me*. Flynn also won a speed class on *Diamond Explosion* and went on to win on *Rincoola Abu* at Wiesbaden later in the month.

At St Gallen in June, Ledingham and *Millstreet Ruby* won a speed class and *Kilbaha* was clear in the first round of the Nations Cup in which Ireland finished fourth. But *Kilbaha* never regained his old sparkle and, instead of lining out for his eighth Aga Khan Cup, he was officially retired at Dublin Horse Show 1999. Aged sixteen, he had competed in thirty-two Nations Cup competitions, had been a member of seven Aga Khan Cup sides, including two winning ones, and recorded back-to-back Derby wins in 1994 and 1995, while finishing second twice and third once. He had given nine years of fine service to Ledingham.

Flynn and *Carraig Dubh* were the army representatives on the team that finished joint-second with the British that year as, for the very first time in the history of the Aga Khan Cup, the Dutch won through. And, with *Rincoola Abu*, the Longford man won the Grade A class in which another of the promising newcomers, Lieutenant David O'Brien from Athlone in County Westmeath, steered *Marlton* into fourth ahead of Quinlivan on

*Killone Abbey*. Flynn was also second in the Accumulator on *Diamond Explosion*, joint-winner in the Baton Relay along with Ledingham on *Millstreet Ruby*, and third behind this army duo in the Power-and-Speed, but it was Ledingham who took the Leading Irish Rider of the Show title.

Ledingham and Flynn went to Athens in September, where they cleaned up with five wins between them and helped Ireland move to the top of the Samsung Nations Cup league table by winning the Nations Cup, and in November Ledingham announced he was calling it a day himself, at the age of forty-one. 'When *Kilbaha* had to be retired at the Kerrygold Horse Show, I knew then that I would have to follow suit since I had no international replacement horse to ride,' the Waterford man said sadly in an interview with Michael Slavin in December. 'He was the nicest horse I had ever ridden. He had size, scope, stride and real spring – I loved him,' the army man pointed out in a simple but touching tribute to his old friend.[19]

*Above*:
Captain John Ledingham and Kilbaha *both retired from the jumping arena in 1999 after a spectacular nine-year career together.*

It was, indeed, the end of another era at the Army Equitation School as the new millennium dawned. But it was also the beginning of a new Ireland as the widespread violence, bitterness and division experienced by the people of Northern Ireland since the 1960s was finally consigned to the history books. The Good Friday Agreement, signed by the Governments of the United Kingdom and the Republic of Ireland in May 1998, was first implemented on 2 December 1999, and everyone on the island looked forward to a brighter future. Minister for Defence Michael Smith put a smile on the faces at McKee Barracks too when boosting horse numbers with additional funding and announcing a forward-thinking All-Ireland Bursary Scheme designed to encourage the development of up-and-coming equestrian talent. So as the Irish Army Equitation School marched towards the new millennium, its future seemed assured. But it would face bigger challenges than ever before as the changing climate of equestrian sport would place a heavy weight on young shoulders in the years to come.

# THE CHANGING OF THE GUARD: MARCHING INTO THE NEW MILLENNIUM

## 2000 to 2009

*'Wearing the army uniform and flying the Irish flag meant everything to me'*
*Commandant Gerry Flynn*

The principal theme of the final decade of this history is the Army Equitation School's massive contribution to the effort that has maintained Ireland's status amongst the elite showjumping nations of the world. The emergence of the Samsung Super League in 2003 dramatically changed the face of international team competition. The eight-nation premiership became the stage for the best of the best, and the inclusion of two further countries when Meydan donned the sponsorship cloak in 2009 has increased the pressure.

In the lead-up to the creation of the Super League, however, Ireland enjoyed a great run of form, beginning with a record-breaking ten team victories in the 1999–2000 season which convincingly clinched the Samsung Nations Cup title.

The nurturing of young talent, both civilian and military, was now a priority and would pay dramatic dividends as, with teams competing at both premier events and some less high-profile fixtures, the next generation quickly cut their teeth. But the new crew at McKee had a particular advantage. David O'Brien, today a Captain and a linchpin of the Irish senior team, but then a young Lieutenant, puts it into perspective: 'We were very fortunate because Lieutenant Colonel Mullins and Commandant Ledingham had retired from riding and channelled all their energies into us – you couldn't find two men with more experience anywhere in the world and we had them all to ourselves for a couple of years, so we learned very quickly.'

Mullins was now Officer Commanding, following the retirement of Lieutenant Colonel Ronnie MacMahon, who moved on to become Head of the Show Jumping Department at the United Arab Emirates Equestrian Federation. Tommy Wade remained Chef d'Equipe of what became known as the 'A' team, while Mullins and others guided developing sides that combined raw young talent with experience to great effect. Mullins's passion had already turned to designing a coaching strategy on behalf of the Equestrian Federation of Ireland (EFI) together with a number of influential people, including Dressage Ireland's Joan Keogh and Liam Moggan from the National Coaching Training Centre (NCTC) at Limerick University. Such was the success of this project that the international governing body, the Lausanne-based Federation Equestre Internationale (FEI), bought the rights for the EFI Levels 1 and 2 training programmes, which have since been rolled out to developing countries worldwide. Ireland continues to benefit from one of the best training systems available. Mullins was appointed to the Board of the NCTC in 2001 and five years later his efforts were recognised by the FEI with a special award for services to equestrian sport presented at the FEI General Assembly in Kuala Lumpur, Malaysia.

In his White Paper on the Defence Forces, published in February 2000, Minister for Defence Michael Smith accurately reflected on the continuing contribution of the Equitation School to the success and development of Irish equestrianism. 'The School has ... not alone been an excellent showcase for non-thoroughbred horses, but its riders have represented Ireland with distinction throughout the world. Through its attendance at national events, the School has provided popular contact between the Defence Forces and the public as well as promoting excellence in equitation and encouragement to horse breeders,' he pointed out.[1] It would continue to do just that as it marched into the twenty-first century.

The knock-on effect of the school's successes at local level was underlined at the very beginning of the year when the organising committee of Lanesborough Fair honoured local man Captain Flynn following his great season in 1999, and he was again a key player in 2000. However, it was rookie Lieutenant Shane Carey who was first out of the McKee starting blocks when recording a double of speed wins, on the Clover Hill gelding *Galteebeg*, on his senior international debut at Compiegne in April. Ferociously

*Above*: Chef d'Equipe Lieutenant Colonel Gerry Mullins with his winning team at Helsinki 2000 – (left to right) Captain Gerry Flynn (Rincoola Abu), Cian O'Connor (Waterford Crystal), Captain Shane Carey (Shannondale), Cameron Hanley (Balaseyr Twilight).

competitive ever since the days when he, and his now fellow-army-officer Lieutenant Danielle Quinlivan, used to wage war on each other in pony classes around the country, twenty-two-year-old Carey was on his way to establishing his reputation as one the great speed specialists of the following decade.

Quinlivan was also in the money at Compiegne with the mare *Cruise Hill*, but it was at Lyon a week later that her year really took off when she claimed the Leading Lady Rider trophy. Meanwhile Flynn and *Carraig Dubh* were second in the Grand Prix at Stadthagen before moving on to Berlin, where they were also runners-up in the Derby.

Alongside Ledingham, Flynn had been a core player in the Irish victory at that first leg of the 1999–2000 Samsung series in Athens the previous September. And the Longford man was again the hero of the second win in Helsinki in July 2000, where he was joined by the considerably less-experienced Carey riding *Shannondale*, Cian O'Connor on *Waterford Crystal* and Cameron Hanley riding *Balaseyr Twilight*. In this second-division Nations Cup just three riders returned in the second round, so Carey was sidelined following an eight-fault first effort. But when O'Connor followed up his opening clear with a single error and Hanley added 12 to the four he had already accumulated, it fell to Flynn and *Rincoola Abu* to save the day, which they did with flawless style. Flynn then went on to scoop the Grand Prix honours with the mare and had lost none of his form by the time he arrived at Drammen in Norway a week later, with exactly the same squad of riders. Buoyed up by their previous success, Carey, O'Connor and Flynn all jumped double-clear and once again Flynn clinched it in his anchorman role, this time riding *Carraig Dubh* and fending off a strong German challenge.

It seemed entirely justifiable to celebrate three successive Nations Cup victories – something not achieved since the 1930s – but as it turned out that would only be the tip of the iceberg. On another glorious July weekend that summer, two teams – one at Lummen in Belgium and another at Falsterbo in Sweden – both triumphed to bring the tally to a fabulous five. The civilian squad at Lummen left the French runners-up a full twelve faults behind them, while the Falsterbo team's winning margin was decidedly narrower – just 0.25 faults; but it was equally commendable because they left the mighty Germans in their wake. Yet again it was Flynn who ensured the final score-line at the Swedish fixture when double-clear on the tough little *Rincoola Abu*. Carey lowered just a single fence in each round with *Shannondale*, while Cian O'Connor improved on his first-round four faults with a zero from *Normandy*.

Despite these extraordinarily good results, the SJAI decided it would not send a team to the Sydney Olympic Games, and the sights were instead turned to taking the coveted Samsung Nations Cup title. It seemed very do-able indeed, with six wins already notched up. Quentin Doran O'Reilly of the *Irish Farmers Journal* noted: 'It is refreshing to hear from the selectors, Chefs d'Equipe and National Executive members alike a steely determination not only to win this big one but to build on the vibrant, youth-rich strengths of our present sides and aim at even greater targets like the European Championships of 2001, the 2002 World Equestrian Games in Spain and the 2004 Olympics.'[2]

The roll continued with another win for a civilian side at Hickstead. But there was disappointment for Flynn when *Rincoola Abu* suffered a colic attack and he had to forfeit his place on the winning Aga Khan Cup team. Two more top

*Below*:
*Captain Shane Carey and* Killossery *blended into a hugely successful partnership.*

*Below*:
Army riders performing
a quadrille in the indoor
school at McKee
Barracks during the
seventy-fifth Anniversary
celebrations in 2001.

*Opposite top*:
Lieutenant David
O'Brien was a young
officer waiting in the
wings during the
seventy-fifth Anniversary
celebrations at McKee
Barracks in 2001.

*Opposite bottom*:
Denise (Sneezy) Foster,
wife of the late Captain
David Foster, receives a
commemorative medal
during the anniversary
celebrations from (right)
Major General Jim
Sreenan and (left)
Commandant John
Ledingham.

placings, at Rotterdam and at Spruce Meadows in Calgary, Canada, rounded up the sensational ten-win tally. After the Samsung Nations Cup final in Rome, Ireland were clear winners of the series with a 78-point scoreline which gave them a 25-point advantage over Germany in runner-up spot.

No sooner was the 1999/2000 Nations Cup season over, however, than the 2000–2001 series began. Lieutenant David O'Brien lined out with *Boherdeal Clover* for his Nations Cup debut at Tripoli in October where the team finished third and the army partnership contributed a first-round clear and just four faults second time out. By the time they came home to win the Grand Prix at Cavan International in November, it was plain to see that the Athlone man and the *Clover Hill* stallion were gelling into a partnership with potential. They had already finished second in both the Millstreet Masters and the Millstreet Indoor Grand Prix earlier in the summer, and the horse, which won the Irish Horse Board's 5 Year Old Championship four years earlier and which was now on lease from owner Paraic Goonan, would prove a great asset to the McKee armoury.

The outbreak of Foot and Mouth Disease, first in Northern Ireland and then throughout the remainder of the country, crippled equestrian activity for the first half of 2001 and sharply curtailed many of the plans to mark the Equitation School's 75th

anniversary. But, in May, Flynn got away to Italy where he secured the first rosettes of the year with *Diamond Explosion* and *Rincoola Abu* at Migliarino Pisano and Pontedera. In June, O'Brien went into over-drive with a hat-trick at Le Mans in France. He now had the ride on *Galteebeg* with which he won the two-phase competition, while with *Cruise Hill* he claimed the honours in both the Power-and-Speed and then the Grand Prix – an exceptional result so early in his international career.

The swap which saw O'Brien getting Carey's first international class-winner resulted in a horse called *Killossery* finding its way to Carey, and this was to prove fortuitous. In all, Carey would go on to clock up a spectacular eighty-nine wins over the next ten years, and a huge number of them were on *Killossery*, which he describes as 'the best I've ever ridden, and a trier every time he goes into the ring'. They won the two-phase class that summer in Madrid, but it was O'Brien and Flynn who contributed to the following weekend's sensational result when four Irish riders won Grand Prix classes at international shows. Riding *Boherdeal Clover*, O'Brien bested the great French horseman Michel Robert at Lisbon in Portugal, while Dermott Lennon and *Liscalgot* – now well-established stars of the senior squad – topped the line-up at Modena in Italy. At Bourg en Bresse in France, a young man called Robert Power steered *Gypsie de Bacon* into pole position in the Seven-Year-Old Grand Prix. Like his sister Elizabeth, this son of Captain Con Power was a highly-competitive showjumper at the time, but Rob went on to

make an even bigger name for himself as a National Hunt jockey when winning the

Aintree Grand National with *Silver Birch* in 2007. Flynn secured the fourth win of that extraordinary weekend with *Carraig Dubh* at Bourg en Bresse.

Irish showjumping was in great shape, and in July, at Arnhem in Holland, Jessica Kuerten, Peter Charles, Dermott Lennon and Kevin Babington claimed the European Team title for the very first time, while Lennon was in the individual shake-up right into the closing stages. Tails were up again, and the victory roll continued with a repeat of the 2000 Falsterbo/Lummen double a week later, on a Friday 13th that was far from unlucky. The result at the Swedish fixture was cemented by double-clear performances from O'Brien with *Boherdeal Clover* and Cian O'Connor riding *Waterford Crystal*, but such was the strength of the side, which also included Francis Connors, that Flynn and *Carraig Dubh* didn't need to come back into the ring in the second round because the mission had already been accomplished. The civilian team success in Lummen was equally convincing, and when they went on to head the line-up at Hickstead as well, it was all but taken for granted that the European championship winning side would just walk away with the Aga Khan trophy at Dublin. Their success, however, left them vulnerable to the smallest slip-up, and despite three second-round clears they could only manage a fourth placing, while Belgium reigned supreme on Irish soil for the very first time.

The army riders were in the ribbons throughout the week, but there was a sorry end to the show for O'Brien when *Boherdeal Clover* took a crashing fall at the triple combination in the Grand Prix. Taken away by horse ambulance, it would be almost ten months before the stallion would be fighting fit and back in action again. Another year of solid team performances, however, secured runner-up spot in the 2000–2001 Samsung series and the winning streak continued with a civilian team victory in Calgary. Flynn and *Carraig Dubh* then joined them to make it a hat-trick at Washington and Toronto. It was the perfect conclusion to the school's seventy-fifth year, as Chef d'Equipe Lieutenant Colonel Gerry Mullins acknowledged. 'It's unbelievable that an Irish team could win the Nations Cup in Washington and now in Toronto … it's never been done before,' he commented with some considerable satisfaction.[3] And in a speech at McKee Barracks in November, Minister for Defence Michael Smith recognised the 'unique national institution' that was the Army Equitation School to which he committed his full support. 'The School set out from modest beginnings on a mission to promote the Irish horse abroad, and this mission has been achieved a thousandfold,' he said.[4]

When Carey broke his wrist during a training session, his irrepressible Officer Commanding, Lieutenant Colonel Mullins, jumped back into the saddle to help his team take the silver medal at the World Military Equestrian Championships in Chile in February 2002; and the following month, Second-in-Command, Commandant John Ledingham, retired. He was already in great demand as a freelance instructor and went on to become a key figure in the High Performance team for Horse Sport Ireland.

The army men got into their stride at Monte Carlo, Eindhoven and Spangenberg before Carey's single time penalty over two rounds contributed to Ireland's third placings in the Nations Cup at Poznan, Poland, in June.

Later that month the team finished fourth at Linz in Austria, where *Boherdeal Clover* showed the one chink in his otherwise impenetrable armour when taking a strong dislike to the water jump, but it was still a great show for the Irish as *Lismore Clover* recorded a double of wins for O'Brien, while Carey was third in the Little Tour Final with *Killossery* and third again in the Linz Championship, this time with *Laughton's Lass*. 'She was a great mare – she had her own very personal technique and she was very strong, but she was highly competitive, incredibly brave and had endless heart,' recalls the Limerick rider, whose own characteristics are not entirely dissimilar.

Marching on to Vichy in France, Carey and *Cruise Hill* pipped Flynn and *Diamond Explosion* in the Derby, while at Deauville O'Brien on *Boherdeal Clover* and Flynn on *Rincoola* took a win and second placing respectively. In July, two teams were sent out to attempt the hat-trick of doubles in the Nations Cups at Lummen and Falsterbo, but it wasn't to be, as they finished eighth at the Belgian fixture and fifth in Sweden. But O'Brien and *Boherdeal Clover* won the SEB Cup in Falsterbo and finished eighth in the Grand Prix, while Carey and *Killossery* topped the Two-Phase and then won the prestigious Falsterbo Derby with the only clear of the competition to take the Leading Rider award. He now had eight international wins under his belt for the 2002 season, but the home circuit was considered equally important and just five days later he was back in Ballina, County Mayo, accepting the Grand Prix winner's rosette with *Laughton's Lass*.

*Above:*
*Captain Gerry Flynn*
*struck up a superb*
*partnership with Harold*
*McGahern's* Cruising
*mare* Rincoola Abu,
*pictured here competing*
*at the Piazza di Siena*
*in Rome.*

At Dublin Horse Show the civilian team was third and O'Brien also lined up third with *Boherdeal Clover* in the Grand Prix – the stallion's horrible fall in the same arena a year earlier now just a distant memory. O'Brien won the Speed Derby and was runner-up in the Speed Championship with *Lismore Clover*. Then, with Mullins as Chef d'Equipe, Carey, O'Brien and Flynn were selected for Gijon in Spain.

Before leaving, they travelled to Millstreet where Quinlivan recorded a win and third placing with *Abby*, Flynn was second in a jump-off on his new ride, *Rathnew*, and Carey won the Masters and was third in the Grand Prix with *Shannondale*. In Spain, the Irish trio had five wins, but the biggest accolade of all went to O'Brien, who scooped an €18,200 windfall for the Minister for Defence when taking the Grand Prix title with *Boherdeal Clover* and topping the Speed Final with *Killossery*. However, with very few points accumulated from the Nations Cups at Gijon, Rotterdam and Zagreb, Ireland was still unsure of qualification for the inaugural Samsung Super League season the following year.

This series, which would raise the Nations Cup game to an entirely new level, was open only to the eight top teams in the world, who would compete against each other at the eight most prestigious venues on the international circuit, including the RDS. Inclusion was essential in order to maintain a prominent profile in the sport in which Irish teams had proven so competitive for so long, while exclusion would mean being branded a second-class nation, no longer capable of cutting it with the best of them.

It came down to a bitter battle with the Swiss, who needed a win in Athens in September in order to squeeze the Irish out. But Switzerland suffered a cruel defeat by just one point at the hands of Germany. Ireland's fifth-place finish saw them qualify by what Chef d'Equipe Lieutenant Colonel Ronnie Mac Mahon admitted was 'the closest of margins'. The challenges ahead, however, were going to be enormous, not just for Ireland's top riders, but also for the Irish horse, whose popularity in international showjumping circles was suffering a further decline. More than ever before, it would fall to the men of the Army Equitation School to fight their corner and prove their worth. It would be no easy task.

The 2003 season got underway in earnest in March when Carey and the eleven-year-old *Master Imp* gelding *Ballycumber* won the Grand Prix at Villamoura, where Flynn placed with *Kilcummin, Cnoc na Seimre* and the eye-catching grey six-year-old *Cruising* mare, *Mo Chroi*. Flynn returned to win the opening Grand Prix on the national circuit at Coilog Equestrian Centre in Kildare in April, and Carey followed suit with *Lismakin* at Sutton in Dublin the following month before travelling to the Royal Ulster show at Balmoral in Belfast. Here he had the historic distinction of being the very first uniformed member of the Irish Defence Forces to jump in the arena which is so closely associated with the cause of Northern Unionism.

A civilian team finished a creditable fourth in the opening leg of the inaugural Samsung Super League series at La Baule in France, and Carey and *Lismakin* were called up for the second leg in Rome later in May, where Ireland secured an even more impressive second-place result. Flynn and O'Brien were also in action in Italy that same weekend over at Pontedera in Tuscany, where they registered a superb hat-trick as O'Brien and *Boherdeal Clover* claimed the Grand Prix title and Flynn topped the Two-Phase and Accumulator with *Rincoola Abu*. O'Brien also recorded two runner-up placings at this fixture, with *Lismore Clover* and *Carraig Dubh*. However, army riders would not see Super League action again until the very end of the season.

There was a superb win by a civilian team at St Gallen, and when this was followed by another victory in Aachen, the Irish were proving themselves more than capable of holding their own in exalted company.

Flynn and Carey lined out in the second-division Nations Cup at Drammen, Norway, in July where Ireland finished fourth and Flynn had a brace of wins with *Rincoola Abu*. There was another fourth-place team finish at Falsterbo, Sweden, where O'Brien scored a double with *Killossery* and *Lismore Clover,* while 2002 Derby winner, Carey, scooped the Speed Trophy honours with *Laughton's Lass*. O'Brien then went on to the World

Military Games at Minderhout in Belgium where he took the individual silver medal with *Lismore Clover* before coming home to win his fourth national Grand Prix of the season with *Carraig Dubh* at Celbridge in Kildare.

The civilian team was equal-third at Dublin Horse Show where O'Brien and *Lismore Clover* were just pipped in their effort to defend their 2002 speed title. The team finished fifth at the European Championships in Donaueschingen, Germany, later in August, where a medal slipped from their grasp in the closing stages, but they clinched a qualifying spot for the 2004 Olympic Games. Ireland was lying a comfortable second on the leaderboard going into the final of the first Super League season at Barcelona in September. Carey and *Killossery* really shone when following their four-fault first-round effort with a brilliant clear. A few weeks later, Irish breeding got a further lift when Carey and *Laughton's Lass*, and *Bornacoola* ridden by Flynn, were part of an all-Irish-bred team that scooped the Nations Cup at Gijon in Spain.

O'Brien and *Boherdeal Clover* won the first leg of the national indoor autumn series in Cavan before heading to the Helsinki leg of the World Cup, where, as lone Irish representative, the army man enjoyed a tremendous run of form with two wins and two

good places. Riding *Lismore Clover*, he was pipped by just 0.66 seconds by Britain's Robert Smith before winning the Speed event ahead of Germany's Franke Sloothaak. Then he shared the Puissance honours with Denmark's Michael Aabo when clearing 2.18 metres with ease, partnering the brave *Cruise Hill*. But a fall for *Boherdeal Clover* in the practice arena led to the decision to withdraw from the World Cup qualifier.

The stallion showed he was none-the-worse for his Helsinki slip-up when taking a third placing at the Belfast International Horse Show which was hailed a huge success in its inaugural year. Then, with a win in the bag for Carey and *Laughton's Lass* at Cavan Indoor International, the McKee drawbridge was hauled up for year's end.

European gold medalist in eventing and keen equestrian enthusiast, The Princess Royal, Princess Anne, paid a visit to McKee Barracks to view the horses and facilities in February 2004. In March, Mullins announced his retirement from the army following a medical check-up which led him to reassess his lifestyle. His sudden departure from McKee Barracks saw the reins taken up by Lieutenant Colonel Gerry O'Gorman, a career army man who, after a short early period at the Equitation School, spent thirty years in transport and logistical operations both at home and abroad. Appointed Second-in-Command was the 1981 individual European eventing bronze medallist Commandant Brian MacSweeney, who, in the years since his departure from McKee, had filled a variety of command, staff and unit appointments throughout the Eastern Brigade and at Defence Forces Headquarters. MacSweeney was now also a level two coach and trained riders in all disciplines. Soon the careers of Lieutenant Brian Curran-Cournane and Lieutenant Geoff Curran would begin an upward trajectory as the army ventured back into the sport of eventing once more, and with considerable success.

Flynn headed out to pick up the first rosettes on the international circuit at Vittel in France in April with *Donadea*, *Newbawn* and *Bornacoola*. He was on the team that finished fifth in Copenhagen, but the army had lost some of its best horses in recent months, including *Rincoola Abu*, who was now back in Longford with owner Harold McGahern and in foal to the stallion *Touchdown*, while O'Brien's winning stallion *Boherdeal Clover* was standing at stud for owner Paraic Goonan.

The 2004 Super League campaign was not such an easy ride as Ireland languished at the bottom of the leaderboard following poor performances at the first three legs. And during an extraordinary series of events, which included the hiring, firing and re-appointment of Eddie Macken as team trainer, it was army men who were called in to calm things down. Colonel Ned Campion, now retired from his Secretary General role at the EFI, was appointed Olympic and Super League Chef d'Equipe while Commandant Ledingham took on the role of intermediary with the riders.

Carey got the first army call-up of the Super League season at Rotterdam in June, having shown excellent form at Bourg en Bresse, where he racked up a win and second placing with *Laughton's Lass* before finishing second in the Grand Prix with *Killossery*. And he played a pivotal part in Ireland's third-place Nations Cup finish at the Dutch fixture, where *Killossery* produced Ireland's only first-round clear. This was the beginning of a claw-back from the abyss for the Super League team, and this army partnership would play a major role in that battle for survival. A win on *Lismakin* and fourth-place finish on *Laughton's Lass* rounded up the Limerick rider's good show at the Dutch venue.

Meanwhile, Flynn picked up just a single time fault with *Bornacoola* in the Nations Cup at Ypaja in Finland, where the team finished third, and the new Officer Commanding, Lieutenant Colonel Gerry O'Gorman, cut his teeth as Chef d'Equipe during this tour. The same army duo, Carey and Flynn, were also on the side that claimed joint-second at Falsterbo, while at home O'Brien was making the most of his time on the national circuit when following his Grand Prix wins at Galway and at Rolestown, Dublin, with a third victory for *Carraig Dubh* at the Limerick and District Show held at Crecora, and staged on the home farm of his fellow-officer, now also promoted to Captain, Shane Carey. In a unique move, the sponsorship of the Crecora Grand Prix consisted of a training package involving Carey and Cian O'Connor, with many more contributing to the cause over the following years as the younger generation worked to put something back into the sport and supported the local charity, Milford Hospice. Not entirely happy that his fellow-offer had outdone him on his home ground where he had to settle for second place, Carey came out to turn the tables with *Lismakin* at Newcastlewest the following afternoon. And Lieutenant Geoff Curran rounded up a great army weekend on the national circuit when winning both the Derby and Speed Derby with *Abby* at the Ward Union Hunt show at Tattersalls in County Meath.

The Super League situation was looking a bit precarious, however, and Carey and *Killossery* were called up for Hickstead where the Irish held the lead at the halfway stage, but slipped to fifth in the final analysis. A win by the civilian team in the Aga Khan Cup lifted Irish hopes, and Carey and *Killossery* kept up their run rate when winning the Power-and-Speed and taking fourth place in one of the toughest Dublin Grand Prix competitions for many years. Italian course designer Uliano Vezzani made no allowances for the appalling ground conditions created by heavy rain, and in an unusual turn of events there were no clears in the first round, so the result was decided by bringing those with the least faults back into a jump-off, in which Carey and his game gelding left the course intact. O'Brien shared the Puissance honours, with a brilliant performance from *Cruise Hill*.

Carey travelled as reserve to the Olympic Games in Athens where, on an extraordinary night in the Markopoulo arena, twenty-four-year-old Cian O'Connor won individual gold on *Waterford Crystal*, while Kevin Babington kept the flag flying high for Irish breeding when joint-fifth with *Carling King*. Ireland was electrified with excitement in the immediate aftermath, and O'Connor returned to a hero's welcome. But that golden summer was followed by a long, dark winter when, in October, a positive dope test for O'Connor's horse was confirmed. In the acrimonious aftermath there was a widespread atmosphere of suspicion and mistrust, and the Equitation School found itself subject to an inquiry into its practices and management, following a request from former officer, Captain Con Power. The inquiry panel, which included veterinary experts Dr Brian Hilbert and Dr Patrick J Pollack from University College Dublin, gave the school a clean bill of health, however, and Lieutenant Colonel O'Gorman commented afterwards that while he was surprised at the turn of events, his reaction was: 'the door is open so feel free to examine whatever you want. To my mind this is the best horse hotel in the world. If I were a horse this is where I would want to be stationed!' he said.[5] O'Connor was stripped of his medal and given a three-month ban by the FEI the following year.

Carey meanwhile returned from Athens to compete in the final leg of the Samsung Super League at Barcelona, where Ireland managed to avoid relegation. Also in September, event rider Curran followed a win with *Kilmessan* in the CNC 3-Star at Park House in Cork with seventh in the CCI 2-Star at Necarne Caste in Fermanagh with *Kilkishen*. The army jumpers scored a hat-trick at Cavan International in November,

*Below:*
*Captain Shane Carey*
*with* African Drum,
*later renamed*
River Foyle.

and the year drew to a close in December when Carey was sixth with *Lismakin* in the Classic and third with *Cruise Hill* in the Puissance at the Belfast Indoor International.

The sudden death of Paul Darragh came as an enormous shock in early January 2005, and his three-in-a-row Aga Khan Cup team-mates, Captain Con Power, Eddie Macken and James Kernan, paid an emotional tribute to their former comrade by acting as pall-bearers at his funeral at Rathfeigh, in Tara, County Meath.

The Irish horse was now desperately struggling to maintain its profile on the international showjumping scene, with only half the number in the top two hundred compared to a decade before as the inexorable decline continued. In eventing, however, Irish-breds remained absolutely dominant, and Lieutenant Geoff Curran made a great start to his 2005 campaign when fourth in the CIC World Cup Qualifier at Ballindenisk in Cork, riding the eleven-year-old mare, *Quick Thinking*, which was on lease from Meath owner, John Swanton. Following Ireland's Olympic effort the previous summer, the *Irish Field* commented that 'Athens underlined something very clearly for the Irish who finished eighth – gone are the days of making up for weakness in dressage by producing something special on cross-country day.'[6] From the outset of his career, it was clear that Curran was prepared to put in the hard slog in order to ensure his horses were competitive through every phase in this sport. At Punchestown the previous spring he made a promising start on the *Master Imp* gelding *Kilmessan* in the 2-Star class, only to take a cross-country fall, but there was no mistake a year later at Balllindenisk, and in May he followed up with a win from the *Cavalier Royale* mare in the O/CNC 2-Star at Tattersalls in Meath. They maintained their form right through the summer with another victory in the CNC 3-Star at Annaharvey in August.

Meanwhile Carey and O'Brien racked up a hat-trick at Modena and Cervia in Italy, while Flynn and *Bornacoola* were third in the Grand Prix at Fontainbleau, France, and runners-up in the Munich Masters. It was a poor start to the 2005 Samsung

Super League, however, when the civilian side finished last at La Baule, and it didn't get any better when Flynn and Carey joined up for Rome later in May. This was a special show for Carey and *Killossery*, however, when they were second in the prestigious Grand Prix. They produced one of only two first-round clears and, pathfinders against the clock, had the quickest time, but were forced to settle for runner-up spot behind Germany's Christian Ahlmann when leaving a fence on the floor. The dynamic army duo were also on the teams that finished fourth in the St Gallen and Rotterdam Super League legs, by which time Ireland had at last moved off the bottom of the leaderboard. But it remained precarious with another fourth-place finish at Hickstead and fifth in Dublin, where Carey and *Killossery* improved from a double-error in the first round of the Aga Khan Cup to collect just five at their second attempt.

They were on the team that finished last at Aachen, plunging Ireland back into the Super League relegation zone, although Carey had two strong second placings at the German fixture. Going to the Super League final, Irish backs were against the wall, and when Carey's father, Sean, died suddenly just after the team arrived for the Barcelona showdown, it seemed that all was lost. But those left standing were not going to go down without a fight, and Carey's characteristic toughness kicked in. He flew home to be with his family, but returned in time for the final battle in which Billy Twomey produced a great performance with *Anastasia*, who had thrown in an unfortunate stop at the last fence in Aachen, but who came up trumps when it really mattered now. Following a first-round four-fault effort, the Cork man and his mare produced an all-important last-to-go clear at the Spanish fixture. Cian O'Connor and *Echo Beach* collected 24 faults, Shane Breen and *World Cruise* made just one mistake over the two rounds and Carey with *Killossery* had one fence down in the first round, but four in round two. In the final analysis, fourth place was good enough to rescue Ireland from the plunge down to the second division. Carey looked totally exhausted at the end of the class, and the emotional turmoil of the previous few days had clearly taken its toll. But with typical determination, and at a time when other riders failed to step up into the breach, he stuck to his guns and delivered. 'The commitment has always been there,' the *Irish Farmers Journal* commented afterwards, 'and nowhere was this more evident than from Captain Shane Carey ... who returned to Spain before the funeral to give as best could be expected for his country and contributed in no small way to Ireland's survival.'[7] Sean Carey had enthusiastically supported his son's career and had enjoyed watching him in action in Barcelona just twelve months earlier. Asked if he had been tempted to remain at home rather than to return to face the seemingly impossible task ahead of the team that week, Captain Carey said, 'No, it was really important and I knew what my father would have wanted – I was proud to be there.'

Later in September, O'Brien lined out in the side that was joint-third in the Nations Cup at Podebrady in the Czech Republic. And when the Belfast Indoor International Show was cancelled, then Flynn's win in the Grand Prix at Cavan International with his future star, the eight-year-old *Mo Chroi*, brought this difficult season to a close.

Nothing could save the Irish from the slip into obscurity in 2006, however. At the Super League opener at La Baule in May, they were seventh, despite a strong performance from Carey and *Killossery*, who followed a first-round five-fault score with a brilliant clear. Second-last again in Aachen, fourth in Rome, sixth in Lucerne, seventh again in Rotterdam and fifth in Hickstead, they improved to third in Dublin, where *Killossery* gave his all yet again, with only one fence down in the first round and just a single time penalty at Carey's second attempt. At the Barcelona final it was pure desperation. Pinned down at the bottom of the leaderboard and two points behind Sweden, the Irish needed to finish at least two places ahead of them to avoid relegation, and Carey's inspired opening clear on *Killossery* gave a glimmer of hope as Ireland stood equal-third at the halfway stage. But when *Killossery* just couldn't hold it together next time out and returned with sixteen faults, and only Cameron Hanley on *Hippica Kerman* managed to keep a clean sheet, it was all over. Robert Splaine, appointed team manager at the beginning of the year, said of his gallant side, 'They put their hearts and souls into this today; you couldn't have asked for even the smallest bit more.' And EFI President, Charles Powell, pointed out, 'We are at a crossroads now, and it is essential that we find the right direction for the months and years ahead.'[8]

All were agreed, however, that the right direction was back to where they had just come from - in the Samsung Super League amongst the eight best nations in the world. So, refusing to dwell on the disappointment, Carey was on the team that began the long fight back with a second-place finish behind Germany in the Nations Cup at Zagreb,

Croatia, just seven days later. The Limerick man collected just five second-round faults with his handsome new grey gelding, *African Drum*, which would soon be renamed *River Foyle* and which would step up to relieve *Killossery*, now aged fourteen, from the heaviest duties in future years. And with his new speed ride, *Hands Free*, who would be renamed *Cashla Bay*, he also recorded two top-place finishes. *Mo Chroi* really began to show her class this season for Flynn when part of the winning team in Copenhagen in May, while O'Brien and *Ringfort Cruise* were on the winning side at Lummen in June. Flynn and Carey joined forces to ensure an emphatic Irish victory at Athens in October where the Longford man steered *Mo Chroi* into runner-up spot in the Grand Prix, in which Carey and *River Foyle* were fourth. Carey also won the Parthenon Cup and the final speed event with *Cashla Bay*, and came home to win the Grand Prix at Kill in Kildare in November. O'Brien on *Ringfort Cruise* won the Grand Prix at Cavan International, where Carey also recorded wins with *Lismakin* and *Cashla Bay*.

In eventing, Curran's star continued to rise through the 2006 season, which began with a double of wins over two consecutive April weekends with the ten-year-old *Kilkishen* at Tyrella in County Down, in preparation for his second-place finish in the World Cup Qualifier in Ballindenisk in Cork, where he also slotted into fifth with *Quick Thinking*. He brought out *The Jump Jet* to win at Kilmanahan in Waterford in May, but things didn't quite go to plan at Punchestown, where he was eliminated for a cross-country fall from *Quick Thinking*, but finished tenth with *Kilkishen*. At Tattersalls in June, however, he steered *The Jump Jet* to a close second-place finish in the CCI 2-Star, helped greatly by his good dressage test, which left him joint-second behind British star Pippa Funnell after the first phase. It was another Briton, Selina Elliott, riding *LB*, who pipped him at the post, however, as he was robbed by the rub of a plank in the showjumping ring. Curran-Cournane was also in the spotlight when fourth with the six-year-old *Ballymoney* in the CCI 1-Star class, and in July Curran was best of the Irish when eighth in the CIC 3-Star in Strzegom, Poland, with *Balladeer Alfred*. The following month he was in the Irish team that finished a disappointing ninth at the World Equestrian Games in Aachen, but in September he finished a creditable fifteenth at the Eventing World Cup final in Malmö, Sweden. And in only their third 3-Star outing, Curran and *Kilkishen* claimed tenth place at the notoriously challenging event at Pau, France, in October.

Curran was lying forty-fourth in the world rankings, one place ahead of World and European champion Zara Phillips from Great Britain, as 2007 began.

This year belonged to Commandant Gerry Flynn and *Mo Chroi*, who started out in April with a second placing in the Grand Prix at Chantilly, and never looked back. They were on the winning sides at both Linz in Austria and Poznan in Poland, and by May it was already being suggested that Ireland's road back to the elite Samsung Super League series might not be such a long one after all. Carey joined Flynn at Poznan, picking up just a single time fault with *Killossery*, as the army played a major role in the fight-back to the top. Despite single clears from both Equitation School riders, there was a disappointing seventh-place finish at Hamina in Finland in June, but the winning ways returned at Drammen in Norway, where Flynn recorded a double-clear with *Mo Chroi*, Carey and *River Foyle* had just one fence down, and Conor Swail clinched it in a third-round head-to-head with Norway's Geir Gulliksen. *Mo Chroi* was now at the very top of her game as she scooped the Norwegian Grand Prix honours. The team won again at Lummen, where Carey and *River Foyle* produced a foot-perfect double-clear. Now Ireland was well out in front in the second-division league, which they needed to win in order to rejoin the elite Super League nations. There was a disastrous last-place finish at Falsterbo, however, despite another foot-perfect performance from Carey, who was selected for the Dublin team along with Flynn. And they gave a great account of themselves, *River Foyle* producing an opening clear, and *Mo Chroi* picking up just one time fault, to leave Ireland just one fault behind the eventual winners from Germany at the halfway stage. With just four faults from both riders second time out, the home side finished joint-third. One commentator wrote afterwards: 'It was a great day for the army which for so many years has been the back-bone of the Irish Aga Khan Cup team and the Irish Chef d'Equipe said he was "particularly thrilled" with the performances of Carey and Flynn whose Irish-bred horses showed more class than anyone might have expected.'[9]

Then, in the ultimate test of class, *Mo Chroi* and Flynn claimed the Dublin Grand Prix title in superb style when facing an impossible target in the nine-horse jump-off. There were four home runners in the race against the clock, including Carey on *River Foyle*, but Flynn followed Georgina Bloomberg's eight-fault path-finding round for the USA with a blistering clear, and the 55.93-second target registered by the great grey mare proved way too fast for the rest of them. Last in, leading rider of the show Markus Fuchs from Switzerland came close when stopping the clock just five-hundredths of a second slower, but he left a fence on the floor and it was The Netherlands' Ben Schroder who was runner-up with the only other double-clear in 56.77. Flynn was the twenty-first Irish rider to take the Dublin Grand Prix title and the first army man to hold the trophy in his hands since Mullins steered *Rockbarton* to victory twenty-one years earlier in 1986.

'I could have gone faster,' the Longford man claimed afterwards with a grin, 'but I didn't want to overdo it because this is only *Mo Chroi*'s first year at international level!' – it was a spectacular result for the ten-year-old bought from Angus and Claire McDonnell in Wicklow when she was just four. Typically, Flynn insisted this victory was not his alone. 'I get huge support ... particularly from my groom, Private Linda Tracey – she adores *Mo Chroi*,' he said.[10]

The team finished fourth in the Nations Cup at Gijon later in September, and second in Prague, where again Flynn and *Mo Chroi* were double-clear. The Dublin champions were just beaten in the Prague Grand Prix, but at Lisbon in September, where the team was second, they triumphed once more before rounding up their sensational season with their fourth Grand Prix title at Vimeiro in Portugal. By the end of October, Ireland's return to the Samsung Super League in 2008 was confirmed and the army's contribution to that achievement was undeniable: Carey held the record for the most appearances during the season, having lined out eight times and

the *Irish Independent* said, 'the star performers were Cian O'Connor, Conor Swail, Commandant Gerry Flynn and Captain Shane Carey who between them produced 31 clear rounds and 10 double-clear performances.'[11] At last they were back at the sharp end.

Now aged forty-three and with twenty years of service at McKee Barracks behind him, Flynn announced his retirement in January 2008. 'His trademark do-or-die style of riding set him apart from the rest ... he represented Ireland in 43 nations cups and was on 16 winning teams, and ... secured nine international Grand Prix wins,' said the *Irish Independent*.[12] He never made any secret of his pride in riding for his country – 'Wearing the army uniform and flying the Irish flag meant everything to me,' he said, before taking up his new role as trainer and rider at the SIEC Equestrian Centre in Turkey alongside his former senior officer, Lieutenant Colonel Gerry Mullins.

Back in the Super League, Ireland finished second in the opening leg at La Baule, where German-based Denis Lynch continued his move to centre stage when winning the Grand Prix with *Lantinus*. Carey and *River Foyle* had just four faults in the first round of the Cup, but sixteen next time out, while *Killossery* showed he still had plenty left in the tank with a hat-trick of speed wins at the French venue. Captain David O'Brien made his 2008 debut riding *Mo Chroí* in Madrid. This season was an extremely difficult one for the man from Athlone because his lovely young wife of less than a year, Tracey, died in a motor accident the previous December, just weeks before the expected arrival of their first child. But he threw himself back into his job at McKee and worked at establishing a relationship with the temperamental mare who had

*Above*:
*Capt Geoff Curran and Kilkishen enjoy their victory gallop after winning the 2008 Eventing World Cup Qualifier at Tattersalls in County Meath.*
(*Tony Parkes*)

bonded so firmly with Flynn. And it was clear his efforts were paying off when they produced a good performance in the Nations Cup at Lisbon in May where the team placed fifth. By the time they registered a second-round clear on their very first Super League outing at Rotterdam in June, where the team battled its way into sixth place, the partnership was clearly cementing, and team manager Splaine said that day, 'It was a terrific fight back from an uncomfortable position at the halfway stage and Captain David O'Brien's second round, in particular, was very special.'[13]

Meanwhile, however, the return to the Super League was proving a big challenge and following another sixth-place result in Aachen and fifth at Hickstead, the Irish were second-last on the leaderboard with just two legs left to run. A much-improved runner-up result at the penultimate leg in Dublin – where Eddie Macken's thirty-eighth appearance on an Aga Khan team and his first in eight years created a big buzz – wasn't enough to pull out of the relegation zone. Splaine was desperately short of rider-power going into the Barcelona final, which would decide whether Ireland would stay up with the big boys in the new-look Meydan-sponsored super-series or be back playing with the minors. His job was further complicated by the absence of both Denis Lynch and Jessica Kuerten, who had helped secure that good Dublin result. Lynch, the sole Irish showjumping representative at the equestrian Olympic Games in Hong Kong, was now suspended, following Ireland's second successive Olympic drug-test disaster, which removed the Tipperary-man from the starting blocks on the final day of the individual competition. So, with his back to the wall again, Splaine turned to the army, who sent Carey and O'Brien out to do battle. Everything was riding on this one last effort, but the task was a simple one – the Irish must finish ahead of Sweden at this final showdown if they were to survive. Carey, who had claimed the Leading Rider prize at Prague shortly beforehand, wasn't called into team action, but O'Brien and *Mo Chroi* joined Cameron Hanley, Cian O'Connor and a new young face on the Irish side, Thomas Ryan, to take fourth place, while the unfortunate Swedes, badly hampered when fielding only a three-man side in the aftermath of the long Olympic summer, were completely scuppered when their first-line rider Jens Fredricsson was forced to retire in the second round. It was mission accomplished, and the army once again had played its part.

Curran, meanwhile, secured the biggest win of his career when beating a high-class field of Olympic hopefuls from seven nations in the World Cup qualifier at Tattersalls, in Meath, earlier in June. Lying fifth after dressage with *Kilkishen*, he rose to third, following a fast cross-country run in which he picked up just eight time penalties, but it was a nail-biting finish in the showjumping ring. The track was big and influential, and Curran thought he had lost any chance of victory when *Kilkishen* kicked out the second-last fence for four faults. But when the leader, Clayton Fredericks of Australia, had a nightmare round to drop to eighth, then Curran moved up to second behind New Zealand star Andrew Nicholson, whose three mistakes on *Lord Killinghurst* dropped him behind the Irishman by a margin of just 0.5 faults. It was agony for the Kiwi, whose survival skills earned him the nickname 'Mr Stickability', but pure joy for Curran, who proved his solidity in all three of the tough eventing disciplines, and who also left British super-champs, William Fox-Pitt and Pippa Funnell, in his wake. 'I'll never sit on one with such a heart,' said Curran of *Kilkishen*, with whom he was subsequently selected for the Olympic team. But a nervy dressage test in the Shatin arena in Hong Kong put paid to their chances and although they moved up twenty places after a great cross-country performance, and made little of the showjumping test, they had to settle for thirty-second place individually in the Olympic line-up.

*Kilkishen* spent much of 2009 out of action with a recurring stifle injury. However twenty-six-year-old Kerryman Brian Curran-Cournane, now also promoted to the rank of Captain, stepped up to the plate on his international debut at Belton Park CIC 3-Star to finish fifth with *Rossbeigh* and seventeenth with *The Sally Rod*. This event was overshadowed by the tragic death of veteran Irish rider Ian Olding, who lost his life in a rotational fall. Curran-Cournane slotted *The Sally Rod* into nineteenth and *Rossbeigh* into twentieth place at Saumur in May, while at home defending champion Captain Geoff Curran was lying ninth after dressage in the World Cup qualifier at Tattersalls, but dropped ten places over the following two phases. There were great Irish celebrations, however, when Cork husband-and-wife partnership Patricia and Michael Ryan took the top two slots.

In showjumping, O'Brien's 2009 year began with good results on *Kiltoom* in Hardelot, France, where Carey and *Cashla Bay* were also in the ribbons – and the two riders moved on to Manerbio in Italy, where they were also in the shake-up. In the new

Meydan FEI Nations Cup series that replaced the Samsung Super League, the threat of relegation now hung over two teams instead of just one, and a last-place finish at La Baule was not the best possible launching pad for the Irish. Joint-sixth in Rome and eighth at St Gallen failed to improve the situation, and team manager Splaine found himself under intense pressure again. At Rotterdam in June, things were looking better when clears from Jessica Kuerten and Cameron Hanley, and four faults from Denis Lynch and O'Brien with *Mo Chroi*, ensured the joint-lead at the halfway stage. But when the army mare hit three fences next time out, and both Hanley and Lynch knocked two apiece, it was Kuerten's double-clear that clawed them back for a fifth-place finish.

Despite this gallant effort, Ireland was still in an extremely vulnerable position, lying second-last on the leaderboard from which two teams would be demoted at the end of the season. And Splaine was left with a further dilemma when, very late in the day, Cameron Hanley asked to be excused from the Aachen team. Once more it was a man in uniform who rode to the rescue, although it was a complex operation to get him to the German fixture. The *Irish Independent* reported that, following a late-night call from Splaine less than forty-eight hours before the event began, O'Brien, en route to Charleville show in Cork, was turned around while the troops and equipment were mustered. But *Mo Chroi* was unavailable as she had injured herself at Rotterdam, so he would have to rely on the considerably less-experienced *Kiltoom*. 'The horse was in McKee Barracks, the lorry was in the workshop, groom Private Sinead Carolan was in Ardee, and driver Corporal Dessie O'Sullivan was in Tipperary,' OC Lieutenant Gerry O'Gorman explained. 'However, the full cast made the Dublin–Holyhead ferry on Sunday afternoon, and after crossing from Dover to Calais, arrived in time for Monday's vet-check.'[14] And O'Brien was hailed the hero when contributing a great effort to the gritty fifth-place finish.

There was still no room for complacency going to the Meydan leg at Falsterbo, where *Mo Chroi* returned to the ring but was not on best form. However, this time O'Brien's team-mates took the strain and secured a brilliant victory. So when a civilian side was third at Hickstead, the pressure was off for the last Meydan League leg in Dublin, where Ireland finished eighth. There was no army representative on this Aga Khan side, but

Carey set the ball rolling for the host nation with a great win from *River Foyle* on the first morning of the show. Once again, Government cutbacks were threatening the school, but as the *Irish Independent* said the following day: 'An Bord Snip has the Army Equitation School in its sights, but public support for the men at McKee Barracks, whose exploits in the early years of the Free State gave Irish people a real sense of nationhood, has been steadily growing. It was early in the morning when Carey took his victory gallop around the RDS main ring, but you could still hear the crowd roaring.'[15] And by the end of the week Carey took the Leading Irish Rider award following his joint-victory in the Puissance and third place in the Speed Championship. Another new name also entered the Dublin results sheets that summer – Lieutenant Michael Kelly from Carrickedmond in Longford won the 6/7-year-old qualifier with the seven-year-old mare, *Major Chance*, which was subsequently re-named *Lough Foyle* as she is out of the same *Cruising* mare as *River Foyle*. An all-round athlete, the twenty-six-year-old former Gaelic games star has already secured a place in Irish sporting history as a member of the Longford team that claimed the Leinster Minor Football Championship for only the third time in 2002. With *Lough Foyle*, Kelly is already fulfilling all three of the vital core missions of the Army Equitation School, which include the winning of equestrian competitions on Irish-bred horses, supporting the national sport horse industry, and acting as a public relations agent for Ireland, the Defence Forces and the Irish sport horse.

The role of the Equitation School today goes well beyond the iconic image of the army man on his horse. Support to policy and strategic development through participation in the national governing body, Horse Sport Ireland, and close associations with national organisations, particularly Showjumping Ireland and Eventing Ireland, are key elements of its function today. Like its fine old partner, the Royal Dublin Society, which continues to ensure Ireland's elevated status in the equestrian world through innovative breeding initiatives and ongoing capital investment in its infrastructure at Ballsbridge, the school is deeply embedded in the heart of the Irish horse industry. It is a vital reference point and resource to the Irish sport horse and its breeders, producers, riders and purchasers, both at home and abroad.

It falls to O'Brien and *Drumiller Lough* to bring this history of the Army Equitation

School to a close. Their silver-medal winning performance at the 2009 World Breeding Federation Championships at Lanaken in Belgium, where top breeders from around the world assemble for the annual assessment of studbook strength and potential stars, confirmed that the Army Equitation School has one of the best six-year-old horses in the world at its disposal. Sired by the Dutch stallion, *Heartbreaker*, and out of an Irish draught/thoroughbred dam line, this bay gelding emerged from a starting field of 240 runners through two super-tough qualifying rounds, and was only just pipped at the post. Bred by Paul Dillon in Armagh, and bought by the Minister for Defence as a four-year-old, he won the six-year-old championship at Dublin Horse Show, and then the six-year-old national title a few weeks later. Commandant John Ledingham, Irish Chef d'Equipe at the Belgian fixture last September, predicts that this horse will be a contender for the 2012 Olympic Games in London. *Drumiller Lough* represents Ireland's best effort to restore the reputation and popularity of the Irish horse in the modern era by blending the cream of our native stock with those from foreign studbooks, and in the hands of O'Brien, who rides very much in the Ledingham mould, he should, if the showjumping spirits smile upon him, have a fine future ahead of him.

He will carry the hopes and dreams of generations of Irish breeders, producers, riders and horse-lovers wherever he goes, while his rider will continue the long tradition of the 'ambassadors on horseback' who set out in 1926 to fly the flag of a fledgling state astride Ireland's most noble and precious asset – the Irish horse.

*Below*:
*Captain David O'Brien and* Drumiller Lough *won the Silver Medal at the World Breeding Federation Championships in Lanaken, Belgium in September 2009.*
(Tony Parkes)

# EPILOGUE

There is a timelessness to the Irish Army Equitation School that transcends horses, riders and even the initial mission of the school itself. Horses come and go, and riders enjoy only a moment in the limelight, but the mission continually evolves according to the needs of the nation and the Irish sport-horse industry.

Since 1926, while the school has adapted to change, its core operational ideal has remained the same – a uniformed rider mounted on a horse bred on an Irish farm and competing at the top level of international equestrian sport. Due to the unique reason for its very existence, the school has outlived the great competition-oriented cavalry units of other countries. Although these other national units gradually disappeared, the Irish Army Equitation School survived and is now the only establishment of its kind in the world.

At its inception, the Equitation School was one of the very few Irish sporting bodies capable of raising the flag of our fledgling nation in world-class competition. In fact, it was the only one that could so clearly identify our country. Down the years, that has changed, and Ireland now competes with distinction at the top level of many sports. In the case of the Army Equitation School, however, the basic 'equipment' for taking part is still uniquely linked to our small island – the Irish horse. That very link is at the core of its continuing role.

Many years ago now, the great mentor of the school, Judge William Wylie of the Royal Dublin Society, prophetically declared that Ireland needed a national equestrian centre for the training of riders and horses to international competition level. In a very real way, the Army Equitation School has realised that ambition, becoming 'a centre of excellence for the sport-horse industry'.

The industry is currently experiencing a period of enforced adaptation and immense change. In line with the worldwide evolution of both equestrian sport itself and the kind of horse needed to participate in it, improved selectivity in our breeding programme has become an imperative, and more focused training of our young riders is a must. For some time now, the Army Equitation School has been closely connected with these important developments and is a driving force in moving them forward. It is no longer just a question of army officers competing internationally, they also play a major role in encouraging and assisting others to realise their dreams and in helping to develop their future potential.

Both serving and retired Army Equitation School officers sit on committee boards of Horse Sport Ireland, Showjumping Ireland, Eventing Ireland and the RDS Equestrian Committee – organisations dedicated to the improvement of the breeding of Irish sport horses and the training of future international stars. As a centre of excellence, the Army Equitation School participates in training and educational seminars run countrywide by the national training organisation Teagasc, organises demonstrations and training clinics for Horse Sport Ireland and, in conjunction with Showjumping Ireland and Eventing Ireland, provides in-house training bursaries for individual riders. The school's facilities are used for coaching junior- and young-rider international teams under the direction of former army riders. It hosts educational visits by the country's horse breeders and has a transition year Work Experience Programme for students in the horse industry. Former school officers have played key roles in developing a National Equestrian Coaching Programme in conjunction with the University of Limerick. It assists Horse Sport Ireland with the selection and enhancement of the breeding herd of mares and stallions, and all of this while continuing to train its own riders and horses up to a level whereby they can support the national team through participation in the Super League of showjumping and the world contests of eventing.

And all the time the school is on the lookout for that special horse that will take the place of great ones like *Limerick Lace*, *Loch an Easpaig*, *Rockbarton* or *Kilbaha*. Through annual purchases, a lease programme and the generosity of patrons like Maurice Cassidy, who has donated four eventing horses, they continue the day-to-day search.

The Army Equitation School continues to play an extraordinarily successful role as a unique public relations agency for the nation, the defence forces and the Irish sport-horse industry. Its 'Ambassadors on Horseback' are a timeless asset, and as it gallops into the future it does so with the Irish flag flying high. Long may it ride!

# APPENDIX 1:

*List of International Riders from the Equitation School 1926–2010*
*and Their Years of International Competition*

| | | | |
|---|---|---|---|
| Cyril Harty | 1926–1938 | Larry Kiely | 1966–1978 |
| Ged O'Dwyer | 1926–1939 | Jim Nicholson | 1969–1978 |
| Dan Corry | 1926–1958 | Patrick Phelan | 1971–1974 |
| Tom Finlay | 1929–1932 | David Foster | 1975–1989 |
| Fred Aherne | 1929–1948 | Con Power | 1975–1980 |
| George Heffernan | 1930–1939 | Brian McSweeney | 1977–1989 |
| Louis Magee | 1930–1954 | John Roche | 1978–1982 |
| Dan Leonard | 1931–1935 | Gerry Mullins | 1978–1996 |
| Jack Lewis | 1932–1948 | Martin Nolan | 1980–1982 |
| James Neylon | 1932–1952 | John Ledingham | 1980–1999 |
| Jack Stack | 1934–1951 | Nick Connors | 1983–1986 |
| Bill Mullins | 1947–1950 | Tom Freyne | 1995–1997 |
| Michael Tubridy | 1947–1953 | Gerry Flynn | 1997–2007 |
| Colm O'Shea | 1949–1954 | Shane Carey | 2000–2009 |
| Brendan Cullinane | 1949–1952 | Danielle Quinlivan | 2000–2002 |
| J J O'Neill | 1950–1957 | David O'Brien | 2000– |
| Kevin Barry | 1950–1956 | Geoff Curran | 2002– |
| Tommy Moroney | 1953–1957 | Brian Curran-Cournane | 2008– |
| Patsy Kiernan | 1954–1958 | Michael Kelly | 2009– |
| Billy Ringrose | 1954–1970 | | |
| Desmond Ringrose | 1957–1959 | | |
| Roger Moloney | 1954–1972 | | |
| Pat Griffin | 1956–1962 | | |
| Sean Daly | 1957–1962 | | |
| Jim Whelan | 1959–1963 | | |
| Eamonn O'Donohue | 1959–1965 | | |
| Ned Campion | 1961–1977 | | |
| Eoin Lavelle | 1968–1970 | | |
| Ronnie MacMahon | 1963–1975 | | |
| Jimmy Quinn | 1966–1971 | | |

# APPENDIX 2:

*Officers Commanding the Army Equitation School*

| | |
|---|---|
| Major Liam Hoolan | 1926–1930 |
| Colonel Liam Hayes | 1930–1932 |
| Colonel Michael Hogan | 1932, 1933–1935 |
| Colonel JJ O'Connell | 1932 (March – June) |
| Colonel Fred Bennett | 1932 (June) – 1933 (August) |
| Major Ged O'Dwyer | 1935–1939 |
| Commandant Tom Finlay | 1940–1945 |
| Colonel Jack Lewis | 1945–1949 |
| Colonel Fred Aherne | 1949–1958 |
| Colonel Jim Neylon | 1958–1968 |
| Colonel Bill Rea | 1968–1971 |
| Colonel Billy Ringrose | 1971–1945 |
| Colonel Sean Daly | 1975–1977 |
| Colonel Billy Ringrose | 1977–1989 |
| Colonel Ned Campion | 1989–1997 |
| Lieutenant Colonel Ronnie MacMahon | 1997–1999 |
| Lieutenant Colonel Gerry Mullins | 1999–2004 |
| Lieutenant Colonel Gerry O'Gorman | 2004– |

*Sergeants Major (SM) and Company Sergeants (CS) at the School*

| | |
|---|---|
| RSM Paddy Dunne | 1926–1936 |
| RSM James Daly | 1936–1949 |
| RSM Walter Smith | 1950–1964 |
| RSM Steve Hickey | 1964–1984 |
| RMS Paddy Waters | 1984–1989 |
| RMS Martin Smith | 1989–2000 |
| CS Jimmy Dwyer | 2000–2002 |
| CS Declan O'Connor | 2002–2005 |
| CS Paddy Byrne | 2005– |

# APPENDIX 3:

*Army Rider Participation on Irish Winning Nations Cup Teams 1928–2010*

## 1928
Dublin: Captain Dan Corry (*Finghin*); Captain Ged O'Dwyer (*Cuchulain*); Captain Cyril Harty (*Craobh Ruadh*)

## 1931
Lucerne: Captain Tom Finlay (*Moonstruck*); Captain Cyril Harty (*Kilmallock*); Captain Ged O'Dwyer (*Rosnaree*)
Toronto: Captain Fred Aherne (*Blarney Castle*); Captain Dan Corry (*Shannon Power*); Captain Ged O'Dwyer (*Turoe*)

## 1932
Dublin: Captain Ged O'Dwyer (*Limerick Lace*); Captain Fred Aherne (*Ireland's Own*); Captain Dan Leonard (*Miss Ireland*)
Boston: Captain Fred Aherne (*Gallowglass*); Captain James Neylon (*Kilmallock*); Captain Dan Corry (*Shannon Power*)

## 1933
Toronto: Captain Dan Corry (*Shannon Power*); Captain Cyril Harty (*Limerick Lace*); Captain Fred Aherne (*Blarney Castle*)

## 1935
Lucerne: Captain John Lewis (*Limerick Lace*); Captain Fred Aherne (*Ireland's Own*); Commandant Ged O'Dwyer (*Blarney Castle*)
Dublin: Commandant Ged O'Dwyer (*Limerick Lace*); Captain Fred Aherne (*Blarney Castle*); Captain Dan Corry (*Miss Ireland*)
New York: Commandant Ged O'Dwyer (*Limerick Lace*); Captain Dan Corry (*Red Hugh*); Captain Fred Aherne (*Blarney Castle*); Captain Jack Lewis (*Glendalough*)
Toronto: Captain Jack Lewis (*Glendalough*); Captain Fred Aherne (*Gallowglass*); Commandant Ged O'Dwyer (*Blarney Castle*)

## 1936
Nice: Captain Fred Aherne (*Blarney Castle*); Captain James Neylon (*Kilmallock*); Captain Dan Corry (*Limerick Lace*)
Amsterdam: Commandant Ged O'Dwyer (*Blarney Castle*); Captain James Neylon (*Miss Ireland*); Captain Jack Lewis (*Kilmallock*); Captain Dan Corry (*Limerick Lace*)
Lucerne: Commandant Ged O'Dwyer (*Blarney Castle*); Captain Jack Lewis (*Glendalough*); Captain Dan Corry (*Red Hugh*)
Dublin: Commandant Ged O'Dwyer (*Clontarf*); Captain Jack Lewis (*Glendalough*); Captain Dan Corry (*Red Hugh*)

## 1937
London: Commandant Ged O'Dwyer (*Limerick Lace*); Captain Dan Corry (*Red Hugh*); Captain Jack Lewis (*Tramore Bay*)
Lucerne: Captain Jack Lewis (*Duhallow*); Captain Fred Aherne (*Ireland's Own*); Captain Jack Lewis (*Limerick Lace*); Captain Dan Corry (*Red Hugh*)
Dublin: Captain Fred Aherne (*Duhallow*); Captain Dan Corry (*Red Hugh*); Commandant Ged O'Dwyer (*Limerick Lace*)
Aachen: Captain Jack Lewis (*Limerick Lace*); Captain Fred Aherne (*Ireland's Own*); Lieutenant Jack Stack (*Red Hugh*); Lieutenant George Heffernan (*Duhallow*)

## 1938
Nice: Captain Jack Stack (*Red Hugh*); Captain Dan Corry (*Duhallow*); Captain Jack Lewis (*Limerick Lace*); Captain Fred Aherne (*Ireland's Own*)
Dublin: Captain Fred Aherne (*Blarney Castle*); Captain Dan Corry (*Duhallow*); Commandant Ged O'Dwyer (*Limerick Lace*)
New York: Captain Dan Corry (*Duhallow*); Captain Jack Stack (*Blarney Castle*); Captain James Neylon (*Clontarf*); Captain Dan Corry (*Tramore Bay*)
Toronto: Captain Dan Corry (*Duhallow*); Captain Jack Stack (*Blarney Castle*); Captain James Neylon (*Owen Roe*); Captain Dan Corry (*Tramore Bay*)

## 1939
Lucerne – Commandant Ged O'Dwyer (*Limerick Lace*); Commandant Fred Aherne (*Ireland's Own*); Captain James Neylon (*Duhallow*); Captain Jack Lewis (*Kilmallock*).

## 1946
Dublin: Commandant Dan Corry (*Antrim Glens*); Captain Jack Stack (*Tramore Bay*); Lieutenant Colonel Jack Lewis (*Clontibret*)

## 1949
Dublin: Captain Michael Tubridy (*Lough Neagh*); Captain Colm O'Shea (*Rostrevor*); Captain Bill Mullins (*Bruree*); Commandant Dan Corry (*Clonakilty*)
Harrisburg: Captain Michael Tubridy (*Bruree*); Captain Colm O'Shea (*Rostrevor*); Captain Dan Corry (*Clare*); Captain Bill Mullins (*Lough Neagh*)

**1950**

Nice: Captain Michael Tubridy (*Bruree*); Captain Louis Magee (*Clontibret*); Captain Colm O'Shea (*Ormond*); Captain Bill Mullins (*LoughNeagh*)

**1951**

Toronto: Captain Michael Tubridy (*Glandore*); Captain Louis Magee (*Red Castle*); Captain Kevin Barry (*Ballynonty*)

**1953**

New York: Captain Kevin Barry (*Kilcarne*); Captain Colm O'Shea (*Clonsilla*); Captain Michael Tubridy (*Ballynonty*)

**1954**

Rotterdam: Captain Kevin Barry (*Ballycotton*); Captain Brendan Cullinane (*Ballynonty*); Lieutenant Billy Ringrose (*Liffey Valley*); Lieutenant Patrick Kiernan (*Glenamaddy*)

**1955**

Harrisburg: Captain Kevin Barry (*Ballyneety*); Lieutenant Patrick Kiernan (*Ballynonty*); Lieutenant Billy Ringrose (*Hollyford*)
Toronto: Captain Kevin Barry (*Ballyneety*); Captain Patrick Kiernan (*Ballynonty*); Captain Billy Ringrose (*Glencree*).

**1961**

Nice: Captain Sean Daly (*Loch Gorman*); Lieutenant Eamonn O'Donohue (*Cill an Fhail*); Captain Billy Ringrose (*Loch an Easpaig*); Lieutenant Ned Campion (*Cluain Meala*).

**1963**

Dublin: Captain Billy Ringrose (*Loch an Easpaig*); Diana Conolly-Carew (*Barrymore*); Seamus Hayes (*Goodbye*); Tommy Wade (*Dundrum*)

**1967**

Dublin: Captain Billy Ringrose (*Loch an Easpaig*); Captain Ned Campion (*Liathdruim*); Seamus Hayes (*Goodbye*); Tommy Wade (*Dundrum*)

**1971**

Ostend: Captain Ned Campion (*Garrai Eoin*); Captain Larry Kiely (*Inis Cara*); Eddie Macken (*Oatfield Hills*)

**1976**

Ostend: Captain Larry Kiely (*Inis Cara*); Lieutenant Con Power (*Coolronan*); Commandant Ned Campion (*Sliabh na mBan*)

**1977**

Dublin: Lieutenant Con Power (*Coolronan*); Paul Darragh (*Heather Honey*); Eddie Macken (*Boomerang*); James Kernan (*Condy*)

Rotterdam: Captain Con Power (*Look Out*); Paul Darragh (*Heather Honey*); James Kernan (*Condy*)

**1978**

Dublin: Captain Con Power (*Castle Park*); Paul Darragh (*Heather Honey*); James Kernan (*Condy*); Eddie Macken (*Boomerang*)

**1979**

Aachen: Captain Con Power (*Rockbarton*); Captain John Roche (*Maigh Cuilinn*); Paul Darragh (*Heather Honey*); Eddie Macken (*Boomerang*).
Dublin: Captain Con Power (*Rockbarton*); Paul Darragh (*Heather Honey*); James Kernan (*Condy*); Eddie Macken (*Boomerang*)

**1984**

Dublin: Captain John Ledingham (*Gabhran*); George Stewart (*Leapy Lad*); Jack Doyle (*Kerrygold Island*); Eddie Macken (*Carroll's El Paso*)

**1987**

Dublin: Captain John Ledingham (*Gabhran*); Commandant Gerry Mullins (*Rockbarton*); Jack Doyle (*Hardly*); Eddie Macken (*Carroll's Flight*)
Chaudfontaine: Captain John Ledingham (*Gabhran*); Commandant Gerry Mullins (*Rockbarton*); Paul Darragh (*Trigger*); Eddie Macken (*Welfenkrone*)

**1990**

Dublin: Commandant Gerry Mullins (*Glendalough*); Captain John Ledingham (*Gabhran*); Edward Doyle (*Love Me Do*); Eddie Macken (*Welfenkrone*)

**1992**

Dublin: Commandant Gerry Mullins (*Lismore*); Peter Charles (*Kruger*); James Kernan (*Touchdown*); Eddie Macken (*Welfenkrone*)

**1994**

La Baule: Captain John Ledingham (*Kilbaha*); Jessica Chesney (*Diamond Exchange*); Eddie Macken (*Schalkhaar*), Peter Charles (*La Ina*)

**1995**

Aachen: Captain John Ledingham (*Kilbaha*); Trevor Coyle (*Cruising*); Peter Charles (*La Ina*); Eddie Macken (*Miss FAN*)
Dublin: Captain John Ledingham (*Kilbaha*); Peter Charles (*La Ina*); Trevor Coyle (*Cruising*); Eddie Macken (*Miss FAN*)
Calgary: Captain John Ledingham (*Kilbaha*); Peter Charles (*La Ina*); Trevor Coyle (*Cruising*); Eddie Macken (*Miss FAN*)

**1997**

Dublin: Captain John Ledingham (*Kilbaha*); Trevor Coyle (*Cruising*); Paul Darragh (*Scandal*); Eddie Macken (*Schalkhaar*)

Zagreb: Captain John Ledingham (*Kilbaha*); Captain Gerry Flynn (*Carraig Dubh*); Cameron Hanley (*Geometric*); Marion Hughes (*Flo Jo*)

**1999**

Athens: Captain John Ledingham (*Lismakin*); Captain Gerry Flynn (*Rincoola Abu*); Dermott Lennon (*Liscalgot*); Cian O'Connor (*Normandy*)

**2000**

Helsinki: Captain Gerry Flynn (*Rincoola Abu*); Lieutenant Shane Carey (*Shannondale*); Cian O'Connor (*Waterford Crystal*); Cameron Hanley (*Balaseyr Twilight*)

Drammen: Captain Gerry Flynn (*Carraig Dubh*); Lieutenant Shane Carey (*Shannondale*); Cian O'Connor (*Waterford Crystal*); Cameron Hanley (*Balaseyr Twilight*)

Falsterbo: Captain Gerry Flynn (*Rincoola Abu*); Lieutenant Shane Carey (*Shannondale*); Cian O'Connor (*Normandy*); Cameron Hanley (*Balaseyr Twilight*)

**2001**

Falsterbo: Captain Gerry Flynn (*Carraig Dubh*); Lieutenant David O'Brien (*Boherdeal Clover*); Cian O'Connor (*Waterford Crystal*); Francis Connors (*Cruiseway*)

Washington: Captain Gerry Flynn (*Carraig Dubh*); Kevin Babington (*Carling King*); Cian O'Connor (*Waterford Crystal*); Robert Splaine (*Coolcorron Cool Diamond*)

Toronto: Captain Gerry Flynn (*Carraig Dubh*); Kevin Babington (*Carling King*); Cian O'Connor (*Waterford Crystal*); Robert Splaine (*Coolcorron Cool Diamond*)

**2003**

Gijon: Captain Gerry Flynn (*Bornacoola*); Captain Shane Carey (*Laughton's Lass*); Harry Marshall (*Splendido*); Clement McMahon (*Gelvin Clover*)

**2006**

Copenhagen: Captain Gerry Flynn (*Mo Chroí*); John Hickey (*Artiq*); Cameron Hanley (*Hippica Kerman*)

Lummen: Captain David O'Brien (*Ringfort Cruise*); Denis Lynch (*Lancelot*), Marie Burke (*Chippison*); Marion Hughes (*Transmission*)

Athens: Captain Gerry Flynn (*Mo Chroí*); Captain Shane Carey (*River Foyle*); Cameron Hanley (*Concept*); Conor Swail (*Rivaal*)

**2007**

Linz: Captain Gerry Flynn (*Mo Chroí*); Shane Breen (*World Cruise*); Ryan Crumley (*Baltimore*), Conor Swail (*Rivaal*)

Poznan: Captain Gerry Flynn (*Mo Chroí*); Captain Shane Carey (*Killossery*); Ryan Crumley (*Baltimore*), Cian O'Connor (*Complete*)

Drammen: Captain Gerry Flynn (*Mo Chroí*); Captain Shane Carey (*River Foyle*); Paul O'Shea (*Jor de l'Elnon*); Conor Swail (*Rivaal*)

Lummen: Captain Shane Carey (*River Foyle*); Marion Hughes (*Transmission*); Cian O'Connor (*Echo Beach*); Conor Swail (*Rivaal*)

**2009**

Falsterbo: Captain David O'Brien (*Mo Chroí*); Darragh Kerins (*Night Train*); Cameron Hanley (*Livello*); Denis Lynch (*Lantinus*)

## INTERNATIONAL CHAMPIONSHIP MEDALS
*Showjumping*
**1979**

Rotterdam: European Championship Team Gold, Captain Con Power (*Rockbarton*); Captain John Roche (*Maigh Cuilinn*); Captain Gerry Mullins (*Ballinderry*); Eddie Macken (*Boomerang*)

**2009**

Lanaken: World Breeding Federation Championship Six-year-old, Silver – Captain David O'Brien (*Drumiller Lough*)

## EVENTING
**1979**

Luhmuehlen: European Championship Team Gold – Captain David Foster (*Inis Meain*); Alan Lillingston (*Seven Up*); Helen Cantillon (*Wing Forward*); John Watson (*Cambridge Blue*)

**1981**

Horsens: European Championship Individual Bronze – Captain Brian MacSweeney (*Inis Meain*)

# APPENDIX 4:

*Major Grand Prix and Derby Wins by Army Riders, 1930–2010*

1930 – Dublin, Captain Dan Corry (*Sliabhnamon*)
1932 – Dublin, Captain Ged O'Dwyer (*Limerick Lace*)
1934 – Dublin, Captain Ged O'Dwyer (*Limerick Lace*)
1935 – Nice, Captain Fred Aherne (*Ireland's Own*)
1935 – London, King's Cup, Captain Jack Lewis (*Tramore Bay*)
1936 – London, King's Cup, Captain Ged O'Dwyer
 (*Limerick Lace*)
1937 – Lucerne, Captain Dan Corry (*Red Hugh*)
1938 – Dublin, Captain Fred Aherne (*Blarney Castle*)
1938 – Lucerne, Captain Jack Lewis (*Limerick Lace*)
1938 – Rome, Captain Jack Lewis (*Limerick Lace*)
1939 – Nice, Captain Jack Lewis (*Limerick Lace*)
1939 – Amsterdam, Captain Ged O'Dwyer (*Limerick Lace*)
1939 – Dublin, Captain Dan Corry (*Red Hugh*)
1946 – Dublin, Captain Michael Tubridy (*Kilkenny*)
1950 – New York, Captain Michael Tubridy (*Rostrevor*)
1951 – London, King's Cup, Captain Kevin Barry (*Ballynonty*)
1952 – Nice, Captain Dan Corry (*Ballycotton*)
1953 – Dublin, Captain Michael Tubridy (*Ballynonty*)
1953 – Rotterdam, Captain Kevin Barry (*Hollyford*)
1955 – Nice, Captain Patsy Kiernan (*Ballynonty*)
1955 – Dublin, Captain Patsy Kiernan (*Glenamaddy*)
1956 – New York, Captain Billy Ringrose (*Loch an Easpaig*)
1961 – Rome, Captain Billy Ringrose (*Loch an Easpaig*)
1964 – Harrisburg, Captain Billy Ringrose (*Loch an Easpaig*)
1965 – Nice, Captain Billy Ringrose (*Loch an Easpaig*)
1976 – Ostend, Lieutenant Con Power (*Coolronan*)
1979 – Wiesbaden, Captain Con Power (*Lough Crew*)
1979 – Deauville, Captain Con Power (*Lough Crew*)
1982 – La Baule, Captain Gerry Mullins (*Rockbarton*)
1982 – Bordeaux World Cup, Captain Gerry Mullins
 (*Rockbarton*)
1984 – Dortmund World Cup, Captain Gerry Mullins
 (*Rockbarton*)
1984 – Hickstead Derby, Captain John Ledingham (*Gabhran*)
1985 – Wolfrath, Captain John Ledingham (*Gabhran*)
1986 – Dublin, Captain Gerry Mullins (*Rockbarton*)
1987 – Helsinki, Captain Gerry Mullins (*Glendalough*)
1988 – Millstreet Derby, Captain Gerry Mullins (*Gabhran*)
1993 – Babenhausen, Commandant Gerry Mullins
 (*Millstreet Ruby*)
1994 – Falsterbo, Commandant Gerry Mullins (*Millstreet Ruby*)
1994 – Hickstead, Commandant Gerry Mullins (*Pallas Green*)

1995 – Falsterbo Derby, Commandant Gerry Mullins
 (*Killone Abbey*)
1995 – Hickstead Derby, Captain John Ledingham (*Kilbaha*)
1996 – Hickstead Derby, Captain John Ledingham (*Kilbaha*)
1997 – Monterrey Derby, Captain John Ledingham
 (*Millstreet Ruby*)
1998 – Altenhof, Captain John Ledingham (*Kilbaha*)
1998 – Drammen, Captain John Ledingham (*Kilbaha*)
1999 – Einhoven, Captain Gerry Flynn (*Carraig Dubh*)
1999 – Tripoli, Captain Gerry Flynn (*Rincoola Abu*)
2000 – Helsinki, Captain Gerry Flynn (*Rincoola Abu*)
2001 – Lisbon, Lieutenant David O'Brien (*Boherdeal Clover*)
2001 – Bourg-en-Bresse, Captain Gerry Flynn (*Carraig Dubh*)
2001 – Le Mans, Lieutenant David O'Brien (*Cruise Hill*)
2002 – Gijon, Lieutenant David O'Brien (*Boherdeal Clover*)
2002 – Falsterbo Derby, Lieutenant Shane Carey (*Killossery*)
2003 – Pontedera, Lieutenant David O'Brien (*Boherdeal Clover*)
2003 – Vilamoura, Lieutenant Shane Carey (*Ballycumber*)
2004 – Athens, Captain Gerry Flynn (*Bornacoola*)
2005 – Cavan, Captain Gerry Flynn (*Mo Chroí*)
2006 – Cavan, Captain David O'Brien (*Ringfort Cruise*)
2007 – Drammen, Captain Gerry Flynn (*Mo Chroí*)
2007 – Dublin, Captain Gerry Flynn (*Mo Chroí*)
2007 – Vimeiro, Captain Gerry Flynn (*Mo Chroí*)


*Three-day-event Wins*

1971 – Punchestown, Captain Ronnie MacMahon (*San Carlos*)
1983 – Punchestown, Captain David Foster (*Inish Meain*)
1989 – European Championship Team Gold Medal, Captain
 David Foster (*Inish Meain*)
2008 – Tattersalls World Cup, Captain Geoff Curran (*Kilkishan*)

# APPENDIX 5:

*The Army's Nations Cup Winning Horses of Renown (in order of purchase date)*

- *Finghin* – bay gelding, breeding unknown, purchased 1/1/26, 10 y.o.
- *Cuchulainn* – chestnut gelding, s. *The Joker*, source Captain Gardiner, Birr, Co. Offaly, purchased 2/7/26, 5 y.o.
- *An Craobh Ruadh* – chestnut gelding, s. *Walmslane*, purchased 15/5/26, 5 y.o.
- *Rosnaree* – bay gelding, s. *Sir Rowland*, source Eamon Rohan, Carrigtwohill, Co. Cork, purchased 14/3/26
- *Kilmallock* – chestnut gelding, s. *Rockman*, dam by *Barroniki*, source Patrick Mahoney, Kilmallock, Co. Limerick, purchased 21/1/30, 4 y.o.
- *Moonstruck* – bay mare, breeding unknown, source John Kelly, Carlow, purchased 18/2/26, 6 y.o.
- *Turoe* – brown mare, s. *Sprig of Mint*, source J Kennedy, Cumberland St, Dublin, purchased 30/10/26, 4 y.o.
- *Shannon Power* – chestnut gelding, s. *Mount Edgar*, dam by Tom Steel, source JJ Foley, Bellefield, Co. Limerick, purchased 22/8/30, 3 y.o.
- *Blarney Castle* – bay gelding, s. *Convert Ruadh*, dam by *Jeannettsy*, source Michael O'Dwyer, Mitchelstown, Co. Cork purchased 12/7/29, 4 y.o.
- *Gallowglass* – chestnut gelding, s. *Iron Hand*, dam by *Reynard*, source Joseph Barry, Fermoy, Co. Cork, purchased 26/3/32, 6 y.o.
- *Limerick Lace* – chestnut gelding, s. *Forest Prince*, dam by *Pach-del-North*, source JB Hogan, Bruff, Co. Limerick, purchased 1/11/30, 5 y.o.
- *Ireland's Own* – brown gelding, s. *Irish Battle*, source J Dickson, Moate, Co. Westmeath, purchased 17/9/31, 5 y.o.
- *Glendalough* – brown gelding, s. *Sir Rowland*, source Terence O'Brien, Midleton, Co. Cork, purchased 11/8/33, 6 y.o.
- *Miss Ireland* – brown mare, s. *King's Herald*, dam by *Cabra Castle*, source Mr Duggan, Mullinahone, Co. Kilkenny, purchased 28/8/29, 4 y.o.

- *Red Hugh* – chestnut gelding, s. *Mellary*, dam by *Glassmalo*, source H Harty, Croom, Co. Limerick, purchased 15/11/32, 5 y.o.
- *Tramore Bay* – bay gelding, s. *Ben Eader*, dam by *Minstrel*, source John Curtin, Rathcormack, Co. Cork, purchased 7/8/31, 3 y.o.
- *Duhallow* – brown gelding, s. *Fairway*, dam by *HRH*, source Major Mitchell, Grangecon, Co. Wicklow, purchased 11/8/34, 5 y.o.
- *Clontarf* – brown gelding, s. *Rosewreath*, dam by *Discovery*, source James McClintock, Portlaw, Co. Waterford, purchased 15/10/33, 5 y.o.
- *Owen Roe* – chestnut gelding, s. *Denis d'Or*, d. *Kitty* by *Crackenthorpe*, source John O'Callaghan, Glanworth, Co. Cork, purchased 22/9/32, 5 y.o.
- *Antrim Glens* – brown gelding, s. *Santovan*, dam by *Sir Rowland*, source J O'Brien, Midleton, Co. Cork, purchased 6/2/37, 5 y.o.
- *Clontibret* – bay gelding, s. *Volta's Pride*, dam by *Lawton*, source Mrs A Kavanagh, Thomastown, Co. Kilkenny, purchased 30/9/37, 3 y.o.
- *Lough Neagh* – chestnut gelding, s. *Cottage Chase*, source Timothy Hyde, Midleton, Co. Cork, purchased 31/3/38, 5 y.o.
- *Rostrevor* – chestnut gelding, s. *Triapster*, dam by *Sandino*, source Mr Galway-Greer, Dunboyne, Co. Meath, purchased 21/7/45, 5 y.o.
- *Bruree* – chestnut gelding, s. *Dick Turpin*, source J White, Liffey Bank, Dublin, purchased 3/8/45, 4 y.o.
- *Clonakilty* – information not available
- *Clare* – information not available
- *Glandore* – information not available
- *Red Castle* – information not available
- *Ballyneety* – bay gelding, s. *Wavetop*, source Major Ged O'Dwyer, Corbally, Co. Limerick, purchased August 1949
- *Clonsilla* – information not available

- *Ballynonty* – bay gelding, s. *Sandyman*, dam by *Pamponious*, source Willie O'Grady, Thurles, Co. Tipperary, purchased 1951
- *Ballycotton* – chestnut gelding, s. *Selection*, dam by McKenna, source Eamonn Rohan, Midleton, Co. Cork, purchased 1948
- *Liffey Valley* – information not available
- *Glenamaddy* – grey gelding, breeding unknown, source Captain Michael Tubridy, purchased 1953
- *Hollyford* – bay gelding, s. *Buxton*, dam by *Free Return*, source Tim Hyde, Cashel, Co. Tipperary, purchased 1953
  Glencree – information not available
- *Loch Gorman* – information not available
- *Cill an Fhail* – information not available
- *Loch an Easpaig* – chestnut gelding, s. *Water Serpent*, dam by *Knight's Crusader*, source Mrs B Lawlor, Bishopslough, Co. Kilkenny, purchased August 1958
- *Garrai Eoin* – chestnut mare, s. *Candleabra*
- *Liathdruim* – information not available
- *Inis Cara* – brown gelding, s. *Golden Years*, dam by *Blue Speck*
- *Cluain Meala* – information not available
- *Sliabh na mBan* – chestnut gelding, s, *Glenasmole*
- *Coolronan* – brown gelding, s. *Midlander*
- *Castlepark* – bay gelding, s. *Exmouth*
- *Rockbarton* – chestnut gelding, s. *Come Fast*, source Tommy Wade, Dundrum, Co. Tipperary, purchased 1966, 7 y.o.
- *Lough Crew* – chestnut gelding, s. *King of Diamonds*, dam by *Battleburn*, bred by James Finnegan, Stoneyford, Co. Kilkenny, purchased 1966
- *Mullacrew* – brown mare, s. *Nordlys*
- *Maigh Cuillin* – chestnut gelding, s. *Nordlys*, dam by *Stalino*
- *Glendalough* – grey gelding, s. *Arctic Que,* bred by Mick Dwyer, Nenagh, Co. Tipperary, purchased June 1985
- *Lismore* – chestnut gelding, bred by Hugh McLaughlin, purchased 1988
- *Gabhran* – brown gelding, s. *Come Fast*
- *Kilbaha* – chestnut gelding, s. *Tudor Rocket*, bred by Timothy O'Sullivan, Newmarket, Co. Cork, purchased *1989*

- *Castlepollard* – chestnut gelding, s. *First Consul*, bred by Michael Gormley, Aughnacliffe, Co. Longford, purchased 1989
- *Shannondale* – bay mare, s. *Laughton's Flight* dam by *Sky Boy,* bred by John Doyle, Borris, Co. Carlow
- *Laughton's Lass* – chestnut mare, s. *John Henry* dam by *Poynton,* bred by John Troy, Strawberry Beds, Lucan, Co. Dublin
- *Boherdeal Clover* – black stallion, s. *Clover Hill* dam by *Regular Guy,* bred by Ms Pamela Miller, Mount Cashel Stud, Mount Cashel, Co. Roscommon
- *Carraig Dubh* – brown gelding, s. *Slyguff Joker,* bred by John Leacy, Ballyragget, Co. Kilkenny
- *Killossery* – bay gelding, s. *Clover Hill,* dam by *Radical (TB),* bred by Killossery Lodge Stud, Kilsallaghan, Co. Dublin
- *Lismakin* – brown gelding, s. *Master Imp*, dam by *King of Diamonds,* bred by Ann Downey, Ballacolla, Co. Laois
- *Rincoola Abu* – brown mare, s. *Cruising*, bred by Harold McGahern, Rincoola, Granard, Co. Longford.
- *Ringfort Cruise* – grey stallion, s. *Cruising*, dam by *Nimmerdor* (KWPN) bred by Harron Eakon Farms, Crossgar, Co. Down
- *Mo Chroi* – grey mare, s. *Cruising, b*red by Claire and Angus McDonald, Newcastle, Co. Wicklow
- *River Foyle* – grey gelding, s. *Cavalier Royale*, dam by *Cruising* bred by Kathleen Gallagher, Ballykelly, Co. Derry

*Three-day-event Winners*
- *San Carlos* – chestnut gelding, s. *Trouville*
- *Inish Meain* – chestnut gelding, s. *Sunny Light*, dam by *Candleabra*, bred by Denis Hickey, Ballyneety, Co. Limerick
- *Kilkishen* – bay gelding, s. *Cavalier Royale*

# APPENDIX 6:

*Of Saddles, Shoes and Scope*

Down the years, the Army Equitation School has depended on saddlers, farriers and vets to ensure that the needs of its complement of horses were catered for in the best possible way. At first some of this expertise came from within the army itself, but in more recent times the work has been commissioned out to private practitioners.

### The Saddlers

Three generations of saddlers served the school. Mick Kelly was the first, and then Dudley Goodwin. They were followed by Murty O'Brien and now Mick Allen. These men did the repair work and kept all of the leathers in the best of order. And all along, Goodwins of Mulhuddart have been suppliers of tack for the horses at McKee Barracks – first Michael, a brother to Dudley, then his son Tony, and now his grandsons, Ken and Damien.

### The Farriers

The school has always had its own forge near the stables. At first the farriers were drawn from within the army itself. The first recorded was Sergeant Dinny Byrne; then came Sergeant Tom Meagher. After him, in 1960, the civilian farrier John Boyne was commissioned to do the work – he was a legendary master farrier who trained many of those who ply the trade around the country today. His son, also John Boyne, has continued the tradition and is the current farrier for the horses in McKee Barracks. One of John Boyne senior's apprentices at the school was a man called Seamus Brady – he went to America and became a legend there in his own right as an expert in 'corrective shoeing'. He was once offered a blank cheque by owner of the great *Nijinski*, Bert Englehart, if he would come and work for him, but Seamus preferred the open road. He travelled all over the US working out of a trailer forge, and because of his unique knowledge he became known as 'God with a hammer'.

### The Vets

Just as with the farriers, early vets were drawn from within the army itself. The last of those was Commandant Mark Heffernan, who was brother to the international rider of the thirties, Captain George Heffernan. After Mark, the work was then commissioned out to private practitioners. Martin Byrne was the first of these, followed by Paddy Kelly and Maureen Prendergast of the veterinary college. Peter Gibbons of County Meath is the current vet at the school. Down the years one of the very important duties performed by the appointed veterinary surgeon was to be on hand whenever the Army Purchase Board went to look at a horse that was for sale.

**Left**:
*Master Farrier John Boyne preparing a horse for competition at McKee Barracks where he shod the Army mounts for many seasons beginning in 1960. His son, John, continues the tradition.*

# NOTES:

## Chapter 1

1 *Minutes of RDS Shows and Sales Committee,* 15 October 1925.

2 *Proceedings of Royal Dublin Society*, 1867–1868: Vol 104, p.100.

3 In interview for this book, 26 June 2009.

4 Wylie, W.E, *The Development of Horse Jumping at the Royal Dublin Society's Shows*, (Dublin; RDS), 1939.

5 *An Cosantóir, Irish Defence Journal,* Army Headquarters, Dublin, Vol. XXXVI, No. 8, August 1976, p.223.

6 Kiely, E., *A Short History of McKee Barracks Army Headquarters*, (Dublin: 2000), p.12.

7 Taped interview between author and Major Ged O'Dwyer in summer of 1993.

8 T*ransport Corps. Memorandum on Development of the Force 1923–1927,* Army Archive, p.20.

9 Toomey, T., *Forgotten Dreams*, Limerick, O'Brien – Toomey, 1995: p.89.

10 Ibid., p.90.

11 Op. cit., taped interview.

12 *The Irish Times,* Dublin Issue of 7 August 1926, p.4.

13 *An t-Óglach*, Dublin, Army Headquarters: vol. 5, No. 5, August 7, 1926: p.13.

14 Ibid., p.12.

15 *The Irish Times,* Sat., 8 August 1926.

16 Dan Corry taped interview, *Irish Field*, 28 July 1984, p20

17 Op. cit., taped interview.

18 Montergon, Capt., *Revue de Cavalerie, 1929 quoted in op. cit., Toomey, Forgotten Dreams*, p.114.

## Chapter 2

1 *Thom's Directory of Ireland*, Dublin: Alex Thom & Co., 1931: p.623.

2 Santini, Piero, *Riding Reflections,* London, Country Life Ltd., 1933 (revised edition 1950): p.2.

3 Op. cit., *An Cosantóir*, p.238.

4 Op. cit., taped interview.

5 Ibid.

6 Montergon, Capt., *Revue de Cavalerie,* 1929 quoted in op.cit., *Toomey*, p.114

7 Military Archive, Minutes from Advisory Group meeting of 15 December 1930.

8 Op. cit., *An Cosantóir*, p.226.

## Chapter 3

1 Op.cit., *An Cosantóir,* 1976, p.235.

2 Ibid., p.223.

3 Ibid., p.230.

4 *An t-Óglach,* vol.V, No. 1, p. 71.

5 Op. cit., *Forgotten Dreams*, p.128.

6 Op. Cit., *An Cosantóir*, p. 223.

7 McGarry, Ferghal, *Eoin O'Duffy, A Self Made Hero,* Oxford University Press, Oxford, 2007, p.196.

8 Op.cit., *Forgotten Dreams,* p.137.

9 O'Clery, Conor, *Phrases Make History Here, Ireland in Quotes,* O'Brien Press, Dublin 1999, p.78.

10 O'Connell, Col. J J, *Who's Who In The Royal Dublin Society's Military Competitions*, RDS Souvenir Bi-Centenary Book 1931, p.49.

11 Op. cit., *Forgotten Dreams,* p.139.

12 Being considered part of the British Commonwealth was a sore point with the De Valera administration and had been part of the cause for his rejection of the Treaty back in 1922.

13 Moynihan, Maurice, *Speeches and Statements by Éamon de Valera*, Gill and Macmillan, Dublin 1980, p.237.

14 Op. cit., *An Cosantóir,* 1976, p.230.

## Chapter 4

1 Kavanagh, Patrick, 'To the Man After the Harrow', *Collected Poems*, Penguin Classics, London 2005, p.35.

2 Op. cit., *Forgotten Dreams,* p.154.

3 Op. cit., *Farmer's Journal,* interview.

4 Op. cit., *An Cosantóir,* 1976, p.224.

5 Gerard, H., *Souvenir of Dublin Horse Show,* Dublin, Royal Dublin Society, 1935, p.9.

6 White, Dr Cyril M., *University Athletics in Ireland 1857–2000,* University College Dublin, 2000, p.13.

7 Op.cit., *An Cosantóir,* 1976, p.223.

8 Op. cit., *Forgotten Dreams*, p.167.

9 Minutes of Conference Meetings of the Minister of Defence's Advisory Group on the Equitation School, 1925–1926, Military Archive.

10 Op. cit., *Farmer's Journal*, interview.

## Chapter 5

1 Ledwidge, Francis, 'Soliloquy', *The Complete Poems of Francis Ledwidge,* Poolbeg Press, Dublin, 1998, p.188.

2 Meade, Liam, *Olympic Aspirations Crushed, A Story of 1936,* Dooradoyle, Limerick, (no date), p.5.

3 The author (MS) was present when Latvia first flew its flag as a declared free nation at any sporting event when their riders, wearing tiny badges of crimson and white, rode at the Helsinki World Cup of 1989.

4 Having survived the war, Captain Brinckmann was instrumental in restoring the sport of showjumping to Germany. He also became a much admired coach and an innovative course builder, who influenced others around the world, including our own Sergeant Major Steve Hickey.

5 Lynch, Stanislaus, 'Dublin Horse Show', *Riding*, September issue 1939, p.94.

6 Ibid., p.95.

7 Military Archives, Minutes of Minister's Advisory Board's Meeting, 19 June 1940.

## Chapter 6

1 Lynch, Stanislaus, *Hunting Poems*, reprint of *Hoofprints on Parchment,* The Kerryman, Tralee, 1984, p.60.

2 Minutes of HJ&REA First Annual General Meeting 1945, p.3.

3 *Irish Independent,* 12 May 1945.

4 Military Archives 'Memorandum for the Government', dated April 12th, 1945.

5 Ibid., April 24th, document s.5775.

6 *Irish Independent*, 22 May 1945.

7 *The Irish Field,* 11 May 1946.

8 *The Irish Times,* Wednesday, 17 July 1946.

9 *The Irish Field,* 17 May 1947.

10 *The Irish Field,* 3 August 1946.

11 Ibid., 19 July 1947.

12 Yeats, W B, 'Easter 1916', *Collected Poems*, Macmillan and Co., London, 1952, p.202.

13 Op.cit., *An Cosantóir*, 1946, p.237

14 Military Archive 3/16581 Report from Quartermaster General to the Minister for Defence, 19 June 1952.

15 Op.cit., *An Cosantóir*, 1976, p.239.

16 *Show Jumping And Horse News,* Vol. 1, Number 8, December 1950, p.259.

17 *The Field, The Country Newspaper*, London, Vol. 196, 19 August 1950, p.285.

18 'What's Wrong with the Army Jumping Team?', *Farming Post*, Agricultural Association of Ireland, Dublin, Vol. 1, No.13, 1951, p.5.

19 'Who Is Running The Irish Army Jumping Team?', *Sunday Independent,* 27 April 1952, p.6.

20 Op. cit., Military Archive 3/16581.

## Chapter 7

1 Shakespeare, William, *King Richard II*, iv. 7.

2 Macgregor-Morris, Pamela, *Show Jumping on Five Continents,* Heinemann, London 1960, p.121.

3 *Irish Times Supplement*, 1 January 1959, p.61.

4 *The Irish Field*, 29 April 1954, p.9.

5 Ibid., 9 June 1956, p.5.

6 *The Irish Field*, Saturday, 22 August 1959, p.6.

7 Ibid., 30 May 1959, p.8.

8 Ibid., 1 August, p.8.

9 *Irish Independent*, 17 November 1961, p.6.

10 Op.cit., *An Cosantóir*, 1976, p.231.

11 *Chronicle of the Horse*, Middleburg, Virginia, USA, Vol. XXVI, No. 22, August 1963, p.19.

## Chapter 8

1 Interview with Lt. Col Ronnie MacMahon

2 SJAI Archive 1963.

3 *The Irish Field*, 25 January, 1964, p. 4.

4 The group included Haughey's close friend Stan Collen, along with P.J. Cooper, event rider Alan Lillingston and Sean O'Cathain. Peter Fitzgerald of the Department of Agriculture was chairman.

5 *Report of the Survey Team, Horse Breeding Industry*, Stationery Office, Dublin, 1966, p.41.

6 Ibid., p.21.

7 *Horse Industry Act, 1970*, Stationery Office, Dublin, p.7.

8 *The Irish Field*, 25 August 1973, p.11.

9 Ibid., 23 June 1973, p.11.

10 Ibid., 3 August 1974, p.22.

**Chapter 9**

1 C. James, *The Irish Horse Yearbook 1977*, Bord na gCapall, Dublin 1977, p.28.

2 A. Douglas, *The Irish Field*, Dublin 1977, 5 March, p.13.

3 M.E. Tinsley, *The Aga Khan Trophy - 50 Years On*, Pontoon Press, Dublin 1979, p.26.

4 A. Fanning, *The Irish Independent,* Dublin 1977, front page.

5 A. Douglas, *The Irish Field*, Dublin 1977, 24 September, p.9.

6 M.E. Tinsley, *The Aga Khan Trophy - 50 Years On*, Pontoon Press, Dublin 1979, p.27.

7 A. Fanning, *The Irish Horse Yearbook 1979*, Bord na gCapall, Dublin 1979, p.6.

8 A. Douglas, *The Irish Field*, Dublin 1978, 4 November, p.13.

9 A. Douglas, *The Irish Field*, Dublin 1979, 19 August, p.9.

10 A. Douglas, *The Irish Field*, Dublin 1980, 31 May, p.13.

11 J. Fagan, *The Irish Field*, Dublin 1980, 30 August, p.11.

12 B. Langrish, *The Irish Field*, Dublin 1980, 27 September, p.11.

13 G. Willis, *The Irish Field*, Dublin 1981, 12 September, p.13.

14 G. Willis, *The Irish Field*, Dublin 1982, 19 June, p.13.

15 G. Willis, *The Irish Field*, Dublin 1984, 12 May, p.25.

16 Editorial, *The Irish Field*, Dublin 1984, 30 June, p.13.

17 G. Willis, *The Irish Field*, Dublin 1984, 11 August, p.21.

18 G. Willis, *The Irish Field*, Dublin 1985, 6 July, p.27.

19 G. Willis, *The Irish Field*, Dublin 1986, 29 July, p.27.

20 *The Irish Field*, Dublin 1987, 17 October, p.13.

**Chapter 10**

1 *The Irish Field*, Dublin 1989, 16 September, p.27.

2 *The Irish Field,* Dublin 1990, 10 February, p.34.

3 *The Irish Field,* Dublin 1990, 9 June, p.33.

4 *Development Proposal, Army Equitation School*, Army Equitation School, Defence Forces, Dublin 1991, September, p.7-8.

5 *The Irish Field,* Dublin 1991, 17 August, p.27.

6 M. Slavin, *The Irish Field*, Dublin 1991, 21 December, p33

7 Lord, Miriam/Dillon, Willie, *The Irish Independent,* Dublin 1992, 18 July, p.1.

8 *The Irish Field,* Dublin 1993, 20 March, p.27.

9 *The Irish Field,* Dublin 1993, 7 August, p.29.

10 Von Wrangel, Alexis, *The Irish Field*, Dublin 1993, 4 September, p.11.

11 *The Irish Field,* Dublin 1994, 6 August, p.31.

12 *The Irish Field,* Dublin 1994, 3 September, p.29.

13 *Irish Independent*, Dublin 1995, 1 July, p.19.

14 *Irish Independent*, Dublin 1995, 11 August.

15 *Irish Independent*, Dublin 1995, 25 August, Sport.

16 *Irish Independent*, Dublin 1995, 11 September, Sport.

17 Finnegan, Mary, "*Irish Independent,* Dublin 1997, August 3.

18 *The Irish Field*, Dublin 1998, 22 August, p.44.

19 *The Irish Field*, Dublin 1999, 23 December, p.39.

**Chapter 11**

1 'White Paper on Defence', Government Publications, Dublin, February 2000, p.48.

2 'The Irish Horse', *Irish Farmers Journal*, Dublin, 15 July 2000, p.21.

3 'FEI Communications Press Release', Lausanne, 10 November 2001.

4 Speech by the Minister for Defence, Department of Defence, 18 November 2001, p.1.

5 'The Irish Horse', *Irish Farmers Journal*, Dublin, 27 November 2004, p.20.

6 *The Irish Field*, Dublin, 21 August 2004, p.68.

7 'The Irish Horse', *Irish Farmers Journal*, Dublin, 17 September 2005.

8 *The Irish Independent*, Dublin, 23 September 2006, Sport 1.

9 'FEI Communications', Lausanne, 10 August 2007, p.2.

10 *Irish Independent*, Dublin, 12 August 2007, p.22.

11 *Irish Independent*, Dublin, 30 October 2007, Sport 1.

12 *Irish Independent*, Dublin, 5 February 2008, Sport 1.

13 *Irish Independent*, Dublin, 17 June 2008, Sport 1.

14 *Irish Independent*, Dublin, 4 July 2009, Sport 1.

15 *Irish Independent*, Dublin, 5 August 2009, News.

# BIBLIOGRAPHY:

*An Cosantóir,* The Army Defence Journal, Dublin, Vol. XXXVI, No 8, August 1976.

*An tÓglach,* Army Archive, Dublin.

Ansell, M. P., *Show Jumping Obstacles and Courses,* Collins Sons & Co. Ltd., Glasgow, 1951.

Bardon, J., *A History of Ireland in 250 Episodes,* Gill and Macmillan, Dublin, 2008.

Barker, David, *One Thing and Another,* Pelham Books, London, 1964.

Berry, Henry F., *A History of the Royal Dublin Society*, Longmans Green and Co., London, 1915.

Bord na gCapall, Reports and Accounts, 1978.

Brooke, Geoffrey, *The Way of Man With a Horse,* Seeley, Service & Co., London, 1929.

Churchhill, Peter, *Practical Showjumping,* David and Charles, London, 1990.

Clayton, Michael, and Steinkraus, *The Complete Book of Show Jumping,* Heinemann, London, 1975.

Clayton, Michael, and Tracy, Dick, *Hickstead, The First Twelve Years,* Pelham Books, London, 1972.

Coldrey, Christopher, *Courses for Horses* (revised edition), J.A. Allen, London, 1991.

Coogan, Tim Pat, *Ireland in the Twentieth Century,* Hutchinson, London, 2003.

Coogan, Tim Pat, *Michael Collins,* Arrow Books, London, 1991.

De Nemethy, Bertalan, *The de Nemethy Method,* Doubleday, New York, 1988.

*Designing Courses and Obstacles,* ed. John H. Fritz, Pelham Books, London, 1978.

De Vere White, Terence, *The Story of the Royal Dublin Society,* The Kerryman, Tralee, 1955.

D'Orgeix, Jean, *Horse In The Blood,* Nicholas Kaye, London, 1951.

Dossenbach, Monique and Hans, *Irish Horses,* Gill and Macmillan, Dublin, 1975.

Dreaper, Judith, *Show Jumping Records, Facts and Champions*, Guinness Books, London, 1987.

Dreaper, Judith, *The Stars of Show Jumping,* Stanley Paul, London, 1990.

Duggan, J.P., *The History of the Irish Army*, Gill & Macmillan, Dublin 1991.

Fell, Alex, *The Irish Draught Horse,* J.A. Allen, London, 1991.

Gerard, Hugh, *Souvenir of Dublin Horse Show 1934,* Royal Dublin Society.

*Horse and Hound Yearbook,* IPC London, 1940–2009.

*Horse Breeding Industry,* Report of Survey Team to Minister for Agriculture Charles J. Haughey TD, 1966, Stationery Office, Dublin.

*Horse Industry Act* 1970, The Stationery Office, Dublin.

*Horses of Ireland,* ed., Quintan Doran O'Reilly, Agri Books, Dublin, 1982.

*International Show Jumping Book,* ed. C. Hallam-Gordan, Souvenir Press Ltd., London, 1968.

*Irish Horse Yearbook,* Bord na gCapall, Tallaght, Co. Dublin, 1978–1981.

*Irish Showjumping Annual,* Merit Publications, Dublin, 1978 and 1979.

Keily, E., *A Short History of McKee Barracks,* Army Headquarters, Dublin, 2000.

*L'Année Hippique,* 1982–2009, BCM, Best, Holland.

Le Chevalier D'Orgeix, *Horse in the Blood – A Show Jumper's Working Notebook,* Nicholas Kaye, London, 1951.

Lewis, Colin, *Horse Breeding in Ireland,* J.A. Allen, London, 1980.

Macardle, D. *The Irish Republic,* Irish Press Ltd., Dublin, 1951.

MacGregor Morris, Pamela, *Great Show Jumpers, Past Present and to Come,* George Allen & Unwin Ltd., London, 1950.

O'Broin, Leon, *W. E. Wylie and the Irish Revolution 1916–1921*, Gill and Macmillan, Dublin, 1989.

O'Donoghue, Florence, *No Other Law, The Story of Liam Lynch and the Irish Republican Army, 1916-1922*, Irish Press Ltd., Dublin, 1954.

*Official Report on Ireland's Participation, XIVth Olympiad,* Irish Olympic Council, Dublin, 1948.

*Official Report on Ireland's Participation in XVth Olympiad*, Irish Olympic Council, Dublin, 1952.

O'Hare, Nicholas, *Heroes On Horseback,* Harkaway Publishing, 2004.

O'Hare, Nicholas, *The Hammering of the Horse Industry,* Harkaway Publishing, Navan, 2009.

O'Hare, Nicholas, and Slavin, Michael, *The Irish Draught Horse from the Earliest Times to the Present Day*, Irish Draught Horse Society, Dublin, 1989.

Personal archive of Noel O'Dwyer.

Personal archive of poet and journalist Stanislaus Lynch (RIP), with grateful thanks to his wife, Margaret.

Personal archive provided by Donal Corry, Naas, County Kildare.

Pollard, Hugh, B. C., *Riding and Hunting,* Eyre and Spottiswoode, London, 1938.

Proceedings of the Royal Dublin Society, 1920– 2009.

Rodzianko, Colonel Paul, *Tattered Banners*, Seeley Service, London.

SJAI Archive, Anglesea Lodge, Anglesea Rd., Ballsbridge, Dublin (now SJI Beech House, Millennium Park, Naas, Co. Kildare).

SJAI Rule Book, 1954.

Slavin, Michael, *Showjumping Legends,* Wolfhound Press, Dublin, 1998.

Smith, Brian, *The Horse In Ireland,* Wolfhound Press, Dublin, 1991.

Smith, Harvey, *Harvey Smith on Show Jumping,* Pelham Books, London, 1984.

Smyth, Pat, *Leaping Life's Fences,* Sportsman Press, London, 1992.

*Standard Jumping Rules*, Royal Dublin Society and Irish Shows Association, Ballsbridge, Dublin, 1948.

Tapani, Count, *Modern Show Jumping,* Stanley Paul, London, 1954.

*The Course of Irish History,* ed. Moody, T. W., and Martin, F. X., enlarged ed., Mercier Press, Cork, 1984.

*The Horse and Hound Yearbook, 1951–1952,* Odhams Press, London.

*The Horse and Pony Yearbook,* Farmstock Press, Dublin, 1993.

*The Horseman's Year,* ed. W. E. Lyon, Collins, London, 1953.

The Horse Show Annual, Royal Dublin Society, Ballsbridge, 1900–1910.

*The Irish Field*, 1926–2009.

*The Irish Horse,* Bloodstock Breeders and Horse Owners Association of Ireland, Dublin, Vol. XII, 1944.

*The Irish Horse,* The Bloodstock Breeders and Horse Owners' Association of Ireland, Cahill, Dublin 1953.

*The Irish Independent* 1926–2010.

*The Irish Press,* August 1944.

*The Irish Times,* August 1944.

*The Light Horse,* D. J. Murphy Publishers, London, 1956.

*The Royal Dublin Society 1731–1981,* ed. James Meenan and Desmond Clarke, Gill and Macmillan, Dublin, 1981.

The Standard Rules of Jumping, RDS, Dublin, 1948.

*Thom's Directory of Ireland,* Alex Thom & Co, Dublin, 1931.

Tinsley, M.E., *The Aga Khan Trophy – 50 Years On,* Pontoon Press, Dublin, 1979.

Toomey, Thomas, *Forgotten Dreams,* O'Brien-Toomey, Limerick, 1995.

*Volvo World Cup, Media Guide,* ed. Ammann, Max, Reklam Poolen AB, Gothenburg,

Sweden, 1979–1998.

Watson, S. J., *Three Days Full*, A Record of International Eventing, Irish Horse Board, Dublin, 1980.

Williams, Dorian, *Show Jumping,* Faber and Faber, London, 1968.

Wylie, W. E., *The Development of Horse Jumping at the Royal Dublin Society's Shows,* RDS, Dublin, 2nd ed., 1952.

# GLOSSARY:

**Derby**: a competition over rustic type fences.

**Dressage**: a riding competition which is judged on the basis of how well a horse and rider perform a set series of controlled movements on the flat.

**Equitation**: term applied to horse sport as distinct from horse racing.

**European Championships**: similar to the world championships except that the twenty-five best competitors after the speed and team phases go through to a two round final.

**Fault**: the penalty awarded by the judges when a horse and rider knock a fence, have a refusal or exceed the time allowed for a round of jumping.

**Global Champions Tour**: a richly sponsored new world competition confined to the top thirty riders on the computer ratings. The tour has up to six qualifying rounds held at prestige venues around the globe. Each round has a minimum of €300,000 in prize money. The final has a prize fund of one million euro.

**Grand Prix**: the most important individual competition at any showjumping tournament.

**Grooms**: soldiers assigned to looking after the army horses.

**Nations Cup**: a showjumping contest for teams of four riders from different countries. It is surrounded by more pageantry and importance than any other event in the sport. The riders jump two rounds over a very difficult course and the best three scores from each round are added together to determine the outcome. The team with the least number of faults wins.

**Olympic Games Medals**: are awarded for both the team and individual performances.

**Pocket**: the area where mounted riders await their turn in the arena.

**Puissance**: a high jump competition featuring a wall with quite easily dislodged coping on top.

**Quartermaster General**: the officer in charge of army expenditure.

**Six-bar**: a line of six progressively higher fences.

**Three-day eventing**: an equestrian competition that includes not only showjumping but also dressage and cross-country riding.

**Time Fault**: one fault is awarded for each quarter of a second beyond the time allowed taken by a rider to complete the course.

**World Championships**: in this competition there is a speed round, a team round and a semi-final out of which the four riders with the best overall scores go forward to a final in which they have to jump each other's horses.

**World computed rankings**: a computerised system of awarding points to riders on the basis of their performances in the principal events at each showjumping tournament they attend. It is worked on a month-by-month basis whereby points gained in a given month in the previous year are dropped and points gained in the current month are added.

**World Cup**: an individual indoor championship to which riders qualify through a series of regional leagues around the world. The overall championship consists of a speed leg, a two-round Grand Prix and a two-round final confined to the best thirty, or so, scorers from the original qualified start list of about sixty.

## ACRONYMS:

**FEI** – Federation Equestre Internationale, the overall international governing body for equestrian sport, which is based in Lausanne.

**HSI** – Horse Sport Ireland, the overall national governing body of equestrian sport in Ireland. It recently took over from the former EFI, Equestrian Federation of Ireland.

**MCP** – Medication Control Programme, the medication and drug control programme administered by the FEI to ensure that no performance-enhancing drugs are used on horses competing in international equestrian sport.

**OC** – Officer Commanding.

**SJI** – Showjumping Ireland, the national governing body of showjumping.

# INDEX:

Numbers in bold indicate that the subject is referenced on this page in a picture caption